THE BATTLE for AMERINDIA

The Story of Catholic North America

Solange Strong Hertz

Cover Illustration by Thomas Brannon

THE REMNANT PRESS * St. Paul

The Remnant Press
2539 Morrison Ave.
St. Paul, Minnesota 66117

2000

CONTENTS

A First Word.. 1
The Old New World... 3

Part One
FOUR CROWNS

CHAPTER I
The Crown of Spain... 14
CHAPTER II
The Crown of Mexico.. 31
CHAPTER III
The Crown of Brotherhood................................... 46
CHAPTER IV
The Crown of Martyrdom..................................... 64

Part Two
THE SIDES OF THE NORTH

CHAPTER V
Terror of Demons.. 82
CHAPTER VI
The Wasp's Nest... 105
CHAPTER VII
Planting the Lily.. 124
CHAPTER VIII
Canadian Diamonds.. 141
CHAPTER IX
More Diamonds.. 159
CHAPTER X
Trampling the Lily... 175

Dedication

For Our Lady of Guadalupe, Crusher of the Serpent

&

St. Joseph of Montreal, Terror of Demons

THE BATTLE for AMERINDIA

A FIRST WORD

Whoever picks up this book expecting to find a history text will be disappointed. Even worse disappointment awaits those looking to find in it a systematic deployment of recorded facts and dates in pages heavily larded with impressive footnotes. Readers desiring such are advised to look elsewhere, for the author has never at any time postured as a historian. Although successive events must inevitably be dealt with as competently as possible in their place, her intention is not to chronicle, but to orientate. What follows concerns Spanish Mexico and French Canada, the United States' two neighbors in North America, the one south of its borders and the other to the north. For the soundest historical reasons both are Catholic nations, and although they have been there longer than the United States and within easy reach, the Catholics of that apocalyptic democracy need very much to think about them in a full Catholic perspective, rather than in the exclusively political light so far supplied by certain occult interests --which is really no light at all.

Ironically enough, both Spain and France contributed heavily to the building of the Masonic republic which would eventually destroy their rule in North America. Without their help, proffered in a desire to weaken their common enemy heretical England, it is doubtful that the thirteen English colonies

1

could have won their independence from their mother country at the time. The massive aid of money, men and materiel given by Louis XVI of France under General Rochambeau is well known, but that supplied by Spain under General Galvez and others continues to go largely unrecognized.

There is, nonetheless, in the National Historical Archives in Madrid an original invoice for eight warships, copper and tin for cannons, 300,000 military uniforms, 1.000 rifles and cannons, 60,000 pairs of shoes, ten tons of gun powder, 80,000 blankets, 80,000 shirts, 3,000 saddles and other sundries amounting to $ 7,730,000. All this over and above a subsidy of a million Turin pounds, not to mention attacking the British forces in Central America and capturing the Bahamas, plus the British emplacements at Baton Rouge, St. Joseph, Mobile. Fort Charlotte and Pensacola. Spain furthermore kept her seaports of Havana and New Orleans open to the rebels, who were unable to receive supplies from the Atlantic due to the British blockade.

So now, on with our tale.

THE OLD NEW WORLD

To establish the proper bearings as far back as possible in time, be it noted that America has been the ground of one of the Serpent's cleverest illusions: People believe it is a new world. Of all expanses on earth, it is not that, and the truth is seeping out the seams of the godless modern science which was set in motion in the days of Galileo to obscure the true history of the universe. Far from new, America may in fact contain some of the older segments of the world which God created in the beginning. When He said, "Let the waters that are under the heaven be gathered together into one place: and let the dry land appear," there emerged under the divine hand a single land mass surrounded by one great body of water, "and God called the dry land Earth: and the gathering together of the waters He called Seas" (Gen. 1:9-10). The very center of the great mass of land at the apex of the world would be the site of Jerusalem, God's Holy City, "the midst of the earth" whence the Psalmist tells us that God, Who "is our king before all ages, ... hath wrought salvation" (Ps. 74:12).

Later shattered by the waters of the Flood, this original mass left jumbled fragments of that catastrophe in Earth's three

3

major mountain systems, two of which, the Rockies and the Appalachians, are found today in North America. Still one whole uni-continent like the first, the second mass of land is now referred to by geologists as a hypothetical Pangaea, the "All-Land." Although its inhabitants, descendants of Noah and his sons, who re-peopled the earth, eventually developed into races and nations, Scripture affirms that until the men of Babel, presumably under the leadership of the evil Cham's descendant Nimrod, began building "the city and the tower" by which they intended to reach heaven, "the earth was of one tongue and of the same speech," its peoples evidently enjoying the same natural unity which had prevailed in adamic times.

There must have been signs, however, that the admirable cohesion in which God had created the earth was giving way, for the city planners betrayed a certain urgency in the accomplishment of their work. "Let us make our name famous," they said, "before we be scattered abroad into all lands" (Gen. 11:4). As we know, God mercifully aborted the artificial world government they were contemplating, first by deciding to "confound their tongue, that they may not understand one another's speech." This is why the place came to be known as Babel, which means "confusion," and in the course of it, "the Lord scattered them abroad upon the face of all countries" (Gen. 11:1-9).

Heber, a descendant of Noah's good son Sem, was the ancestor of the Hebrews and would have taken no part in the building of Nimrod's prideful empire. Scripture says furthermore that one of Heber's sons was called Phaleg, a name meaning "division," because "in his days was the earth divided" (Gen. 10:25). He was the prophetic figure of that division Our Lord said He would bring into the sinful world in the latter days, and which is the necessary preliminary to any outpouring of redeeming grace. The rupture of Pangaea was therefore the material manifestation of the divine chastisement which miraculously confused the first human language until then spoken by all men. For a time, the fragmentation of land and language put an end to the secular society undertaken at Babel "to make our name famous" without reference to God, for sin by its very nature shatters unity. It did so in Eden and has continued to do so ever since.

That such a division actually occurred should be suspected after the most cursory examination of a terrestrial

4

globe, where the contours of the existing continents can be seen to complement one another. Allowing for the continental shelves extending into the oceans, were the continents to be squeezed together, they would fit with fair precision into one whole, like pieces of a gigantic jigsaw puzzle, an appreciable void occurring only where the ancient continent of Atlantis is believed to have sunk into the sea between North and South America and Africa. When the primordial mass of dry land divided, the nations which had already scattered far and wide from Babel "into all lands" were gradually set adrift on their respective pieces of earth and left to develop their own particular characteristics in their own way, producing a variety of cultures to be "discovered" generations later by explorers from other parts.

In the light of revelation, the origin of the Amerindian tribes is therefore easily explained without concocting either elaborate migratory theories or the fiction of polygenism. In America, since the dispersion from Babel, the original American Indians conserved to varying degrees what was left to them of the civilization of the men of the Tower, whose technology in some respects gives considerable evidence of having advanced far beyond ours. Scripture specifically characterizes them as probers of the heavens, who had furthermore already learned to replace natural substances by artificial ones of their own manufacture (Gen. 11:3). Some of the Amerindians, especially the Aztecs and the Incas, were still highly civilized at the time of Columbus. Rather than believe they had "evolved" faster than their neighbors, as Darwinian pseudo-scientists would maintain, it is far more reasonable to suspect that somehow they succeeded best in preserving the elements of the culture they had brought here with them. Their origins lost in pre-history, the stepped pyramidal temples of Mexico and South America are too like the ziggurats of ancient Sumeria not to suggest that Babel's more ancient tower may have been the common inspiration. Nor is there any better way of accounting for the multitude of stories dealing with creation, the fall of man, the Flood, the rainbow and the babelian diaspora which are found both in Scripture and at least vestigially in so much Amerindian folklore.

The Aztecs in particular had a highly developed priesthood which, for all its demonic cruelty, possessed a ritualized expiatory worship closer to Abel's sacrifice than to Cain's unbloody offering of "the fruits of the earth" (Gen. 4:3). For centuries, the ancient Serpent had a relatively free hand in

5

the American hemisphere, cut off as it was by two gigantic bodies of water from the divine interventions made in the other half of the globe, and apparently he exacted worship patterned as closely as possible on that of the true God. Whatever the facts of the matter, the early Spanish missionaries were not faced with a cultural void on arrival. Setting themselves to purging the existing civilization of its satanic elements, they began slowly but surely incorporating it into Christ's kingdom. As we shall see, this was not to be the case on the eastern seaboard of North America.

+

Divinely inspired as Columbus' mission may have been, to contend that Columbus was the first to discover America is to fly in the face of the evidence. With the vast knowledge of the ancients he possessed, he himself would have been the first to disclaim the idea, especially after finding European relics in Guadaloupe on his second voyage. Nor could he have believed the world was flat. Never known to speak Italian, and certainly no Genoese, he may have come to Europe only after the fall of Constantinople in 1453. If this be true, he would have spent his formative years steeped in the tradition of the second-century geographer Claudius Ptolemy, who knew perfectly well that the world was round, besides knowing how to get around it.

Ptolemy's teaching had never been abandoned in Byzantium, and even in the West only the most ignorant entertained the possibility of a flat earth, so contrary is this to the evidence of any naked eye scanning any horizon. And so contrary to Scripture, where Isaias characterizes God as "He that sitteth upon the globe of the earth" (Is. 40:22). The Pythagoreans taught in the sixth century B.C. that it was round, and eventually Aristotle proved it beyond dispute by computing its circular shadow on the moon during an eclipse. Such was the majority conviction ever after, as can be seen from a mid-thirteenth miniature of the Emperor Augustus enthroned and holding a globe of the world, the well-known *orbis terrae.* A similar globe dates from the eleventh century.

Following the great Eratosthenes, the Greek geographer-historian Strabo, in the first century A.D., went so far as to declare it possible to sail from Spain to the Indies, an opinion on which Columbus was to rely heavily. As for the existence of

6

America, it would be tedious to list all the classical authors who wrote about the land now known by that name. Diodorus of Sicily, Horace, Virgil and Pliny are only a few of those who spoke of "the great western islands" or "the land beyond Thule" or "the western lands." So commonly anticipated was their discovery that Seneca incorporated a famous prophecy into the second act of his tragedy *Medea,* which ran: "In time to come the day will arrive when the Ocean will break the bonds of nature and a majestic land will be revealed to men. And to them Tethys will reveal new worlds, and no longer will Thule be the farthest point of inhabited regions." Columbus cited this passage in his *Book of Prophecies,* and his son Fernando, in his annotation of *Medea* stated, "This prophecy was achieved by my father, the Admiral Christopher Columbus in 1492."

Plato, in his *Critias* and *Timaeus,* speaks at length of Atlantis in accounts accepted as historical by great minds like Aristotle and Theophrastus and their successors. He describes the defeat of the Atlantean empire by the Athenians, followed by a giant earthquake lasting a day and a half, which finally plunged the huge island into the sea. In the twentieth century, the great French hieroglyphist Fernand Crombette would be able to pinpoint the actual date of the disaster as April 1226 B.C. The resultant mud and shallows spawned the vast expanse of seaweed called the Sargasso Sea, which for centuries would block off the direct route to America across Atlantis, which till then had commonly carried constant traffic between the two hemispheres. Only in Columbus' day, as Seneca had predicted, did "the ocean break the bonds of nature" sufficiently to permit passage once more, an occurrence of which the Admiral was well aware.

In apostolic times, St. Clement, in his Letter to the Corinthians, refers to "the other world" as common knowledge, and even the great St. Paul tells the Colossians that they have received the same Gospel "as it is in the whole world" (Col. 1:6). Not conclusive evidence surely, but it is part and parcel of the references to those "worlds beyond the ocean" taken for granted in the writings of St. Hilary, St. Ambrose, St. Thomas Aquinas and his teacher St. Albert the Great, the Venerable Bede, St. Jerome, Tertullian, Macrobius, St. Isidore of Seville, Rabanus Maurus and many lesser ecclesiastical authorities, on down to seculars like Averroes, Dante, Roger Bacon and Sir John Mandeville. St. Augustine had held the same opinion as

7

probable. Everyone seemed to know that America was there. When it came to details, differences of opinion centered mainly on the probable existence and nature of its inhabitants. Like the space age's hypothetical extraterrestrials, "Antipodeans" were supposedly cut off from God's grace because they were descended from other stock than Adam and Eve. This was not seldom voiced, but the notion was roundly condemned as early as the eighth century by Pope Zacharias. Whoever lived there, America belonged to Christ the King along with the rest of the world.

Most remarkable among early references to America are those which tell of the discovery of Europe by Americans, who apparently still occasionally sailed eastward in Our Lord's time. Citing Cornelius Nepos, the historian Pliny averred that some of these arrived in Germany in ancient times. The first were said to have come by way of Atlantis, but after the catastrophe, according to Theopompus of Chios, others actually crossed the Atlantic Ocean to mount a military invasion, only to return in disgust after a good look at the primitive Europeans on the other side of the pond! Among successive waves of immigrants, some nevertheless elected to remain. The Basques of Spain, whose language is related to no other European tongue, have long been regarded as of Amerindian origin. In 1153 and 1189, Americans were greeted in Lubeck, and even as late as 1508, years after Columbus' discovery, boatloads were reported landing in Brittany, where, according to Cardinal Bembo, one of the men was taken to Rouen.

If Columbus was too learned to believe he was the first to discover America, he would also have suspected he was not the first Christian to set foot there. It is known that he inclined to a popular belief that America and not the Mediterranean was in fact the continent on whose soil the Garden of Eden originally stood. Given that the old Serpent had continued to rule America for centuries, there is no reason to assume that his rule was never at any time contested. There is persistent and venerable testimony that the great battle for Amerindia between the Woman and the Serpent actually began not many years after Our Lord's Ascension. According to some authorities and mystics, His parting prophecy to His disciples, "You shall be witnesses unto Me ... even to the uttermost part of the earth" (Acts 1:8) began taking place almost immediately.

8

The Hispanic historian Veytia, in fact, grounds his *Historia General* on the premise that Christianity was introduced into America only twelve years later, when the whole world was apportioned among the Apostles for evangelization. He had good authority behind him, for St. John Chrysostom, Theophylactus and Pope St. Gregory were among those holding that the Gospel had indeed been preached miraculously to the whole world before the destruction of Jerusalem. The immediate sense of Our Lord's prophecy, "This gospel of the kingdom shall be preached in the whole world for a testimony to all nations, and then shall the consummation come" (Matt. 24:14), certainly supports this view, if the destruction of Jerusalem is regarded as a first consummation, prefiguring the final one to come.

It was once common opinion that the Apostle St. Thomas had evangelized America, as well as the Indies. Writing to Columbus from Burgos on August 5, 1495, Jaime Ferrer de Blanes says, "Divine and infallible Providence sent the great Apostle St. Thomas from the West to the East to promulgate in the Indies the holy Christian law; and you, Senor, He dispatched by the opposite way from the East to the West, so that according to the divine will, you have reached the uttermost parts of upper India for the purpose of letting the descendants hear what the ancestors have neglected of the preaching of Thomas in order that the word may be fulfilled, 'Their sound hath gone forth into all the earth' (Rom. 10:18)." The Protestant historian Prescott relates that Piedra Hita, chronicler of the Muyscas, was satisfied that St. Bartholomew had paid a visit to Peru, and it is likely that these two Apostles had divided America between them. Many tales accumulated among the Amerindians concerning a *santo* whose doctrines, relayed to them by their ancestors, were immediately recognized in the preaching of the post-Columban missionaries.

Not to be disregarded is the testimony of that extraordinary seventeenth-century mystical Apostle of America, Venerable Maria de Agreda. In Part III of the masterpiece dictated to her by Our Lady, *La Mistica Ciudad de Dios,* Book VII, Chapter 13, she gives an account of how St. Peter, acting on Our Lady's advice, partitioned the world among the Twelve Apostles. India is clearly allocated to St. Thomas, and India Citerior to St. Bartholomew. "But according to what I was given to understand, the Apostles not only preached in the provinces

9

which St. Peter allocated to them at the time, but in many others adjoining them as well, and more remote. And it is not hard to understand this, because many times they were taken up from some parts to others by the ministry of angels, and this happened not only to preach, but also to consult with one another, especially with the Vicar of Christ, St. Peter, and more so to be brought into the presence of the Blessed Mary, whose favor and counsel they needed in the difficult undertaking of planting the Faith in kingdoms so varied and in nations so barbarous.

"And if, to give Daniel something to eat, the angel lifted the prophet Habakuk from Babylon, it is no wonder that this miracle took place with the Apostles, flown wherever it was necessary to preach Christ and give evidence of the Divinity and plant the universal Church for the healing of all mankind." She also finds a precedent in the New Testament, where we are told "how the angel of the Lord, who picked up Philip, one of the seventy-two disciples, set him down in Azotus from the road to Gaza as recounted by St. Luke (Acts 8:40). And all these marvels, besides countless others we know nothing about, were appropriate for sending a few poor men to so many kingdoms, provinces and nations possessed by the devil, filled with idolatry, errors and abominations, as was the whole world when the Incarnate Word came to redeem it."

Venerable Maria's revelations are certainly not articles of faith, but traditionally she is the miraculous catechizer of the Indians of New Spain. If we accept her testimony, delivered under pressure of religious obedience to a Spanish inquisitorial commission, she herself was also flown many times by angelic ministry from her cloister into what is now the U.S. Southwest to prepare the natives for the coming of missionaries who would baptize them. In her hometown of Agreda, she was able to describe perfectly the topography of the new territory, as well as the individual characteristics of the Franciscans laboring there. When questioned in their turn, her charges on the other side of the Atlantic could not only describe their teacher equally well, but produced rosaries which she had brought them from Agreda and taught them how to say. Her apostolate multiplied the miraculous conversions which had begun taking place in Mexico a century before through the agency of the image of Our Lady of Guadalupe, when Indians came to the Faith by the millions. It is therefore not hard to believe that even greater marvels occurred during Apostolic times.

Archaeologists may evaluate Maria de Agreda's testimony as they will, but Las Casas, the great Councilman of the Indies who sailed with Columbus, wrote of convincing vestiges of St. Thomas' presence found in Portuguese Brazil which form part of a larger body of evidence which cannot be ignored, however it is assessed. Very ancient traces of Christianity which cannot be imputed to the legacy of Babel have been found all over the Americas. Many crosses, like the Square Cross in Paraguay and the one in the Temple of the Cross at Palenque in southern Mexico, have been found in the Bahamas, Yucatan and Peru. Amerindian religious celebrations displayed rites strongly reminiscent of Baptism and the Holy Eucharist, along with fasts and other penitential practices and the use of a "holy" water. Auricular confession to confessors bound to secrecy was not unknown, nor were consecrations of kings, exorcisms, processions, pilgrimages and the blessing of new houses. Celibate priesthoods and convents of nuns existed in Mexico, Central America and Peru.

The devil ever aping God's Church? Perhaps. But an unexplainable "something" had retarded the decay of civilization among certain Amerindians like the Aztecs and Incas, who, for all their abominations, never came close to sinking into outright savagery. According to Veytia, America had been evangelized a second time in the ordinary course of events in the fifth or sixth century. One of the most widespread and persistent legends concerns the hero-god Quetzalcoatl, as he was called by the Aztecs. The Toltecs called him Tolpitzin, the Zapotecs, Wixipecocha. In Yucatan he was KuKulkan, in New Granada Bochica and in Peru Viracocha, but everywhere the descriptions are similar. Spanish historians from Las Casas and Sahagun on down collected tales from all quarters which agreed in their main lines: the god was large of stature and fair-skinned, with black hair and a full, round beard, wearing a long flowing robe and occasionally a miter. He leaned on a sort of crozier or cross. He and his companions, who vary in number from fourteen to twenty, practiced celibacy and were given to penance and abstemiousness. They taught a law of love, leaving among the people monastic institutions of some kind, with the three religious vows.

11

Obviously a foreigner, Quetzalcoatl came to reform the existing religion in America's central regions at a time conjectured to be anywhere from the ninth to the twelfth century, but according to some his ministry took place rather in the sixth. Eventually he departed, but the people never ceased expecting his return. Who was he? It is conceivable that he may actually be known to us under the name of some canonized saint, but whoever he was, he must have been largely responsible for arresting or at least delaying the fall of the southwestern tribes, whose culture remained the highest in America. After his departure, his missionary work and personality gradually merged in the minds of the people into the original Quetzalcoatl, the "plumed Serpent" who figured in their pantheon of gods as their Lucifer or Morning Star. Much like the holy St. Nicholas, Bishop of Myra, who was gradually transformed into the clownish "spirit of Christmas" called Santa Claus, the unknown apostle of Meso-America supplied one more mask for the devil.

Contrary to popular belief, however, serpent worship as such had never been official in Mexico. Although representations of him abounded, no altar was actually raised to him, and in order to spawn the cruelty, immorality and misery which gradually made its way into Amerindian society, he had to act through the established "gods." If the interventions of Our Lady of Guadalupe and Venerable Maria de Agreda were not sufficient proof of the divine predilection for Mexico, it could certainly be found in the miraculous way in which the great Aztec hegemony was gladly and willingly handed over to a handful of conquistadores, without so much as a single shot being fired. For the grateful Montezuma II, Quetzalcoatl had returned at last.

Subjugated by Cortes and reigning supreme for the first time over his neighbors, he had assembled his entire court to remind them solemnly of a prophecy his sister Princess Papantzin had received ten years previously when she had been revived after burial. "It was shown to her in vision and foretold by a messenger who was sent to her from another sphere," runs the account in *The Virgin and the Serpent God* by Helen Behrens, "that white men would come from the other side of the great water. These men are now here, and it is our duty to adhere to the divine will, acknowledging as our sovereign the King of Spain. I hope you will grant me the favor I am about to ask of you, which is to obey the King of Spain in the future as the legitimate sovereign of all. To him you will pay the tribute you have paid to me since I became your ruler. I too will pay him, because I have the obligation to do so, since I too am his vassal."

Montezuma is said to have spoken with tears in his eyes. He would have capitulated in no other way than in a firm belief that the Spaniards would lead his people to the true God. It was generally assumed that Cortes had come because he too knew the prophecy. Not that Papantzin's prophecy was the first angelic communication in this regard. There had been one to King Nezahualcoytl of the kingdom of Texcoco in 1464, related by the native historian Fernando de Alva Ixtlixochitl. This monarch was the author of sixty poems of praise to commemorate a mystical experience of love for the Creator of all things, with which he had been favored after a forty-day fast. He died saying, "How deeply I regret that I am not able to understand the will of this great God, but I believe that the time will come when He will be known and adored by all the inhabitants of this land."

That blessed day is yet to come. So far the white man knows but a fraction of the true history of America, whose evangelization was to begin so many times, and must begin once more in earnest, if Christ the King is to rule over her with full royal honors.

PART ONE

Four Crowns

Chapter I

THE CROWN of SPAIN

The American Revolution did not begin in thirteen British colonies in 1776. By that time it had been in progress for some three hundred years. The American Revolution began in Hispaniola, Christopher Columbus' first permanent colony on Santo Domingo, in other words, as soon as the Faith had taken root in the New World. Neither then nor later did the trouble start with the natives, who greeted the newcomers with flowers, fruit and fervent hospitality, soon joining them in the strains of the Salve Regina. Columbus wrote to the Spanish monarchs Ferdinand and Isabella, "They are the best people in the world, and I have great hope in Our Lord that Your Highnesses will make them all Christians."

The trouble began with revolutionaries imported from the very bowels of Christendom, already at work among Columbus' own men and losing no time in infecting the Amerindians with their disease. Brought here from Europe was the old power struggle between Christ the King and the Architect of the Universe, which began in heaven and continues to this day. In other words, the Great Apostasy which began with the Renaissance simply passed into its American phase, for when the Faith arrived in the New World, it was inevitably accompanied by the powers of darkness which always move in its shadow. Drawn into the conflict, the natives were destined to play a role far more important than appears on the surface. During Columbus' first return to Spain, a revolt was mounted against his deputy Diego de Arana by his own subordinates, with the help of subverted Indians, which led to the massacre of the entire Spanish garrison. A more serious revolt occurred five years later, the pattern tending to repeat itself as the Conquest progressed.

As soon as Columbus returned with his great news, the Church was faced with a theological difficulty, for the biblical account of the re-population of the world by Noah's three sons after the Flood made no mention of another whole continent of human beings. Some churchmen doubted that Amerindians had souls. The problem simmered until Pope Julius II, who called the Fifth Lateran Council, officially declared them sons of Adam and Eve, at the same time implying that they were descended from the reprobate Babylonians, who had existed apart from Noah and his family and had been ignored by the sacred texts. This hypothesis is now being startlingly confirmed by recent archaeological finds, for it is now generally conceded that what Columbus accomplished was in fact the rediscovery of the ancient Amerindia dating from the days of Babel. Because he made possible its incorporation into Christ's Mystical Body, those who were promoting his canonization under Pius IX wished to accord him the title of Apostle of America in the temporal order.

Leaving Constantinople after its fall in 1453, he would have been conversant with the teachings of Ptolemy, fully aware of the lands that lay beyond the remains of the old sunken Atlantis known to Plato and the hermetic sages. The West had lost this knowledge. Evidence is now turning up all over the Americas that the Indians had their origins in Phoenician, Libyan, Spanish, Celtic, Egyptian and other peoples, who were present on the continents centuries before the Christian era. How else explain the pyramids in Mexico, the burial mounds in West Virginia, the dolmens in New England, the gigantic "landing fields" in South America, not to mention the numerous idols and phalli connected with the worship of Baal and Astarte found in Vermont and New Hampshire? How explain the inscriptions in modified ogams and Egyptian hieroglyphics, of whose source the Indians themselves are ignorant?

15

We have God's word for it that there is nothing new under the sun (Eccles. 1:10), and these artifacts, scattered in mysterious profusion throughout the world, are now being recognized as vestiges of an ancient master culture which once prevailed over the whole earth. In this light, the God-excluding world government engulfing us in modern times takes on more and more the aspect of a horrendous dejà vu of the Kingship of Satan, which began with Cain, came to power at Babel before being scattered throughout the earth, and is now anticipating a resurgence under the Antichrist. Essential to its success is the myth of evolution, devised to keep men ignorant of their true history by persuading them that they were only lately groping hominids, who are now on their way to omnipotent control of the universe. It would never do for them to suspect that their brave new City of Man is simply one more rehash of the devil's community planning.

Plastic society began at Babel, where men exhibited a preference for building materials of their own concoction, rather than from God's natural substances: "And they had bricks instead of stones, and slime instead of mortar." God, looking on and seeing them "one people and all have one tongue," predicted, "They have begun to do this, neither will they leave off from their designs till they accomplish them in deed" (Gen. 11:3-6). And so they continue to this day, the modern alchemists and magicians now using simultaneous-translation devices to overcome the regrettable confusion of tongues which God mercifully visited on them to slow their efforts to build a City without Him.

But the truth will out. Sociologists bowing to the evidence are beginning to voice the suspicion that so-called "underdeveloped" peoples languishing in the lower stages of evolution have actually degenerated from higher cultures. This can actually be seen happening where residual Christians systematically deprived of truth gradually lose connection with their past. This takes place to varying degrees, but the trend is always downward. Far from starting out as "primitives," Adam and Eve conversed familiarly with God and were endowed with a wealth of intellectual gifts and physical aptitudes which are now unhappily lost to their descendants. We become "primitive" to the degree that the force of the original sin they bequeathed us remains unopposed in individuals and society, with all the disastrous spiritual and bodily effects multiplying only too easily in a descending culture.

Such must have been the state of the "savages" who joyfully welcomed Columbus, although they had in no way reached the depravity possible only to corrupted Christians. Their downward acceleration had been miraculously arrested by the Flood, and now, by Baptism into the Incarnation of the Son of God, they would be privileged to partake of the rejuvenated life of Christendom. Only by acceptance of the Incarnation and all it brings in its wake can human degeneracy be reversed. Redemption, begun in this life and brought to fruition in the next, is what the Catholic rediscoverers had to offer. America, the land of the Serpent, was on the way to becoming Amerindia, a land given back to its people. This is what the Serpent had to prevent at all costs.

+

If Amerindia was in fact the half of the globe over which he had until then held undisputed sway, exacting the bloodiest homage from his hapless subjects, then he had cause for alarm, for events completely beyond the order of nature began transpiring in Mexico a mere 39 years after the arrival of the Catholic Columbus. Already ten years before, when Montezuma, in fulfillment of a native prophecy, had voluntarily handed over his Aztec empire to the Conquistador Hernando Cortes, it was becoming clear to the devil that this ancient nation at the exact geographical center of the New World's two great continents was destined to be the theater of a major onslaught against his rule. If modern etymologists are correct in contending that America is actually an Amerindian word meaning "land of the Serpent," it would seem that the Woman whom God had set in opposition to him in Paradise was taking the offensive by challenging him on his very own ground.

Appearing without warning in 1531 on Tepeyac Hill near Mexico City, in the missionary bishopric of the saintly Fray Juan Zumarraga, she accosted an aging Aztec named Singing Eagle during the octave of what would become the Feast of the Immaculate Conception. Addressing him by his baptismal name of Juan Diego, she told him in his native tongue, "Dear little son, I love you. I want you to know who I am." And she told him she was "the Ever-Virgin Mary, Mother of the true God

17

Who gives life and keeps it in existence. He created all things. He is in all places. He is Lord of heaven and earth. I desire a church at this place, where I will show my compassion to your people and to all people who sincerely ask my help in their work and in their sorrows. Here I will see their tears; I will console them and they will be at ease. So run now to Tenochtitlan and tell the Lord Bishop all that you have seen and heard." As pledges for the Bishop, she produced not only Castilian roses in the dead of winter, but a miraculous picture of herself on Juan's rough tilma, which survives to this day as a fount of miracles and has become Mexico's national icon. Tepeyac happened to be the site of an ancient shrine to Teotenantzin, the Aztec "Mother of God." Why Our Lady chose that particular spot for the first of her flood of appearances in modern times must remain her secret until the full import of her intervention in the New World is grasped. After her visit, eight million Indians were converted to the Faith almost overnight, but it would be foolish to believe that this was for their benefit alone, for she had appeared vested as the Woman of the Apocalypse, whom St. John beheld "clothed with the sun and the moon under her feet ... and being with child," at the very time he "heard a loud voice in heaven saying: Now is come salvation and strength and the kingdom of God and the power of his Christ: because the accuser of our brethren is cast forth, ... the old Serpent who is called the devil and Satan, who seduceth the whole world" (Apo. 12:1-2,10,9).

In other words, Our Lady had come to America to announce the Serpent's impending doom and Christ's universal reign. Appearing also to Juan Diego's uncle, Bernardino, she instructed him to address her as the Blessed Image, the Ever-Virgin, Holy Mary of "Guadalupe." No less than twenty popes have urged devotion to her under this title, and, in 1754, Benedict XIV proclaimed her Patroness of Mexico. He not only made her feast day on December 12 a holy day of obligation, but raised the shrine built at Tepeyac to the same rank as the Lateran Basilica in Rome. The image was crowned by Leo XIII, and in 1945, on the fiftieth anniversary of this event, Pius XII, in a worldwide broadcast, declared Our Lady of Guadalupe to be Empress of the Americas, although the U. S. Council of American Bishops would continue to solicit her patronage until the title of the Immaculate Conception.

As it turns out, however, Our Lady made no reference whatever to Guadalupe, the Marian shrine in Spain which Columbus visited before embarking on his great adventure. What sounded like "Guadalupe" to the Spaniards was "*te coatlaxopeuh*" to the natives, which meant "Crusher of the Serpent." In other words, three centuries before appearing to St. Catherine Labouré in the rue du Bac with her foot on the Serpent, Our Lady revealed herself to the Amerindians as the Woman whom God had told the devil in Eden would one day "crush your head, and you shall lie in wait for her heel" (Gen. 3:15). Furthermore, by telling the old Bernardino that she was "the All-Perfect and Perpetual Virgin Mary," she virtually proclaimed herself as the Immaculate Conception, three hundred years and more before the dogma was defined by Pius IX or confirmed by Mary herself at Lourdes.

At the outset, the Spanish and Portuguese monarchs were undisputed claimants to the new territories, which Pope Alexander VI confided to their trusteeship with apostolic aims in view, much as Pope Adrian IV had entrusted Ireland to the Catholic English king three centuries before. The French Huguenots, the English and the Dutch, with some Swedes and others who intruded later into American history, began as little more than filibusters with no legal standing under existing international law. Yet, as we know, these heretics, sworn enemies of Christ's Vicar, nonetheless succeeded in planting a small confederation on the eastern flank of North America, which became the powerful United States, a manmade nation founded without religious ties or principle, in whose Constitution neither Christ the King nor God the Father is mentioned.

Small wonder that the Serpent would actually figure on the flags of these colonizers who, knowingly or unknowingly, were enlisted in his infernal majesty's cause. One designed before the Revolution by Benjamin Franklin at the time of the Albany Congress featured a fractured snake above the words "JOIN or DIE." In 1775, appeared the famous Navy Jack, along with the banner of the Minutemen of Culpeper, Virginia, which were followed in 1776 by the Gadsden Flag. All three display the Serpent, coiled or stretched at length, proclaiming his defiance at the safest possible distance from Tepeyac on the opposite side of the continent, in the words, "DON'T TREAD on ME!"

For whom could such a message have been ultimately intended but the Mother of God, appointed his irreconcilable enemy in Eden? The Serpent did not figure in the national flag eventually adopted by the United States, which seems to have been inspired mostly by the red-and-white striped ensign of the old East India Company, but he doesn't have to. His real presence is projected effectively enough both at home and abroad in the serpentine dollar sign which denotes the nation's currency. He is found, it is true, on the Mexican flag, but there he writhes helplessly in the talons of his natural enemy, the eagle, who for all we know may represent the Singing Eagle who, baptized and sanctified, became St. Juan Diego. The Serpent may not be finally dispatched, but he is always under control from on high.

+

That so soon after the conquest Juan Diego was on his way to Mass when Our Lady accosted him, proves how seriously Hernando Cortes took his royal mandate to provide the natives access to the Faith. A soldier both fiery and decisive, he had in fact to be restrained from using force to this end by Fray Bartolomeo de Olmedo, the Mercedarian priest who had landed with him on Good Friday in 1519, and who reminded him that compulsion could not effect what only prayer, teaching and good example could do. True freedom of conscience was not the invention of Vatican II. Even before the miracle of Guadalupe, there had already been one million conversions like Juan Diego's in the ordinary course of evangelization.

Not only were the Spanish missionaries enlightened and zealous, but the natives were only too eager to be released from the worship of a blood-thirsty god who demanded thousands of human hearts torn out annually in his honor. The avalanche of conversions which took place as soon as the Indians heard about the Woman were nonetheless beyond natural explanation. Her request for a church at Tepeyac was received so enthusiastically that a simple chapel arose on the spot within thirteen days. Whatever passive resistance to the Gospel had remained on the part of the Indians vanished overnight on hearing that it was to one of them, and not to a Spaniard, that she had said, "It is altogether necessary that you yourself should undertake this entreaty and that through your own mediation and assistance my purpose should be accomplished."

Clearly, the new religion was to be their very own. The Woman spoke their tongue, and her portrait showed her dressed as one of them, even to the waistband which among the Aztecs denoted pregnancy. Not restricted to Mexico, the extraordinary spiritual transformation was soon experienced in all the Americas and in every sphere of Spanish influence. It was under the banner of Our Lady of Guadalupe that the young Don Juan of Austria, his expedition financed by Amerindian gold, won the decisive victory against the Turks at Lepanto in 1571. Under the new Marian inspiration, the sixteenth century thus found the might of Spain deployed on two fronts, one the counterpart of the other, for while the Aragonese repelled Islam in Europe, Castilians were bending their efforts to spreading the Faith in America.

At first, there was some confusion about methodology, because some of the missionaries could not see why the same procedures used for converting Turks would not serve for Christianizing Indians, but in the midst of the controversy a missiology was worked out which has never been surpassed for attachment to principle joined with hard-headed realism. In the ensuing three hundred years of Spanish colonial rule, social institutions were forged which are now reckoned among the most efficient and benevolent the world has ever seen. Magnificent vestiges of them are still evident in the legal and social systems throughout the Americas, even in the United States.

Whereas England tended to empty her jails and poorhouses into her colonies, thereby ridding herself of what she considered derelict elements of her home population, the Catholic powers sent their best, supporting them from home, not only materially, but spiritually, with the prayers of their convents and monasteries. Not a few of the colonists were saints. Not only were holy missionaries commissioned to teach the Faith, but these produced saints among the natives to perpetuate it. Bl. Kateri Tekakwitha ("The Lily of the Mohawks"), Bl. Juan Diego, St. Felipe de Jesus, and St. Martin de Porres, followed by many more, are outstanding proof of their zeal and God's blessing.

The English government had no interest in converting the natives, but evangelization was official policy on the part not only of Spain and Portugal, but of France, whose presence in the New World was legalized when their sovereign, Francis I, persuaded Pope Alexander's successor, Clement VII, to rule that the old papal mandate applied only to lands already discovered and not to those yet to be discovered by Catholic kings. France thus laid valid claim to the northern reaches, acquiring a particularly thorny part of the Church's vineyard in which to work. The Spanish nun Ven. Maria de Agreda, bilocating from her convent to catechize North America, had in fact been directed by Our Lord to concentrate her efforts on the Indians of the West, for these were open to conversion, whereas those on the eastern seaboard, the worst of whom may have been descended from survivors of the old Chamite empire of sunken Atlantis, would offer fierce resistance, having been persuaded by the devil that to become Catholic meant losing their identity.

It would have been extraordinary indeed if the history of Amerindia had not been to some extent shaped by the Amerindians themselves. At little risk of over-simplification, it can be said that without the help of the eastern Indians, the English could hardly have maintained their illegal toehold in the New World, and heresy would have enjoyed negligible indigenous support. As divine justice would have it, English domination spelled doom for the Indian once he had outlived his usefulness, for the lot of those who were not exterminated was the government reservation. The numbers who managed to disappear into the general population under anglicized names have yet to be tallied.

Had the Catholic powers been able to settle their differences at home and cooperate in excluding England from America, what is now the United States would presumably still be subject to His Most Apostolic Majesty the King of Spain. The one true Catholic Faith would be the religion upon which the government rests, and Spanish would be spoken without prejudice to Amerindian dialects, as is the case today in Latin America. As it is, the English experiment ended by toppling every Catholic throne in Christendom.

+

But we are getting ahead of our story. Against the brilliant record set by the Spanish conquest, the Serpent's only available weapon was calumny, but even this would not have served had the Spaniards not been such merciless critics of their own endeavors. Had they not informed on themselves in persistent reports to the Crown, clamoring for rectification of abuses, there would be no firsthand accounts of alleged mistreatment of the natives for biased chroniclers to draw on. That there were abuses is indisputable fact, the inevitable consequence of fallen human nature. Greed for gold often superseded zeal for souls, but the Catholic Spaniard had the grace to feel guilty about it. Even as he sinned, he confessed it and admonished his brothers.

Of all the Indians' many champions among the clergy, none was more vociferous or indefatigable than Fray Bartolomé de las Casas, "Father of the Indians." His representations to the King and to his superiors, written with a view to shocking them into prompt action, are judged by historians today as impassioned overstatements only partially borne out by the facts. Even Voltaire pronounced them "exaggerated." As it was, Las Casas' *Brevissima Relacion de la Destruccion de las Indias*, published in 1540, caused the sensation he intended in Spain. It produced immediate results, but unfortunately, long after the abuses were corrected, it continued to supply the major documentation for the vicious "Black Legend" of Spanish cruelty, which has been used so effectively to discredit the Catholic monarchies. It persists to this day wherever English is spoken, not only in song and story, but as gospel truth in textbooks and soap operas.

Carefully overlooked is the glaring fact that such mordant criticism was actually encouraged by Catholic authority with a view to checking its own excesses. Beyond mere self-criticism, it was a dutiful Catholic examination of conscience. Without royal permission, Las Casas' book or others like it would never have seen the light of day. As Fr. Philippe André-Vincent, O.P., points out in *Las Casas, Apôtre des Indiens*, such freedom of expression could have sprung only from an exceptionally vigorous Christianity, from "authority uncontested in its principle." Nothing remotely approaching it was permitted by the Protestant governments of the day, whose authority rested on despotism, and whose own injustices, rooted in Calvinist pessimism, led not to mere exploitation of the Indian, but to outright extermination wherever feasible.

No instance in Spanish colonial history can rival the outrages perpetrated first by the British and then by the United

23

States in the name of public policy. The Indian side of USan history was hardly a subject for argument, for there was no moral authority to appeal to for redress under a Constitution where Church and state were rigorously separated. What defense has morality against political expediency in such a commonwealth? In a Catholic monarchy, on the other hand, far from drawing the royal ire, Las Casas not only remained in good standing in his religious order, but was retained to the last as a valuable counselor by both the Emperor Charles V and King Philip II.

Largely under his influence and that of another Dominican, the theologian Francisco de Vitoria, all use of force was excluded in spreading the Gospel, and as much as possible in purely secular areas. They maintained that the colonization of the New World was not a matter of conquest but of penetration, which could be justified only by the right of communication existing between all human beings by nature. Contrary to Vitoria and most theologians of his day, Las Casas went so far as to deny even the possibility of a just war against the Indian, even to protect Spanish lives and property. Spain's was an apostolic monarchy!

He liked to quote Queen Isabella's Testament of 1504, wherein she declared that her "principal intention" in accepting governance in the New World was "to try to draw these peoples and convert them to our Holy Catholic Faith, and to send to the said islands and lands prelates, religious, clerics and other learned persons to instruct the inhabitants in the Catholic Faith, to teach and endow them with good morals and to apply all due diligence therein." She begs the King, her daughter and her son-in-law to see to it that after her death the Indians are in no way harmed, but "well and justly treated, and that should they suffer harm, they remedy it; so that in no wise what is urged upon us and commanded in the said concession be departed from."

The "said concession" referred to by the Queen was of course the famous Bull of Demarcation *Inter caetera,* whereby Alexander VI entrusted the larger part of the New World to the kings of Spain: "We of our own motion, and by the fullness of Our Apostolic powers, do give, grant and assign to you, your heirs and successors ... all the firm lands and islands found or to be found, discovered or to be discovered towards the West and South, drawing a line from the Pole Arctic to the Pole Antarctic, that is, from the North to the South." Lands east of this line, running a hundred leagues beyond the Azores, were assigned to Portugal. According to Fr. André-Vincent, the Bull is subject to different interpretations: "[Was it] an Act of arbitration or a simple consecration of an agreement between two partners in a conquest of zones of influence? The Pontifical Act may be read as a concession of the right of eminent domain over lands in the process of integration into world Christianity, or as a simple recognition and outlining of the responsibilities of the great naval powers of Christendom in spreading the Gospel."

Whatever the interpretation, the primary objective remains unmistakably missionary. This was the context in which Las Casas viewed it, for, in his crucial Tratado *Comprobatorio*, he emphasizes that the Pope was constituted by Christ "Lord of the world, wielding universal and sovereign power, enabling him to resist kings, sanctify princes, command all kingdoms and guide the whole world by bringing it the moral law and the rules of the Faith.... Thus the Apostolic See had the power to delegate the kings of Castile yonder, and to choose them to be foundations of the churches which would be established there in view of magnifying the Holy Name, to be apostles and preachers, heads, pastors and, in a way, prelates and curates. In a word, to be the architects of everything both spiritual and temporal."

In the sixteenth century, slavery was still recognized as part of the common law of non-Christian peoples, for which no apology was required or expected. Apart from the abuses it so frequently gives rise to, slavery as an institution had been sanctioned by God when Noah, as second head of the human race after Adam, declared Cham's impious eldest son Chanaan "a servant of servants ... unto his brethren" (Gen. 9:25). The patriarchs were all slave owners, and that the Mosaic law countenanced the practice is proved by the numerous prescriptions regulating the conduct of both masters and slaves. Under the new law of grace, St. Paul, like St. Peter and Our Lord Himself, neither condoned nor condemned the system, but simply recognized it as one of the many regrettable social legacies bequeathed by fallen nature.

He exhorted slaves to "obey in all things your masters according to the flesh ... in simplicity of heart, fearing God," (Col. 3:22) ... "doing the will of God from the heart" (Eph. 6:6), at the same time instructing masters to do to their slaves "that which is just and equal: knowing that you also have a Master in heaven" (Col. 4:1). Having converted the runaway slave Onesimus, St. Paul sent him back to his master Philemon, to whom he writes, "Do thou receive him as thy own bowels," who "departed for a season from thee that thou mightest receive him forever: Not now as a servant, but instead of a servant, a most dear brother ... both in the flesh and in the Lord" (Phil. 12, 15-16).

Emancipation proclamations cannot abolish slavery, which, for all its being dictated by economic necessity, flourishes today in sophisticated forms no less cruel than those of the past. To be sure, slave owners often abused their authority, but so do parents. The classical definition of slavery was the obligation to work for another for life without free consent, and this definition still holds. There was no question of "owning" a person body and soul, as the American Abolitionists contended, but only of owning his labor. Prisoners taken in war could be enslaved, or criminals reduced to it as a form of punishment. The Church has never declared slavery intrinsically evil. In point of fact, many of her theologians even accepted Aristotle's notion that some peoples are slaves by nature.

This makes all the more remarkable Isabella's refusal to permit enslavement of the Indians. When Columbus sent a shipment of them to Spain in 1492, she called a meeting of canon lawyers to discuss the morality of selling them, from which resulted the royal Ordinance of July 6, 1500, forbidding enslavement of an Indian on pain of death. No Protestant colonizers, notably the English, ever followed her lead. In 1537, six years after the apparition at Tepeyac, Pope Paul III settled once and for all the debate over whether or not Indians had souls, by affirming, in the Bull *Sublimis Deus*, "man by his very nature is capable of receiving faith in Christ, and all who participate in human nature have the aptitude to receive this same faith." Depriving them of goods or liberty was strictly forbidden, and a second Bull laid an excommunication reserved to the Holy See upon any persons enslaving Indians.

+

Spain's Council of the Indies enforced the Papal Bulls as much as lay in its power, but this was not easy, for it was not Spain which had brought slavery to the New World, where it

26

had been an integral part of the culture for centuries and was not quickly eradicated. Building on recommendations handed down by both spiritual and temporal authorities, however, a serious study of Indian psychology and sociology was undertaken, which soon transformed Spanish colonial policy. Initially regarding the Indian as a peculiar type of European peasant, the Spaniards had first tried to place him in tutelage under an *encomienda* (commission) system, patterned roughly on the old familiar serfdom of feudal times; but by 1542, a series of radical new laws was passed which granted full political status to the native institutions by infederating them directly to the Crown without benefit of any intermediate framework. The Hapsburg kings of Spain never regarded Mexico as a colony, or as in any way inferior to the mother country. She was an organic part of the monarchy, her provinces figuring as *reinos* on a par with Aragon and Castile. No other colonial power in the world has ever matched this ideal.

When Las Casas became Bishop of Chiapas, he would not allow his fellow countrymen to appropriate the Indians' lands or property unless these were sold or otherwise freely relinquished to them, instructing his clergy to refuse the Sacraments to anyone found infringing the natives' rights. His father had sailed with Columbus on his second voyage, and he prided himself on having been the first priest ordained in the New World. Holding that the Conquistadores who had taken up arms against the native monarchs of Mexico and Peru had been guilty of serious crimes of *lèse majesté*, he labored on both sides of the Atlantic to repair the havoc he felt they had caused. Even so, the abuses he excoriated were a far cry from the massive injustices perpetrated later in the United States, and it is generally acknowledged that he was guilty of many exaggerations. There is nothing in Spanish history to compare with the "Trail of Tears" inflicted by the U.S. on the Cherokee Nation, whose sovereignty had been guaranteed by a formal treaty and confirmed by a Supreme Court decision.

Las Casas even went so far as to maintain that the Spaniards had no right to interfere forcibly with the human sacrifices offered by pagan Amerindians, detecting in these, as would Joseph de Maistre two hundred years later, a perverted but profound religious instinct which did not flinch from surrendering to their deities what they deemed most precious! The sole remedy, he insisted, was conversion. The Second

27

Vatican Council liberation theologians claimed Las Casas as an early champion of the Rights of Man and freedom of conscience, but nothing could be farther from the truth. For him, Indians in the abstract did not exist, but only the Indian with natural rights to be protected. For him, the Rights of Man were nothing other than the natural law which must be respected as part of the rights of God. Neither cruel nor sentimental, Spanish law regarded the Indian as a man to be governed with a view to his eternal salvation, steering a realistic course midway between adulating him as Rousseau's "noble savage" and despising him as the British frontiersman's "dirty dog." The law was not always obeyed, but it is of record.

Las Casas learned by experience the folly of relying on social planning to impart the Faith, for having once headed an *encomienda* himself, he had been forced to acknowledge that preoccupation with his charges' temporal needs led him to neglect their souls. In his official capacity as Procurator, he tirelessly upheld the primacy of the spiritual, with no scruples about reminding the King that the acquisition of wealth was the last purpose of colonization. He is a standing reproach to the Marxist missiology, which, in the name of human rights, deems it inadvisable to preach Christ to pagans before investing them with the benefits of modern technology—or to preach Christ at all. Unconcerned with any *populorum progressio*, he assumed that where the Faith really takes root, "all these things shall be added unto you" (Matt. 6:33) as a matter of course.

Despite his deep respect for the complex psychology of the Indians, so delicately equilibrated to their unusual environment, Las Casas never fell into situation ethics or into modifying the Gospel message to suit their natural proclivities. Like St. Thomas, he regarded them as the Mystical Body of Christ in potentia, awaiting the fullness of truth and fully entitled to all of it. In the prologue to his *Historia de las Indias*, he writes, "As there is one faith in Christ, as the law of the Gospel and the Christian religion are unchangeable, as there is one doctrine of faith revealed by Christ, promulgated by the Apostles, received and preached by the universal Church, as there is one rational human species spread throughout the world, so therefore has divine wisdom established one way of spreading this same law of the Gospel and faith in Christ; and at no time should it be changed or modified."

Thus, three hundred years before the Second Vatican Council, he set himself in radical opposition to its dictum that "accommodated preaching of the revealed Word ought to remain the law of all evangelization." No doubt he would have had special difficulty in seeing why, to accomplish her task of saving souls, the Church "must rely on those who live in the world, are versed in different institutions and specialties and grasp their innermost significance in the eyes of both believers and unbelievers." (Gaudium et Spes, 44) Throughout his long life, he had had ample occasion to witness the disaster caused by pursuing supernatural objectives in collaboration with the children of this world, always so much wiser in their generation. When have the Church and the world ever had common goals?

When Paul VI, the first occupant of St. Peter's throne to set the Petrine foot on the Serpent's old preserve, addressed the United Nations in New York City, he told that august assembly, "We must get used to thinking of man in a new way." Not many years later, John Paul II, the second Pope to visit the New World, would tell Catholics assembled in the Church of the Assumption in Mexico City, "You cannot be faithful and attached to secondary things, valid in the past but already outdated." They must be faithful, said His Holiness, "to the Church of today." Exactly wherein the Church of today differs from the Church founded by Jesus Christ "yesterday and today and the same forever" (Heb. 13:8) remains unclear, but fairly clear is the fact that the Church of today furthers the Serpent's evangelization throughout "developing" countries by collaborating with the world.

It helps to remember that, with the support of his King, Las Casas won the right of religious to penetrate into new territory ahead of the military, and even to preclude its help if necessary. In the interior of Guatemala, he and his clerics won the hostile "Land of War" to Christ, without recourse either to "those who live in the world" or soldiery of any kind. Not that he scorned temporal help, or the use of force on principle. He did not deem unjust the war going on at the time against the Turks in Europe, but the Turk was an aggressor, whereas the Indian was not. Nor, in his wildest accusations of secular interests, did he remotely suggest any separation of Church and state, beyond insisting that each serve God in its proper sphere. In the purest Thomist tradition, for him the temporal existed to serve the spiritual, and his writings imply that any European whose presence in the New World was not ordered ultimately to its evangelization had no business there at all! That this was Queen Isabella's conviction is incontestable, and it was probably warmly shared by Columbus.

Chapter II

THE CROWN OF MEXICO

Under the tutelage of Our Lady of Guadalupe, Spanish rule in America had been extraordinarily enlightened. In a day when the King was regarded as the Christian father of his subjects, his reign was unabashedly paternalistic, which meant that there was little or no government enterprise on the part of those whose only duty was to govern. Private initiative was allowed the fullest play compatible with royal permission. Cortes financed his own expedition, and it is well known that Columbus' first voyages were underwritten personally by Queen Isabella and others, who used no funds from public coffers. As long as settlers of all ranks recognized universal Catholic principles, the results were the happiest, in marked contrast to Protestant colonies, where hardly a pretense was made of bringing the blessings of civilization to the natives unless these were willing to submerge their identity.

Withal, as Bishop Francis Kelley writes in *Blood-Drenched Altars,* "The Conquerors never forgot that they were Spaniards and subjects of the King. What they could claim for him they always did claim .... Even the Church is second to the King in all things but one. And that became the actual position of the Church when the policy of encouraging private enterprise diminished and more government control was inaugurated." As long as "the absolute rule of the court of Spain was extended over all her American colonies, ... the Church went along with the rest. Concessions relative to the choice of bishops enjoyed by Spain herself were, by Papal decree, extended to her possessions in the New World.... What was Spanish became Spanish-American.... The royal patronage was all powerful.... This great power on the whole was for a long time well and wisely used. Good ecclesiastical appointments were made. Zeal for souls was encouraged and education favored. The royal authority felt its obligation for the spreading of the Faith. It stood firm against complaints that the Indians were being educated and thus made equal to the Spaniards."

Mexico profited vastly, as did all the Americas. A minimum wage law had been established at the very beginning by Cortes, with fixed hours for work, one morning hour being set aside for religious instruction and one afternoon hour for siesta, with no work on Sundays or holy days. The Indians were to a large extent self-governing, electing their own village authorities. Thomas Gage, an English traveler to Mexico in 1625, exclaims over the number of Indian Dons in the city of Chiapa, one of them the Governor, and rich. To an Englishman, the Spaniard's near total lack of racial prejudice was incomprehensible. In Gage's day, the land was already teeming with *mestizos*, Indians of mixed blood, for intermarriage had never been in any way discouraged.

Here again, this recognition of the equal rights of the natives before God was a far cry from the practice of the heretic nations, who with rare exceptions maintained a strong racist policy, until the Indians were driven out or otherwise decimated by disease, alcohol or firearms. In formerly Catholic territories, Indians are still recognizable quantities; whereas where the Calvinist ethic prevailed, they are scarcely to be distinguished outside reservations. In 1930, the Indians of the U.S. were estimated as 3% of the population, these for the most part in the once-Catholic southwest. In Mexico, the percentage of full-bloods was 20%. These statistics constitute an unanswerable retort to the tales of Hispano-Catholic "cruelty."

In *The Changing Indian,* Oliver La Farge, President of the Association of Indian Affairs, wrote in 1942, "There is more than paradox in the fact that the American Indian has become an alien in a country once in his possession. And more than irony in the fact that he is looked upon as a social problem where his ancestors reigned supreme." In 1696, a descendant of Montezuma became Viceroy of Mexico. "It will be a long time," remarked Bishop Kelley, "before a full-blooded descendant of Sitting Bull becomes President of the United States!" Or, as the Indians themselves say today, "If only Plymouth Rock had landed on the Pilgrims instead of the other way around!"

In *The Founding of New England,* James Truslow Adams summed up the Protestant attitude honestly enough when he stated that the whites there traded with the Indians, fought them, occasionally preached to them and then as far as possible exterminated them. The Dutch East India Company went further, officially declaring it "morally impossible to convert [Indian] adults to the Christian faith." That the "Christian faith" being offered them was not the true one may speak well for the Indians. In any case, the judgment was a far cry from the maxim coined by Champlain, the French Catholic Governor of Canada, where Indians were particularly hard to convert. He maintained, "The salvation of a single soul is worth more than the conquest of an empire."

+

Spain literally exhausted herself in the stupendous effort of colonizing and civilizing the New World. Joseph Schlarman, author of *Mexico, a Land of Volcanoes,* reported in 1950 that 14,000 Navajo children under USan rule were without schools. This was not the case when our South and West belonged to Spain and education was the exclusive responsibility of the Church. Before Jamestown and Quebec were founded, a school had been started by the Minims at St. Augustine, Florida. In this apostolate, there labored some of the Church's greatest religious lights. The Franciscan Venerable Antonio Margil, founder of a college at Zacatecas which furnished missionaries to Texas and California, was declared by Pope Gregory XVI in 1836 one of the foremost saints of the two Americas. High nobility like the Flemish Franciscan Pedro de Gante, a close relative of the Emperor, were among them. He founded a vocational school attended by 1,000 Indian boys.

St. Juan Diego's own good Bishop, Juan de Zumárraga, with the help of Mexico's first Viceroy Don Antonio de Mendoza, had imported a printing press by 1544, which immediately began producing catechisms and classics of all kinds, "because," as His Excellency explained, "so many people know how to read!" This was indeed so, for in every town boasting a church, there was a little school alongside where both boys and girls were taught. The New World's first press had probably arrived eighteen years earlier, and before the end of the century, seven printers were hard at work pouring out dictionaries, histories and textbooks on law, medicine, theology, philosophy and other subjects. The very first volume printed on the Continent is said to have been *La Doctrina Cristiana*, by Pedro de Cordoba, edited by the founder of America's first Dominican monastery, Domingo de Betanzos.

Books were badly needed, for a mere thirteen years after Cortes took Mexico City, Bishop Zumárraga had founded Santa Cruz College in Tlatelolco, the first institution of higher learning anywhere in the old land of the Serpent. "Among the faculty," writes Edward Gaylord Bourne in *Spain in America*, "were graduates of the University of Paris and such eminent scholars as Sahagun, the founder of American anthropology, and Juan de Torquemada, himself a product of Mexican education, whose *'Monarquia Indiana'* is a great storehouse of knowledge of Mexican antiquities and history. Many of the graduates of this college became *alcades* and governors of the Indian towns." Santa Cruz served as a model for many other universities, their capstone being that of Mexico City, founded in 1533 and now the largest in the world. This was 119 years before the founding of Harvard, whose modest curriculum, oriented almost exclusively to the production of Protestant divines and certainly not to educating Indians, offers a sad comparison.

According to Bourne: "In number, range of studies and standard of attainments by the officers," the Spanish institutions "surpassed anything existing in English America until the nineteenth century." It was not long before America was making return contributions to European culture with pioneer works like Toribio de Motolina's *Historia de los Indios de Nueva Espana*, Duran's *Historia* on the same subject, and what is probably the greatest work on Indian sociology ever written, the *Historia de las Cosas de Nueva Espana* by the aforementioned Bernardino de Sahagun. These firsthand sources, with those of Las Casas and the international lawyer Vitoria, are not even names to USan students today, immersed as they are in the "black legend" and other myths relayed to them in both public and parochial schools.

It is part of the legend that the old native Indian culture was obliterated by the Spaniards, but the truth is that without them, no trace of it would have survived. It is to enlightened churchmen like Sahagun that we are indebted for the preservation of priceless manuscripts and other lore. The saintly scholar Juan Gonzales worked on the translation of the great Nahuatl manuscript known as the *Codex Mendoza*. Acting as Zumárraga's interpreter with St. Juan Diego at the time of Our Lady's apparition, he received a vocation to the priesthood and spent the remainder of his life as a missionary researcher, beloved by all and dedicated to the declared policy of Church and Crown to educate the Indian, even as he converted him.

This objective was often thwarted by adventurers and entrepreneurs with other aims, but no official effort was ever made to hispanize the Indian. He proved an extraordinarily apt pupil, however, and what complaints there were came from the Spaniards. One Geronimo Lopez, incensed at the teaching of Latin to the Indian, charged he was speaking it "like another Cicero, and every day the number grows!" Allowing for a degree of hyperbole, this must have been true in many cases, for Indians actually went to Europe to teach in universities there. By 1803, when Alexander von Humboldt visited Mexico, he was amazed to find that "no city of the new continent, without even excepting those of the United States, can display such great and solid scientific establishments as the Capital of Mexico."

If many Mexican Indians are illiterate today, clearly "from the beginning it was not so" (Matt. 19:8). Space forbids dwelling on the countless hospitals, orphanages, law courts, mercantile establishments, industries, and other institutions which functioned under the gentle influence of Our Lady of Guadalupe, or on the admirable economic regulations designed to eliminate middlemen, speculators and usurers. The Church was simply at work civilizing the New World, as she had the Old, and in the process here and elsewhere, she produced saints. The first canonized native of America was a Mexican, San Felipe de Jesus de las Casas, a young Franciscan cleric in minor orders, who was crucified at Nagasaki in 1597. He was the first of the twenty-six protomartyrs of Japan to die, but not before foretelling the future destruction of the city, which took place on August 9, 1944, when the powerful USan Air Corps dropped their third atom bomb on its civilian population. Beatified only thirty years after his death, San Felipe was declared the Patron of Mexico and canonized in 1867.

+

The Serpent had to put a stop to this. The Church's authority weakened along with the deterioration of Spanish rule, and the same slow retrogression which was taking place in the Old Christendom inevitably followed suit in the New. Under cover of agitation for the Rights of Man, Mexico, the very heart of Amerindia, would also be swallowed up in the Great Apostasy masquerading as political revolution. Christ the King, first turned into a Democrat, would be gradually transformed into the revolutionary Christ the Worker.

On January 29, 1979, John Paul II, touring Oaxaca, would inform cheering crowds of Indian farmers that in view of their rights, "It is necessary to act quickly and with intensity. It is necessary to effect bold transformations which are profoundly innovative. It is necessary to initiate without delay urgent agricultural reforms.... And if the common good requires it, there must be no doubt about expropriation itself, carried out in the proper manner." His Holiness closed his speech with an expression which his predecessor, Paul VI, had used once before in the New World in his address to the United Nations: "So be it!" Or, as the USan Masons would say, "So mote it be!" How was this point reached? Obviously, the Serpent accomplished in Mexico what he had accomplished in Eden and elsewhere: By dint of setting the spiritual and the temporal in false opposition, he ended by obliterating their distinctions.

The very virtues and successes of the Church were used against her, for in her thirst for souls, it was relatively easy to bring her into conflict with the secular elements of a society whose primary objective was gold. Spain's colonials were certainly guilty of many abuses, which must not be minimized, but they have been sufficiently dwelt on by her enemies, as well as by herself. Here is the other side: The Serpent's readiest tool for driving a wedge between seculars and religious turned out to be the Papal Bull against slavery. Negro slavery never took deep root in New Spain, but Indian slavery had always been a native institution, intimately bound to Indian culture and worship. That the Spaniard tried to eradicate it at all can only be attributed to his Faith.

THE BATTLE FOR AMERINDIA

As Bishop Kelley points out: "Worldly wisdom would have told the Spaniard to make more slaves and exploit the rich resources for his profit as a conqueror. It would be necessary only to bring over more Europeans, educate and train them for the purpose intended, and leave the natives in their fear and ignorance, while allowing them to keep their blood-stained idols, with rebels against the rulers handed over for victims instead of their neighbors and their own children; all the while shutting official eyes to cannibalism.... If such a plan did not appeal to the pious folks at home, especially to Philip II, there was an alternative, later to be adopted by the English.... By every dictate of the god of selfishness and greed, Spain made a fool of herself in the New World."

When Spanish officialdom sided with the Church and put all its weight behind the Bull, it signed its own death warrant. Human nature being what it is, the secular elements who found themselves trammeled in their efforts to get rich quick were easily led to demand a government free of ecclesiastical encumbrances. In 1542, when the King reinforced the Bull with the "New Laws," there were indignant outcries from colonists who maintained that slavery was an economic necessity on which the Crown's revenue depended. The clergy refused absolution to slave owners; mine owners threatened to shut down the mines. The Viceroy told them, "The liberty of the Indians was more important than all the mines in the world, and that the revenues which the Crown might receive from them was not of such nature as to require the violation of laws both human and divine." The liberation of 150,000 slaves, not counting women and children, ended slavery for the Indians, but it put anti-clericalism squarely in the political saddle, for now the Church was blamed for anything that went wrong.

+

Revolt had long been in the air by the time it flared out openly. It was sparked, incongruously enough, by fidelity to Spain. Mexican patriots, indignant at Napoleon's invasion of the mother country, wished to sever relations with the French usurper's government in Madrid. Needless to say, the dormant forces of revolution are always quick to take advantage of such opportunities, and a leader was soon found in one Don Miguel Hidalgo, the worldly parish priest of the town of Dolores. Enjoying a long-standing reputation for greater concern for his

37

parishioners' material well-being than for their spiritual welfare, he would fit easily into today's Marxist-Christian ranks.

Abetted by a well-to-do, dissipated *mestizo* named Don Ignacio Allende, he convinced the Mexicans that the French dictator was also planning to take over Mexico, which they should rise up to keep intact for the lawful Spanish sovereign Ferdinand VII. Gathering a small army under the banner of Our Lady of Guadalupe, Hidalgo "shamefully mixed religion in what should have been a purely political campaign. In fact, he knowingly used religion to give an appearance of respectability to the outrages committed by his frenzied and irresponsible followers," relates Schlarman. The battle cry *"Viva la religión! Viva nuestra Madre Santissima de Guadalupe!"* became soon enough *"Viva la Virgen de Guadalupe y mueran los gachupines!"* (Long live the Virgin of Guadalupe and death to the *gachupines,* a pejorative nickname for Spaniards.) This called forth an appropriate counterrevolution, and eventually Fr. Hidalgo and his friends were court-martialed and shot, but today they are venerated as national heroes and fathers of their country.

The campaign which pitted the Mexican against the Spaniard ushered in the second phase of the Serpent's master plan, for until then Mexico had voiced no grievances against the Spanish government, but only against Napoleon. From now on, however, it would be the Spaniard who would be blamed for everything. Hidalgo was followed by two more rebel priests, Morelos and Matamoros, who headed a tedious succession of revolutionaries too numerous to mention, who would play incessantly on the prejudices of the multitude, leading them to believe the destruction of the Aztec empire by the Spanish lay at the root of all the Indians' woes. Spaniards reacted violently, with *mestizos* taking one side or the other, and the revolutionary pot was rapidly set to boiling.

An antique image which had belonged to one of Cortes' conquistadores, known as *Nuestra Senora de los Remedios,* was propagated as the patroness of the Spaniards, in opposition to Our Lady of Guadalupe, now represented as exclusively on the side of the Mexicans. For a time, the rival images were actually forced into confrontation, the first popularly referred to as *La Gachupina,* and the latter as *La Criolla,* the Creole. Thus racial hostility was injected into the devotion which had proved to be the very source of New Spain's political and religious unity. Anyone believing that this kind of crude propaganda has lost its effectiveness has only to mark the unwearying appeals demagogues still make to Our Lady of Guadalupe as advocate of a democracy of the people.

Or he may visit the impressive Museum of Anthropology in Mexico City, where the most revolting pagan artifacts are venerated as relics of the allegedly superior cultus obliterated by the ruthless Spaniard. It is not surprising that today the charming little *santos* once sold in every gift shop have now given way to grinning idols, and that dark rumors are heard of the resurgence of human sacrifice in the mountains of Oaxaca. Visitors with strong stomachs or a taste for the occult may choose to wander through the home once occupied by the artists Diego de Rivera and his wife Frieda Kahlo in a fashionable suburb of Mexico City. It has been turned into a national shrine, where photos of Marx and Lenin share the premises with giant *papier-mâché* demons and paintings of disembodied hearts by Frieda. The walls of the house are a brilliant blue, and a stone serpent lies coiled under the shrubbery in the patio. The flamboyant mosaics by Juan O'Gorman and others covering the exterior walls of the University of Mexico are also evidence of the "cultural" revival in progress, depicting as they do the Serpent's gradual recovery of Mexico, effected by the long arm of Freemasonry extended in friendship from the United States.

+

Upon Spain, as upon the other Catholic nations, the occult power of Masonry was loosed in full force after the debacle of the Jesuits in the eighteenth century. As Voltaire had predicted to his friend Dr. Helvetius, "Once we destroy the Jesuits, we'll have our way with the infamous thing," i.e., the Church. Once the Order was disbanded, Freemasonry entered the Spanish dominions by way of France and Napoleon's invasion, although even before that it had been progressing secretly despite the vigilance of the Inquisition. Clandestine lodges had been established in Mexico in the very teeth of Pope Clement's Bull *In eminenti,* which excommunicated all Freemasons. In 1789, the memorable year which witnessed the adoption of the U.S. Constitution and the outbreak of the French Revolution, there were French Masons in the retinue of the Viceroy Don Juan Pacheco y Padilla, who gathered at a watchmaker's shop on San Francisco Street in Mexico City. The Viceroy's chef Jean Laussel, later apprehended by the Inquisition, had in fact catered the first Masonic St. John's Day dinner ever celebrated in Latin America.

Brother Enrique Gomez, Grand Master of the York Grand Lodge of Mexico City, says in the January-February 1978 issue of *The Craftsman:* "Many of the founders of Freemasonry in Latin America were priests, bishops, even archbishops, and almost all the leaders of those independence movements were Freemasons and nominal Catholics. For example, Miguel Ramos Arizpe, a priest, was a prominent Scottish Rite Mason, who fought at the side of the Mexican Liberals during the War of Independence.... Some say that Fr. Miguel Hidalgo, the father of Mexican independence, was a Freemason, but we have no definite proof of this. We do know that many of the revolutionary leaders, as for example Ignacio Allende, were Freemasons, and in the history of Latin American Independence movements the names of our Masonic brethren are among the most prominent....

"Coming closer to our time, we find the leaders of the Reform movement in Mexico, Benito Juarez, Ignacio Ramirez, Porfirio Diaz and most of their supporters all Freemasons. All finally proved both Popes, Clement XII and Benedict XIV, completely justified in their attitudes towards the fraternity, because the Reform in Mexico and the reform in other countries did strip the Church of its temporal power and a good deal of its wealth.... It may surprise you to learn that today in Mexico no church or religious organization is permitted to own any property whatsoever. Every church, Catholic or Protestant, every synagogue, every convent in Mexico is the property of the Mexican government, which in turn allows the congregations to use the property for their religious practices."

Before this happened there had of course been repeated attempts on the part of the conservative elements to set things straight in Mexico, and, ironically enough, the movement which was to win independence from Spain turned out to be one of them. It began as a horrified reaction to the turn events were taking in the mother country, where on New Year's Day 1820, Col. Rafael Riego marched on Madrid and compelled the weak Ferdinand VII to swear allegiance to the anti-ecclesiastical Constitution of Cadiz voted by the Cortes. "Masonic clubs and secret societies plotted his overthrow. The army itself was shot through with Masonic doctrines.... Liberals and Masons came out of their holes and flocked to Riego's banner," writes Lesley Byrd Simpson in *Many Mexicos*. "Juntas patrioticas" were organized by Masonry in cafés. At the same time, according to the historian Mora, the Scottish lodges had entered Mexico in 1813 for the express purpose of introducing there also the Constitution of Cadiz.

The final impetus came from no other person than the last Spanish Viceroy Don Juan O'Donojú, a name which no American could fail to recognize as the Hispanic form of the well-known Irish moniker O'Donoghue. A creature of the new Cortes, he was generally believed to be a Mason. His first act on arrival was a proclamation to the people inviting them to choose a ruler of their own if they were in any way dissatisfied with his administration! "The persons that accompanied him," writes Bishop Kelley, "joined the existing lodges and formed new ones, all under the Scottish Rite." It was their purpose "to propagate the liberal principles established in Spain, and among these, the fundamental point, to exclude the clergy from all participation in the education of the young.... Thereupon, the Freemasons became a powerful influence, which we will see in action in all the succeeding events."

+

Mexican liberals who longed for independence and conservatives who wished to remain free of the anti-clerical measures being put through in Spain had already joined forces under the leadership of Agustin de Iturbide, a handsome, cultured, high-principled army officer, who had categorically refused to join Hidalgo's revolt. A former seminarian, son of a Basque father and a Mexican mother, he sponsored the "Plan of Iguala," which proclaimed equal treatment for Creoles and *gachupines*, and the supremacy of the Catholic religion, to be enforced by the army. The Plan also declared total independence, but under a constitutional monarchy, inviting King Ferdinand VII or one of his brothers to leave Spain and ascend the throne of Mexico. Unfortunately there were no takers. The plan itself was nevertheless accepted by Spain in the Treaty of Cordova, and Mexican independence was formally declared on September 28, 1821. For want of a royal incumbent, Iturbide himself was prevailed upon to become

41

Emperor—by the unanimous will of the people, says the Mexican historian and statesman Francisco Bulnes.

Iturbide was crowned in the Cathedral of Mexico City on July 21, 1822. The United States enthusiastically recognized the new independent government, along with those of South America. The next year the Masonic President James Monroe declared all of America free, and warned that henceforth any foreign power attempting to interfere or establish rule in the Western Hemisphere would be regarded as inimical to the U.S. Although at the time he was simply responding to the wishes of the aged Thomas Jefferson and the British Foreign Secretary Canning, who were bent on checkmating the plans of the Russian Czar and the French to help suppress the American rebellions, Monroe's words were blown up out of all proportion into what is now the dogmatic Monroe Doctrine.

One of the engineers of Iturbide's rapid rise had been the charming Joel Roberts Poinsett, a Mason from Charleston, South Carolina, who apparently had unlimited funds at his disposal. Best remembered for introducing into the U.S. the large red flower called the poinsettia, which has since become identified with the Christmas season, he played a far more significant role as special agent to Mexico and later as Secretary of War. Failing to bend to his will the conservative Iturbide once he had become Emperor, Poinsett began immediately working against him through Masonic channels. Controlling the new Congress, "the Scottish Rite lodges arranged everything in their meetings that was to be proposed and what of the proposals were to be agreed upon by the minority," writes Bishop Kelley.

The lodges had Iturbide surrounded. He was unable to put his Plan of Iguala into effect, and within a year his new constitutional empire had collapsed, ostensibly the work of General Santa Anna and other malcontent opportunists. Iturbide was executed. After making his Confession, he had declared from the scaffold, "Mexicans! At the very moment of death, I commend to you love of peace and the observance of our Holy Religion. She alone can lead you to glory.... Observe subordination and render obedience to your rulers. To do what they order is to do the will of God...." He then recited the Apostles' Creed and the Act of Contrition, kissed the Cross and laid down his life. His ashes rest in Mexico City's Cathedral, in the chapel of the aforementioned San Felipe de Jesus, patron of his country.

Now that Congress reigned supreme, Mr. Poinsett could set to work in earnest in a nation where in effect the United States had declared no foreign power had any rights other than itself. Till then the only kind of Masonry known in Mexico was the Scottish Rite imported from France, of which King Ferdinand himself was a figurehead Brother. As we have seen, the Scottish Rite was against the Church and Spain, but its membership was largely composed of aristocrats, who were determined to retain control of their country, regardless of its form of government. To break the power of this holdover from monarchical days, Poinsett brought with him a charter for the establishment of a rival York Rite (that of the previously quoted Brother Enrique Gomez), which would be republican and proletarian in character and would gradually displace the "Scots" in number and influence.

The gambit succeeded. With the help of Fr. Arizpe, Minister of Justice and Ecclesiastical Affairs, not to mention the encouragement of the USans next door, five York lodges were formed, generating a rush of membership from below. At the next election, an alleged plot to restore Spanish rule was uncovered which provided all the excuse necessary for expelling all *gachupines*. (Among innumerable evil consequences, this spelled the end of Fr. Junipero Serra's work in California.) In 1824, the same year that another Mason, Simón Bolívar, broke the Spanish power in South America, the Republic was proclaimed in Mexico, with General Guadalupe Victoria (a political stage name) as its first President.

Iturbide's rule had thus begun a long series of one-man democratic regimes which would rise one after the other in a country which from highest antiquity is monarchical to its roots. Its "republics" have been so in name only, resting as they always do on one man and a one-party system and being usually of short duration. In Mexico, as everywhere, democracy is a diabolical fiction. Even now, if the people were able to express their true will at the polls, a government not unlike the one envisioned by Iturbide might possibly result.

+

With Iturbide's fall, Masonry's influence continued to increase rapidly, its power base having now shifted from France overseas to Mexico's voracious American neighbor just north of the border. Soon all the Americas would slip from Spain's failing grip, as the illuminatus Thomas Jefferson had anticipated, when he gloated in a letter from Paris, "These countries cannot be in better hands. My fear is that they are too feeble to hold them till our population can be sufficiently advanced to gain it from them piece by piece." At the time of Hidalgo's first abortive rebellion, the U.S. was already feeling "sufficiently advanced," for as Secretary of State under Madison, Monroe received Hidalgo's emissary in Washington.

The Spanish ambassador to the U.S. reported to the Viceroy, "Mr. Monroe told him that the United States would aid the revolution in the Mexican provinces with all their power and that they would sustain it to the point not only of furnishing arms and ammunition, but in addition with 27,000 good troops, which they would soon have for the purpose." If the Mexicans would adopt a Constitution like that of the U.S., "they would then admit these republics into the Union, and with the addition of the other American provinces, it would become the most formidable power in the world!" To the everlasting credit of the revolutionary emissary, he departed in fury at the Yankee arrogance.

According to Bishop Kelley, it was Joel Poinsett who was "the real founder of our strange Mexican policy of constant and inconsistent meddling in the affairs of our southern neighbor. He went so far that there were riots against him in Mexico City. He was venomously hostile to the religion of the Mexican people." By assisting the radicals who ousted Iturbide, he became "the real leader of a force containing a few 'intellectuals' like himself, but in the main made up of mulattos and *mestizos*, mixed breeds intent on pillage, unfortunates trained by years of revolutions to know no other way of making a living."

After Iturbide's execution, Poinsett returned from a trip to the States as Minister Plenipotentiary, with full diplomatic regalia. "In 1827, the Grand Lodge of Mexico in collaboration with him adopted a resolution ... suggesting that the York Rite should immediately 'redouble its efforts' to make its principles effective in Mexico 'in accordance with the terms in which it is conceived,' namely, 'improvement in the moral condition of the people by depriving the clergy of its monopoly on public education, by increasing educational facilities and inculcating social duties by means of the foundation of museums, art

44

conservatories and public libraries, by the establishment of educational institutions for classic literature, science and morals.' " In other words, the stage was set for the systematic destruction of what remained of Mexican Christendom.

There was a serious attempt on Spain's part to recover Mexico in 1829, but it was decisively defeated by Iturbide's traitorous General Santa Anna, who eventually wound up President after betraying in rapid succession the Republic's first four incumbents, and who declared himself Perpetual Dictator with the title Most Serene Highness. His Vice-President was Gomez Farias, a York Rite friend of Poinsett, who is credited with the first open persecution of the Church as official policy. By a series of decrees virtually turning parish priests into government officials, a quasi-union of Church and state was effected which enslaved the former to the latter. Religious vows were declared dissolved, clergy barred from teaching, and confiscation of Church property begun. The ancient and glorious University of Mexico was shut down, its chapel turned for a time into a bar.

The self-seeking cross-purposes of these two men greatly facilitated the aims of USan imperialism. In his book on Santa Anna, José Valades describes him as "emotional, ambitious, turbulent, selfish, flashy, a good showman, reckless in affections and free with money, a Catholic and a Mason as it suited his purpose, a military playboy to whom all of Mexico was a military playground." As for Farias, Mme. Calderon de la Barca, a Scotswoman married to the Spanish ambassador to Mexico, characterized him in 1840 as a man opting for "rapid and radical reform," who "detests Spaniards, and during his presidency endeavored to abolish the privileges of the clergy and the troops, suppressed monastic institutions, who is without respect for the most sacred things ... and the cause of the civil war now raging." As we shall see, the short-lived, ill-fated Crown of Mexico was about to pass to other heads.

Chapter III

THE CROWN OF BROTHERHOOD

In the 1870's, a young Freemason from Brooklyn, who was purser on an American merchantman plying its way to Mexico from New Orleans, was entrusted with the delicate task of smuggling a Mexican Brother back into his own country, where there was a price on his head. When the ship anchored offshore at Vera Cruz and the rebel began swimming into port, he was detected by the harbor patrol. Frantically splashing his way back to the boat, he was thrown a line and was being hauled up just as the authorities were coming alongside.

What happened next is unfolded in a little volume called *Low Twelve,* published in 1907 and describing itself on the flyleaf as "A Series of Striking, Truthful Incidents illustrative of the fidelity of Free Masons to one another in times of disorder and danger." Its author, Edward S. Ellis, P.M. of Temple Lodge No. 5 of Trenton, N. J., relates how, "seizing the wet swimmer by his frowzy hair and giving him a heavy blow behind the ear, the purser threw him to the deck, and with an oath pounced upon him and grabbed him by the throat. 'You drunken dog! You hound, I'll teach you to jump ship, I'll teach you to try to drown yourself!' he cried. Then, leaping to his feet, the purser gave orders to put the man in irons and, turning to the astonished soldiers, asked them what he could do for them."

Convinced they had made a mistake, the patrol withdrew, and after dark the fugitive was secretly rowed ashore down coast. The returning revolutionary was Porfirio Diaz. A former seminarian, descendant of the conquistadores with Zapotec blood on his mother's side, he was destined to become dictator of Mexico and remain in power for an unmatched thirty years or more. Brother Ellis tells how the Masonic papers featured the honors the grateful Diaz later publicly bestowed on his former benefactor after becoming President, adding that "an American Mason, the friend of President Diaz, was holding a responsible office under the Mexican government."

Ellis allows, "Just who the real hero was is not disclosed, but on statements made to *The Eagle* it seems certain that his identity is known to some." More of this anon. The facts, he assures his readers, are amply vouched for by leading Brooklyn Masons, one Jerome Farley being credited with the revival of the old tale, the point of which is "how the fate of the Mexican Republic once hung on the Masonic honor and fidelity of a Brooklyn man." Another point is the power and cunning being directed by that time against the staggering remnants of Christ's Kingdom in His New World.

Back in the 1820's, the Spanish authorities had granted generous tracts of land in what is now Texas to Moses Austin of Connecticut and his son Stephen, a member of a Louisiana lodge, who drew other American settlers after them. Numbering 20,000 by 1833, they repaid their hosts by instigating a revolt which ended by setting up the whole territory as an independent republic, the insurrections at San Felipe and San Antonio having been directed personally by Stephen. This was not entirely fortuitous, for back in 1822 it was reported to President Victoria that Joel Poinsett had pointed to a map and indicated the USan intention of absorbing "all of Texas, New Mexico and Upper California and parts of Lower California, Sonora, Coahuila and New Leon."

The Mexican ambassador in Washington correctly predicted, "My opinion is that some agents from New Orleans are intending to plant colonies of Anglo-Americans in Texas ... for the purpose of acquiring an influence and majority in the population and forcing the inhabitants to declare that they desire to be annexed to the United States." The Mexican government asked for Poinsett's recall, and for that of his disgraceful successor Anthony Butler, but it was unable to enforce its rule where USan Americans had settled. Striking brutally at the Alamo and Goliad in an effort to defend sovereign rights which had been clearly recognized by the Austins, the Mexicans were decisively defeated under Santa Anna at San Jacinto in 1836 by General Sam Houston, former governor of Tennessee and a Masonic brother of President Andrew Jackson.

Texan independence a *fait accompli,* it was formally recognized by the U.S. the following year, with Houston as the first President of the new "nation." Under the circumstances, Mexico would not grant recognition, and when Texas petitioned for admittance into the Union as planned, Mexico warned she would declare war if annexation took place. President James Polk, another Mason from Tennessee, recently elected on an annexation platform, nonetheless admitted Texas to statehood in 1845. Admitted the same year was the Florida territory, which had been ceded by Spain to Jefferson for $5,000,000 on the specific condition that all claims to Texas be abandoned. Exhausted by her interior struggles, Mexico did not declare war as threatened, but merely broke off diplomatic relations.

There the matter would have rested, had it not been for the subsequent USan initiatives leading to the Mexican War. They opened a chapter of U.S. history so disgraceful that decent citizens can hardly confront the facts without wincing. The pretext used for war was the relatively minor dispute over Texas' southern boundary, both the U.S. and Mexico claiming the strip of land between the Rio Grande and the Nueces River. Polk offered Mexico $25,000,000 if she would accept the Rio Grande boundary and give the U.S. New Mexico and California! Refusing to see the USan envoy, the Mexicans sent what forces they could muster to confront General Zachary Taylor, who was advancing with three thousand men through the disputed strip.

When the Mexicans captured a small body of reconnoitering cavalry on the land they still held claim to, Polk declared war on his own authority without waiting for Congress, on the grounds that Mexico "invaded our territory and shed American blood on American soil." Even before war was declared, General Taylor had already invaded Mexico proper. Matamoros, Monterey, Saltillo and Victoria fell one after the other, and, as Commander-in-Chief, President Polk ordered

General Winfield Scott, a Mason from Virginia, to land at Vera Cruz and march on the capital, assisted on land and sea by two Catholic military leaders, General James Shields and Admiral Raphael Semmes. Invasion spelled the end for Mexico, compelled to capitulate before internal and external enemies beyond her strength to resist.

Meanwhile, following the same strategy used by the Texans, American settlers in California were on the verge of declaring their independence under the leadership of yet another Mason, Col. John Fremont, who was ostensibly exploring the Rocky Mountains for the U. S. Government. As soon as the war erupted, and before the news of the California gold strike had leaked out, he immediately "liberated" the whole territory, availing himself of the able help of Stephen Kearney, the Catholic USan general who had already "liberated" New Mexico, and of Commodore Stockton, whose naval squadron was lying offshore awaiting orders from Washington. Thus at the close of 1846, when Our Lady appeared at La Salette, the Stars and Stripes was flying over all the land Mexico had refused to sell under pressure.

As soon as her political turmoil permitted proper representation at the conference table, Mexico concluded the Treaty of Guadalupe Hidalgo with the U.S. Not far from the spot where Our Lady of Guadalupe had appeared to Juan Diego, the signing took place on the Feast of her Purification, February 2, 1948, the fateful Year of Revolutions, which saw nearly every nation in Christ's Kingdom fall, or nearly fall, to secular democracy. By the Treaty's terms, in return for $15,000,000, an additional expanse of over 525,000 square miles of Mexican soil once consecrated to Christ disappeared into the maw of the voracious artificial nation constituted by Masonry for the very purpose of expelling the Son of God from the governments of men.

The huge new acquisition would supply the terrain for the states of California, Nevada, Utah, and the greater part of Arizona, with portions of Wyoming, Colorado and New Mexico, all now returned to the Serpent under cover of the New Order of the Ages. The Serpent was well-served from all sides, for the Mexican War provided valuable training for the USan generals to use against one another in their own Civil War, which was even then brewing. Ulysses S. Grant, William T. Sherman, George McClellan, George Meade, Robert E. Lee,

Stonewall Jackson, Pierre Beauregard and the President of the future southern Confederacy, Jefferson Davis, all took part in the Mexican War as members of the armed forces. Some of the leadership, like Sherman, were Catholics; others, like the Episcopalian Robert E. Lee, assumed they were; and yet others, like Beauregard, were Masons as well as Catholics.

Not all were equally enthusiastic about the cause for which they were fighting. After the conflict, Stonewall Jackson, like Jefferson Davis and some other southerners, nearly became Catholic as a result of personal contacts with Mexicans. Abraham Lincoln, a Congressman at the time and possibly a Catholic apostate, did himself a modicum of credit by voting for a resolution thanking the military for their gallantry "in a war unnecessarily and unconstitutionally begun by the President of the United States." Unfortunately, when he was President not many years later, he would declare war on his own countrymen to keep them in the New Order of the Ages at gunpoint.

General Grant, an irremediable Yankee, who had been a pupil of Lee's at West Point, blamed the Mexican War on the southerners. In his *Memoirs,* we find: "The occupation, separation and annexation were, from the inception of the movement to its final consummation, a conspiracy to acquire territory out of which slave states might be formed for the American Union.... I am aware that a treaty, made by the Texans with Santa Anna while he was under duress, ceded all the territory between the Nueces and the Rio Grande, but he was a prisoner of war when the treaty was made, and his life was in jeopardy." Whatever interests were served, even for Grant the whole affair boiled down to "a war of conquest, a political war, and the administration conducting it desired to make capital out of it."

+

Needless to say, the cessation of hostilities did not put an end to the New Order's pursuit of its Manifest Destiny. USan speculators had been buying up land in what still remained to Mexico of Arizona and New Mexico, and the railroad interests were clamoring for a clear path to the Pacific in the south. In 1853, when William Walker set himself up as President of an independent Southern California and annexed Sonora, President Franklin Pierce ordered him to desist, but a year later, the impoverished Santa Anna government in Mexico was driven to sell the remaining 45,535 square miles to the U.S. for $10,000,000. The transaction, known to history as the Gadsden Purchase, was named for the U.S. Minister to Mexico that year, the railroad promoter James Gadsden, who was a South Carolina-Florida Mason. A tawdry tale, but thus was America the Beautiful "crowned with Brotherhood from sea to shining sea" and wrested bit by bit from Christ the King through the machinations of the Craft and a great rail system uniting the Atlantic and Pacific.

In 1898, an American battleship, the Maine, mysteriously blew up in the harbor at Havana while on a goodwill visit, supplying sufficient provocation for the Spanish-American War. Already prostrate, Spain offered to arbitrate, but was summarily refused. Before it was over, Cuba found herself "liberated," with the USans in full possession of Puerto Rico, Guam and Mexico's former sister colony in the Philippines, where Masonic revolutionaries under Dr. José Rizal, a Chinese-Spanish Filipino educated in Europe, had long been at work, with help from the U.S. After World War II, American Masonry, whose figurehead in the Philippines was then Brother Douglas MacArthur of Manila Lodge No. 1, spread thence by further right of conquest to Japan, a nation heretofore closed to Freemasonry by imperial decree, and where the Mexican martyr San Felipe was crucified for the Faith. In the normal course of events, Japan would have been the next sphere of Spanish Catholic influence, and the Serpent could not have been unaware of it.

As long as the Monroe Doctrine remained in force, no European government dared interfere in Latin America's problems, which began proliferating without obstruction. Out of the plots and counterplots roiling from the shambles left in Mexico by the war with the U.S., emerged Benito Juarez, an ardent, intelligent, full-blooded Zapotec Indian. One of the Church's deadliest enemies, he had been befriended in childhood by a Franciscan Tertiary, who had educated him and sent him to the seminary in Oaxaca, where he distinguished himself by "exceptional diligence and particular application." Falling under the influence of the lodges, however, he forsook the seminary in 1828 to study law and was soon cramming his head with the effusions of the French libertarian Auguste Comte and especially Diderot, whose hope it had been "to see the last king strangled with the guts of the last priest."

On his elevation to the governorship of Oaxaca, Juarez enacted a series of anti-Church laws which were later incorporated into the famous *Ley de la Reforma* of 1857. Its administrative paragraphs were patterned on the U.S. Constitution, but the sections dealing with religion were inspired directly by the French Revolution. Imposed by the usual fiercely dedicated minority upon a people 95% Catholic, and violating their deepest traditions of government, the *Ley* kept the revolutionary pot boiling. By this time, Juarez had risen to the Presidency of the Supreme Court. The following year he declared himself President of Mexico in Guanajuato, just as General Zuloaga, a more conservative revolutionary, assumed the same office in Mexico City. When Abraham Lincoln simultaneously entered the White House, and Juarez's friend Thomas Corwin was appointed U.S. ambassador to Mexico, the stage was set for action.

Zuloaga's Foreign Secretary Manuel de Bonilla relates that when the USan plenipotentiary John Forsyth presented his official congratulations, acting on orders from President James Buchanan (a Pennsylvania Mason), he "broached a discussion ... to arrange an agreement in virtue of which Mexico would cede to the United States, for a sum of money to be determined, a considerable part of its national territory and the free passage across the Isthmus of Tehuantepec in perpetuity. When these propositions were rejected as hurtful to the good name and detrimental to the vital interests of Mexico, the same Minister of the U.S. changed tactics and began to stir up embarrassments for the administration, provoking disagreeable questions, offending on every possible occasion the national susceptibility, initiating or demanding unreasonable indemnities, generally unfounded ... and presented in caustic and offensive language."

The U.S. thereupon shifted its support to Juarez and his faction, whose leaders Forsyth "even kept in his own home ... so they might plot in safety, and even concealed in his home the silver taken from the altars of the Cathedral in Morelia." By this time, political stability for Catholic Mexico was an impossibility, for the confiscations and "nationalization" of Church properties begun by Farias and consummated under Juarez had reduced the country to chaos. All Mexican institutions were the work of the Church, painstakingly perfected over three centuries, which meant that almost overnight not only chapels, missions and convents fell into ruins, but schools and universities, libraries, hospitals and asylums, orphanages, banking houses, arts, architecture and charitable projects of all kinds simply disappeared.

Business and industry were wrecked and the national treasury bankrupt, for the impoverished taxpayers were now called upon to assume the burden of public institutions which until then the Church had supported either from the King's bounty or from those who could afford munificence. Disposing at first of vast sums from the plundered properties, Juarez had nonetheless dispatched the goose which laid the golden eggs. Like every Mexican revolutionary from Farias to Plutarco Calles, he was not above playing on the traditional enmity between the Judeo-Masonic English and the Catholic Spanish, created by the Reformation, in order to pick up some small change.

His Secretary of the Treasury, Matias Romero, confessed, "I favored the establishment of a Protestant community as planned by Mr. Henry Riley ... who eagerly sought to establish a Mexican National Church in competition with the Roman Catholic.... He proposed to buy one of the finest churches, the main church of the Franciscan convent, which had been built by the Spaniards, located in the best section of the City of Mexico.... With the hearty support of President Juarez, I sold the building, which had become a national possession after the confiscation of Church property, for a mere trifle, if I remember rightly, about $4,000.... Dr. Butler bought about the same time another part of the same convent of San Francisco, where he established a Methodist church in a very creditable building."

Thus the revolution draws support from the heretic's frantic fear of the supernatural power of the True Faith, with which he knows he cannot coexist. As Bishop Kelley points out, this explains why Latin American politicos have continued "fighting the Spaniard" long after Spain had been expelled. With the Spaniard gone, they began bartering for outside help by destroying their priceless legacy of Spanish culture. After the national patrimony was liquidated, they were reduced to negotiating heavy foreign loans, which they could not repay, to bolster the shattered economy. Finally, to satisfy the foreign creditors who soon controlled them, they turned on their Spanish religion, the Apostolic Faith.

World history is nothing but the religious warfare which began with Cain and Abel, but few of the combatants are allowed to suspect it. To the majority of Mexican liberals, Masonry was little more than an indispensable tool to personal power, its ideals never truly their own. Baptized Catholics almost to a man, many after a lifetime of oppressing the Church called for the Last Sacraments at the moment of death. Juarez was no exception. He had his son educated by a priest, and when his daughter contemplated a civil marriage, he cried indignantly, "My daughter is a decent girl, and civil marriage is a brothel contract!" Yet at the behest of his masters, he had enacted civil marriage into law for his countrymen. During the cholera epidemic in Oaxaca in 1850, Juarez confessed his sins, received Holy Communion and took part in the public processions imploring the divine clemency, even as he plunged the nation into a material and spiritual bankruptcy which would become the concern of all Europe.

+

With no immediate prospects of meeting its foreign obligations, the Juarez regime passed a law in 1861 suspending payments for two years, prompting the Emperor Napoleon III of France to take action in conjunction with Spain and England. While the U.S. was busy with its own Civil War, the three powers defied the Monroe Doctrine and landed troops at Vera Cruz, confident that the Confederacy would easily win her war of secession against the Union. This appeared most probable at the time, for not only did the Southerners have an airtight legal case under the Constitution, but they were solidly united in their cause and had by far the best generals. When the tide unaccountably began to turn, Spain and England withdrew, rather than tangle with the USan colossus, but Napoleon proceeded as planned to reestablish a monarchy in Mexico, a project which was enthusiastically supported by the best conservative elements of Mexican and European society, not to mention His Holiness, the reigning Pius IX .

The choice of a monarch had fallen on the Catholic Archduke Ferdinand Maximilian of Hapsburg, the blond, charming and handsome younger brother of Emperor Franz

Joseph of Austria. His claim to the throne was of the best, for he was a direct descendant of the Holy Roman Emperor Charles V and of Ferdinand and Isabella, and the papal decree conferring this part of the New World on the Spanish monarchs had never suffered repeal. Maximilian's wife, the beautiful Carlota, was the daughter of King Leopold I of Belgium. When, after lengthy negotiation, a junta of prominent Mexicans formally offered the crown to Maximilian, hopes were high for a truly Catholic restoration in the New World. The young monarchs traveled to Mexico by way of Rome, where Pius IX bestowed a solemn blessing on their apostolic mission, delivering an impressive sermon on its importance before assembled dignitaries in the Sistine Chapel.

That summer of 1864 they were crowned in America's greatest cathedral in Mexico City under the auspices of its Archbishop, amid wild acclamations. From Rome on the following October 18, Pius IX wrote the young Emperor, "We shall not cease daily to direct our humble prayers to the Father of light and the God of all consolation, to the end that, all obstacles being overcome, the counsels of the enemies of religious and social order turned to nought, political passions calmed, her full liberty restored to the Spouse of Jesus Christ, the Mexican nation may be enabled to hail in the person of Your Majesty, its father, its regenerator and its greatest and most imperishable glory."

According to the historian Bulnes, "The majority of the acts of submission to the Empire were voluntary. The majority did not then believe that Intervention compromised Independence, and the remainder, excepting the energetic liberal group, were willing to lose even independence to secure respect for property rights, for human life, for personal liberty, the inviolability of labor, sleep without nightmares, authority without brutalities, law without license, courts free from influence and without venality.... The leaders and officers of the republican army deserted their ranks.... The arrival of the Archduke gave the death blow to the republican cause.... The extreme liberals went on presenting themselves in great number, many of them convinced of the advantages of an opulent and truly liberal monarchy in place of the old republic, deformed, false, tyrannical, miserable, Jacobin, anarchic."

Despite such an auspicious beginning, Maximilian ruled only a meteoric three years almost to the day, falling victim in

1867 to hidden forces utterly beyond his strength and control, some of which unfortunately lay in his own mild, romantic character. Unable to grasp the psychology and aspirations of the people, he had, for instance, made his solemn entry into the capital dressed in civilian clothes in order to appear more "democratic," to the great disappointment of many of his subjects, especially the Indians, who looked for another glorious Montezuma decked out in royal finery. One of those modern monarchs enamored of liberalism, he believed implacable enemies could be turned into friends by simply giving in to them. Before six months were out, he actually endorsed Juarez's confiscatory decrees against the Church, in an effort to placate the radicals.

Despite anguished protests from the Papal Nuncio, he declared that henceforth clerical salaries would be paid by the state, and finally he alienated his staunchest supporters by dismissing loyal monarchists from his service and replacing them with militant liberals. The great University of Mexico he reopened, but only to close it definitively in 1865. Such blunders, which strengthened the hand of his adversaries, would have been sufficient to topple his throne without the giant opponent crouching in the wings. Unfortunately for Maximilian and the Catholic cause, the friendly Confederacy next door lost the American Civil War, leaving the powerful Union consolidated as never before, with plenty of war material and unemployed generals left over. Abraham Lincoln had vowed no more war, but after his assassination there was no guarantee that the U.S. would not take up arms against the distraught neighbor who had thumbed its nose at the Monroe Doctrine.

General Philip Sheridan, a Catholic, was in open communication with the resurgent Benito Juarez and already massing troops on the Texas border. In his *Memoirs*, Sheridan relates, "During the winter and spring of 1866, we continued covertly supplying arms and ammunition to the Liberals, sending as many as 30,000 muskets from Baton Rouge arsenal alone, and by midsummer Juarez, having organized a pretty good-sized army, was in possession of the whole line of the Rio Grande, and in fact, of nearly the whole of Mexico down to San Luis Potosí." The USans maintained these maneuvers were necessary to prevent a body of die-hard Confederates from escaping and joining Maximilian. The excuse was a good one, for the sympathy existing between the new Mexican monarchy and the Confederacy was common knowledge.

On the anniversary of Our Lady's apparition at La Salette in 1863, when Southern hopes were still high, the Confederate agent Edward Hardy had written Emperor Franz Joseph, "An Empire having been proclaimed, a war with the United States is inevitable; and next in importance to the pacification and reconciliation of the people of Mexico is a recognition of the Southern Confederacy and an alliance offensive and defensive with it." He suggests that one of the aims of the new government might be, "If war, then the recovery of the state of California, and if the Southern States will allow, of the territory of New Mexico; both of which were necessarily ceded to the United States under the Treaty of Guadalupe Hidalgo." He felt that "Mexico should be an integrity from Oregon to Honduras," and believed "the South would rather see California a possession of the Empire than of the Northern States."

In a famous letter to Jefferson Davis that same year, Pius IX had in effect recognized the existence of two distinct nations in the U.S. The Confederate diplomat Dudley Mann, writing to His Holiness' Secretary of State, reported, "In all intelligent British circles, our recognition by the Sovereign Pontiff is considered formal and complete.... It is believed that the earnest wishes expressed by His Holiness will be regarded as little less than imperative commands by the vast portion of the human family, which esteem him as the Vicar of Christ." At the same time, King Leopold had written his son-in-law Maximilian, "Once you are firmly established in Mexico, it is probable that a great part of America will place itself under your rule." This was, of course, the Catholic dream.

Near the close of the Civil War, the *Richmond Sentinel* published an article allegedly from the pen of Jefferson Davis, suggesting that, "In the event of being unable to sustain our independence, we should surrender it into the hands of those from whom we wrested or purchased it, into the hands of Britain, France and Spain, rather than yield it to the Yankees.... In the dread event which it contemplates, our people would infinitely prefer an alliance with European nations on terms as favorable as they could desire, in preference to the domination of the Yankees." *The New York Times* rumored that the crown of the Confederacy had actually been offered to Captain Bonaparte of Baltimore, a relative of Napoleon III.

Whatever the truth of these insinuations, Catholic aid to Mexico from the States was a long-standing Union phobia. It must be remembered that in those days the bulk of the Catholic population was not in the North as it is now, after the massive steamboat immigrations; it lay in the South, whose culture reflected Catholic values far more than the evangelical. Not forgotten up North were the Irish San Patricios, who during the Mexican War had deserted USan ranks to fight on the side of their Mexican co-religionists, with the blessing of their doughty Fr. Eugene McNamara. Remembered also were the draft riots which had been instigated at the beginning of the Civil War by recalcitrant Irish Catholics, who had no quarrel with the South. General Rufus King, U. S. ambassador in Rome at the time, related how "many Catholics refused to fight for the North. Thousands of others deserted altogether."

+

Were Mexico to succeed in extricating itself from the coils of the Serpent, the whole continent might well be re-won for Christ the King. Maximilian's venture therefore had to be stopped at all cost. The Monroe Doctrine began swinging its fists. William Seward, Secretary of State in the Lincoln Cabinet, dispatched General Schofield to France with clear orders: "I want you to get your legs under Napoleon's mahogany and tell him he must get out of Mexico!" He very nearly authorized Lewis Campbell, USan plenipotentiary to the Juarez government residing in New Orleans, to place the U.S. Army and Navy at Juarez's disposal so that the Mexicans might, said he, "be relieved of all foreign intervention!" There was little need for alarm, however, for like Napoleon III and most of Europe, Maximilian had assumed the Confederacy would win and leave an enfeebled Union, and after the conflict, he mortally underestimated its powers of recuperation. Privately holding republics in contempt and knowing them to be intrinsically unstable, he believed they would fall apart if one played along with them. He completely misjudged the temper and strength of the U.S., especially the arrogance of its expansionist bloc. Above all, he never grasped the scope of the role of Masonry, which supplied the hard-core leadership for the "liberation" of all Latin America: Brother Simón Bolívar in Venezuela, Colombia and Ecuador; Brother Sucre in Bolivia; Brothers Mariano

Moreno and Manuel Belgrado in Argentina; Brother San Marin in Uruguay, Paraguay and Peru; Brother Bernardo O'Higgins in Chile; Brother José Marti in Cuba, etc.

To the last, Maximilian attributed his misfortunes to the perfidy of the unfortunate Napoleon III, who had put him in power only to desert him by recalling the French troops from Mexico when threatened by the North American giant and the wrath of the lodges. The French Emperor was himself a Mason, but "all know," writes Cardinal Rodriguez of Chile, "that Orsini was charged by the lodges in 1858 to make attempts on the life of Napoleon III, accused of infidelity to his oaths, and that from that time the sectarians never ceased to obtain from him new concessions, with new threats against his life." With the indispensable French backing gone, the weak, indecisive Maximilian was wise enough to consider abdicating, even as Carlota sped to Europe to make a fruitless personal appeal to the now-ailing Napoleon, whose own regime would fall three years later.

On her way to see the Pope, who had been deeply wounded by her husband's betrayal of the Church's interests, she lapsed into the madness which remained with her till death. Rather than leave Mexico, Maximilian, with characteristic personal nobility, decided it behooved him to see the tragedy through to the bitter end and to fight on despite the French withdrawal. Although bravely led, his forces were no match for their enemies, armed as these were with excellent USan muskets. Partisanship with the Emperor had furthermore been ruthlessly discouraged by the savage Juarez, who ordered any and all captured imperialists strung up on the nearest trees as examples to others.

Betrayed by Col. Miguel Lopez, one of his most trusted officers, Maximilian was executed at Queretaro with two faithful generals. He wrote the distraught Carlota, "I die without agony. I shall fall with glory, like a soldier, like a conquered king. If you have not the power to bear so much suffering, if God soon reunites us, I shall bless the divine and paternal hand which has so rudely stricken us. Adieu! Thy poor Max." To the firing squad, he said, "Soldiers of the Republic, the unpleasant duty is before you of carrying out the orders of your superiors, and of shooting unto death us three military prisoners. The highest act of a soldier is to obey his officers. No possible stain can come on any of you for shooting us. Always do your duty, and the great God, our common Father, will provide for you. Upon the command of your officer to shoot, aim at the heart of each of us."

Maximilian had been offered a chance to escape from prison, but, a true aristocrat to the last, he had refused on learning that the two others condemned with him could not be included. His last recorded words were: "I pardon all and pray they will also pardon me. Would that my blood might help this country. Long live Mexico! Long live her independence!" So, in the final analysis, Maximilian I of Mexico must be classed among the revolutionaries fighting in Christ's ranks who in every age think they can restore order by serving two masters in the name of political expediency. A century later he would have been a Christian-Democrat. Today might find him a Christian supporter of the New World Order. As for Mexico, the spiritual heart of Christ's Kingdom in the New World, by his death she took her place among the regicide nations of Christendom, after the example of England and France.

A token Mason like Napoleon, Maximilian had accepted help from dark forces in his bid for power, not the least of whom were the Rothschilds. His brief reign, which in many ways resembled that of the Confederate counterrevolution next door, was built on compromise, a terrain on which the children of light are no match for children of this world. In neither case were the strong supernatural cudgels of the integral Faith brandished against the enemy, but worst of all, in neither case was the leadership entrusted to the Immaculate Mother of God, who alone has power from on high utterly to crush the Serpent. After Maximilian's death, the Republic was immediately reinstalled, and Benito Juarez, protected by his powerful friends across the Rio Grande, lost no time in re-assuming the Presidency.

+

A decade later the presidential office would be filled by one of Juarez's generals, who was none other than the Porfirio Diaz, with whose escapade this chapter opened. The Ellis anecdote does not tell us that Diaz was a refugee from the Lerdo regime, which followed that of Juarez, or that he was living in New York. The name of the American ship, on which he returned disguised as an eccentric Cuban doctor, was The City of Havana. Its captain was Alexander Coney, who happened to be a close friend of the Diaz supporter Col. Juan de la Luz Enriquez of Vera Cruz, and Diaz's reentry was carefully planned. It would have been at Tampico that the incident could have occurred. At Vera Cruz, Diaz disembarked disguised as a laborer carrying a bale of cotton, and thence he began his climb to power under the indispensable direction of the lodges. Until that support was withdrawn from him in his old age, he ruled Mexico unchallenged.

In this "strong man" the Mexicans found for a time the monarch, albeit without a crown, they had looked for in Maximilian. For a time, his dictatorship satisfied Mexico's perennial Catholic hunger for a king. The Emperor in his brief reign had reminded the nation how good it was to be governed in peace, and Diaz, descendant of the conquistadores, caught his cue. As we have seen, he was a Mason. Appointed for life Sovereign Grand Commander of the Supreme Council of the Scottish Rite in Mexico, and much esteemed by the Brotherhood, the *New Age* for October 1909 called him "the most remarkable man of the century," and declared a year later, "It is Masonic principles which have inspired rulers like President Diaz in Mexico and Victor Emmanuel in Italy to make every effort to lift their people out of the dense morass of ignorance and superstition into which they had fallen under the long dominion of the Romish priests."

As always, Masonry is quick to take credit for anything which succeeds, but to this day it has never become truly Mexican in the sense that it became English or American. It seems to have a natural affinity for the devil's old Atlantean empire, vestiges of which are now found mostly in England and on North America's east coast. What Francisco Bulnes says about Mexico applies to a degree to all countries once truly Catholic: "In Mexico, Freemasonry has never been the respectable corporation it is in other countries. Since 1824, the incentive to join its ranks has been to obtain government posts. All the high public officials became Masons in order to court popularity and were obliged to give the preference to Masons in the assignment of government positions.

"They also sought under cover of their association to transgress laws, especially in the line of peculations, without incurring the corresponding penalty. The Masonic program was: 'The country to satiate the gluttony of the Masons!'

Descending from this level, already quite low, Masonry went still lower, until it reached the point of having its dignitaries act as private detectives for President Diaz, doing all the dirty work that is part of a Caesarian system. Nothing disparaged Masonry in Mexico more than this. In 1885, a point was reached when it was considered an insult for a decent person to be pointed out as a Mason."

As in France and Italy, for a long time Mexican politicians have seen no contradiction between being a Catholic in private and a Mason in public, in a land where everyone was aware of the true state of affairs. It was perfectly understood, moreover, that no candidate could enjoy long tenure in office without retaining the approval of the Masonic USans to the north. In a way, Diaz himself summed up the entire history of modern Mexico when he remarked, "Poor Mexico, so far from God, so near the United States!" He was among the wiliest of the lot, yet he too fell from power when his masters cut his leading-strings. He had had four years of good seminary training, however, which never quite left him. He never dared take Juarez's old anti-clerical laws off the books, but he neglected to enforce them.

For many blessed years during Diaz's incumbency, the Church found herself free to go about her normal business of saving souls unmolested, despite the fact that officially there was no more God in Mexico than there was in the United States. Although highly educated, Diaz was no wool-gathering intellectual. He was a hard-headed organizer who could bend all factions to his purposes. He settled none of the deep-seated problems which continued to fester beneath the surface of Mexican life, but, by inviting in foreign capital, he was able to satisfy his masters and create an illusion of solid prosperity. He fathered several illegitimate children in his youth, but both his wives were pious Catholics. In the official census, he described himself "as an individual and as head of his family, a *catolico, apostolico, romano.*" He died in Paris with the Sacraments.

Brother Enrique Gomez, quoted in the previous chapter, freely admitted, "Catholic Freemasonry? There is no such thing, but Catholic Freemasons? Thousands of them!" He declared: "No Mason who has not lived in a Latin-American country and participated in a Lodge in one of those countries can have the foggiest idea of the paradoxes and incongruities one finds there. I cite as one example the notice that appeared last year (1977) in a prominent Mexican newspaper of the death of one Alfonso Chong Chang, a Mexican Brother of Chinese descent. It read, 'Mr. Alfonso Chong Chang died yesterday at 10:15 in the bosom of our Mother the Holy Roman Catholic and Apostolic Church, comforted by every spiritual help and the Papal Benediction.' Appearing at the head of this notice was our emblem, the Square and Compasses with the letter G."

No need therefore to marvel that it was a Mexican Bishop, the powerful Mendez Arceo of Cuernavaca, who at the Second Vatican Council proposed for the first time open reconciliation between the Church and her declared enemy. Since the Vatican has now ruled that Catholic laymen may in fact join the Brotherhood, the double allegiance described by Brother Gomez should be entirely acceptable.

Chapter IV

THE CROWN OF MARTYRDOM

The Feast of Christ the King was instituted in 1925 by Pope Pius XI to reinforce the doctrine that "not only private individuals, but also rulers and princes, are bound to give public honor and obedience to Christ. It will call to their minds the thought of the last judgment, wherein Christ, Who has been cast out of public life, despised, neglected and ignored, will most severely avenge these insults; for His kingly dignity demands that the State should take account of the commandments of God and of Christian principles."

Although then as now ignored by the generality of Christian peoples, these words of *Quas primas* had been anticipated in Mexico in 1911, when at long last a National Catholic Party was formed under the leadership of the Archbishop. The fall of Porfirio Diaz ushered in a prolonged revolution, and some attempt had to be made to re-inject Catholic principles into the government. The party's membership soon grew to about a half-million, and had become vocal through the influential periodical *La Nación.* Organized in accordance with the principles laid down by Leo XIII's social encyclicals, the party campaigned for honest elections, vocational unions, proper landholding and the enforcement of Sunday rest.

During its brief existence, it managed to elect twenty-nine federal judges, four senators and four governors, and to win control of the legislatures. Its support secured the presidency for the well-meaning visionary Francisco Madero, a decent millionaire *hidalgo* of Portuguese-Jewish descent, whose family had been Catholic for generations. At one time contemplating religious life, he lost his faith while studying in Paris and ended up as a spiritist vowed to ouija boards and vegetarianism. His was one of the few elections which may actually have reflected the will of the people in a land where democracy has never been more than politely recognized fiction. The candidacy of such a man, however, was typical of the sort of compromise a hopeless contradiction like "Christian Democracy" was bound to foster in order to survive as a party. After eighteen months in office, he was assassinated—"his trouble being," says Bishop Kelley, "a trouble that afflicts half of the world. He took democracy for the principle, when it was at best only a means to an end."

After much turbulence, power was seized by one of Diaz's generals, the Indian full-blood Victoriano Huerta, who seems to have planned a regime similar to the former strong man's. He was a Catholic with many faults, but inclination to persecute the Church was not among them, and he might have succeeded, had it not been for the dedicated hostility of the USan President Woodrow Wilson, Masonic architect of the United Nations' forerunner, the League of Nations. For information on Mexico, Wilson relied on financial advisers, who persuaded him that Catholicism was always bad for business. When his personal messenger to Mexico, John Lind, a fanatical anti-Catholic who knew how to play on the prejudices of the "Presbyterian priest" in the White House, reported to him, "Prostitution and the Catholic Church are the chief causes of the Mexican trouble," Lind was instructed to announce that if Huerta were deposed, "President Wilson would look with favor upon an immediate loan to Mexico."

Huerta's popularity at the polls Wilson chose to dismiss as the result of irregularities. Aware that USan ships were unloading ammunition in Tampico for his rivals Carranza and Zapata, Huerta ordered the port blockaded, whereupon Wilson, arguing that Tampico was an open port, sent two cruisers to enforce delivery. On Holy Thursday, nine uniformed U.S. Marines were arrested trying to get oil from the forbidden zone and were taken to the Huertist General Zaragosa, who released them within an hour with apologies. This became the "Tampico incident," when the squadron commander, Rear Admiral Mayo, chose to regard it as "an insult to the American flag" and demanded a 21-gun salute to Old Glory in reparation. Huerta offered to apologize, but would not salute the flag unless a return in kind was made to the Mexican flag. That failing, he suggested the matter be submitted to the international tribunal at The Hague, as provided by Article 21 of the Treaty of Guadalupe Hidalgo.

When Wilson explained the problem to Congress, he neglected to mention the latter proposal. Informed that a German ship would soon dock at Vera Cruz with ammunition for Huerta, he ordered the U.S. forces to capture the vessel and occupy the customs office. Although Huerta forbade formal resistance, at 1:20 pm on April 21, 1914, the USan ship Prairie opened fire on Vera Cruz, an unprotected city, and Marines landed. Along with the townspeople, the cadets of the Mexican Naval Academy undertook the city's defense with one 25 mm. gun. Nineteen USans were killed and seventy wounded. One hundred ninety-three cadets and other Mexicans lost their lives, with an unknown number of wounded, in what is known in Mexico today as the Vera Cruz Massacre. The ancient Serpent, deprived of his altars, still knew how to exact his quota of sacrifices!

There followed abortive attempts on the part of the South American ABC powers (Argentina, Brazil and Chile), but Wilson instructed the mediators that "no arrangement can have prospects of a lasting settlement unless it includes the elimination of General Huerta and the immediate installation of a provisional government acceptable to all parties." Huerta was therefore forced to resign for the common good. Asked to make a statement two years later in El Paso, where he lay dying of an illness contracted in the U.S. prison at Fort Bliss where he had been confined without trial, he refused. "To what end? I die in peace with God and man. I forgive all who have injured me, most fully the President of the United States, for he never understood; and I ask pardon of all whom I have wronged. The rest I leave to God, into Whose hands I entrust my poor family."

His last words were, "If any money is realized on anything I possess, let the poor have a share."

Carranza became President. The two nations nevertheless continued to hover on the brink of war. Not only did Mexico begin passing laws curbing foreign ownership of her resources, but in 1916 the disappointed office-seeker Pancho Villa killed a trainload of USan mining engineers traveling through Chihuahua. When he and two hundred and forty Roughriders followed this up with an open attack on Columbus, New Mexico, his country was subjected to a humiliating punitive expedition of 10,000 men under General Pershing. USan troops did not leave Mexico until 1917, when only the imminence of USan entry into the First World War put a sudden end to hostilities.

Huerta's surrender brought on three years of particularly bloody conflict, in which religion for the first time figured openly as the central issue. For this development, credit is due to the short-lived Catholic Party, whose potential for damage to the enemy is best gauged by the following accusation, leveled at it by the Masonic magazine *The New Age* in October 1913: "The Roman Catholic political party in Mexico has been managing the Revolution originated by General (Felix) Diaz, and it will attempt to gain control of the destinies of Mexico. It will, of course, try to repeal the Laws of Reform and again unite Church and State in that unhappy country." In other words, the Serpent's worst fears were aroused, but like its counterparts in the rest of the world, Christian Democracy was once more doomed to failure in Mexico, the victim of its own internal contradictions.

+

Soon the Catholic Party found itself outlawed under the new Constitution of 1917, whose Article 130 proscribed any group "whose name contains a word or indication that connects it in any manner with a religious confession." Till then, the persecution of the Church had often been brutal, but its expressed aim had been only to bring her members under state control in accordance with democratic principles. From now on, destruction of the Faith itself was an avowed objective. With the rise of Marxism, Christian Democracy would give way to the further contradiction of Christian Marxism, leaving only

Christian Atheism to be looked forward to. As it was, education became a government monopoly, and churches retained no property rights or legal status whatever. Religious services were strictly confined within church walls, outside of which all public manifestations of public piety were forbidden. Juridically, the Church had ceased to exist.

These provisions were not immediately enforced, but true to the established pattern, events began rolling to a climax about two years later. In May 1920, the bullet-riddled body of President Carranza, who had braved the ire of his masters by requesting Congress to alter the persecutory provisions of the Constitution, was laid to rest in Mexico City. Bishop Kelley relates how later, "when his portfolio was received by his family, they found in it a Crucifix and a little religious medal. On the latter was the inscription: *'Madre Mia, Salva Me'*— Mother Mine, Save Me!" Obviously one more case of merely skin-deep Masonic affiliation for political purposes.

"The makers of the revolutions, bad in action, hoped to be decent at the end, even to the point of compromising with the Church.... Comonfort, Juarez, and even Lerdo, tried to enforce an anti-clerical Constitution which hampered, but did not destroy, the Church. Diaz held to that Constitution but did not enforce it. Madero was openly and avowedly for religious liberty. Huerta did nothing to indicate a change from the plans of Diaz. We have seen Carranza struggle to change the Constitution of Queretaro.... I cannot but see, in each successful Mexican revolutionary leader, a fear of the consequences of the loss of religious influence over the lives of the Mexican people. They could shout maledictions and rob without remorse, but when safely in power—or unsafely as it prove—they all cast longing eyes in the direction of the bleeding Christ, as if begging Him, in spite of their sins, not to leave their country and themselves to the mercy of the evil forces with which they had been playing."

In December 1920, the Presidency was filled by General Obregon (Spanish form of O'Brien), under whom persecution unto blood became public policy. Bombs exploded at the archepiscopal doors in Mexico City and Guadalajara. Two months later, a red flag was hoisted onto one of the spires of Morelia Cathedral, where fifty Catholic protesters were killed by the police. In November, another bomb, said to have been placed by one of Obregon's staff, exploded in the national sanctuary among flowers set before the image of Our Lady of Guadalupe. The picture miraculously escaped damage, although a heavy metal crucifix at the same spot was twisted totally out of shape and can still be seen today.

This in a land where 19/20 of the people are Catholic! Those protesting, or simply trying to defend themselves, as happened the next year when the CYO in Mexico City was attacked by a mob of a thousand socialists, were denied police protection. In 1923, the Apostolic Delegate was expelled for daring to bless the site of a proposed monument to Christ the King on private property on the Cubilete, near Guanajuato. He had agreed to do so on the strength of his belief that President Obregon was personally not unfriendly to the Church. Bishop Kelley would bear this out, for he relates how he knew firsthand that Obregon had tried to reach an understanding with the Bishops, but was, "like the rest, afraid of some power that had a grip on him, and hating it."

This may have been the case with yet another baptized Catholic, the infamous Plutarco Calles, who figured for so many years as the power behind the political scene and assumed the Presidency after the malodorous election of 1924. Arriving at a time when the religious issue was razor-sharp, he brought to the office a ruthlessness unhampered by moral principles of any kind. A professional revolutionary who began political life as a city treasurer in Guaymos, where he was dismissed for fiscal shortages, he had wound up as Governor of Sonora. His character is easily judged by his action as Police Chief of Agua Priete, when he ordered a laborer hanged by barbed wire from a railroad bridge for shouting "Down with Madero!" Apparently driven by consuming lust for personal wealth and power, rather than any direct hatred of the Church or dedication to any particular ideology, he nonetheless launched the worst persecution yet seen.

During Calles' administration, the battle between Church and state approached paroxysm, for the Serpent had by that time recruited every possible ally. Not the least of these was Protestantism, which from the beginning had a been a quiet but steady supporter of revolution throughout all the Latin countries. S.G. Inman of the Committee of the League of Free Nations explains this natural sympathy: "When the Mexican Revolution began, the Protestant churches threw themselves into it almost unanimously, because they believed that the progress of the

Revolution represented what these churches had been preaching through the years, and that the triumph of the Revolution meant the triumph of the Gospel. There were some entire congregations who, led by their pastors, volunteered for service in the Mexican government."

Jean Meyer, author of *The Cristero Rebellion,* wrote in 1976: "Both Obregon and Calles favored evangelical proselytism and openly supported the YMCA and the missions. In 1922, 261 American missionaries were assisting 773 Mexican colleagues in 703 places of worship frequented by 22,000 faithful. In 1926, the Methodists had 200 schools, and their bishop, George Miller, expressed praise for the cooperative attitude of President Calles.... This proselytism, always based on the twin themes of the immorality of the celibate priests and the rapacity of the higher clergy, who kept the parish priests at starvation level, was quite effective in the north and in the pioneering areas of the hot lands, but elsewhere it provoked reactions which were often violent, and which became increasingly frequent after 1926, as Protestantism grew in strength. To the Catholics, it was obvious that the Government was collaborating closely with the Yankee missions, and that it was working for the great 'decatholicization' hoped for by Theodore Roosevelt as a prelude to annexation. The Catholic politicians would have given much to have been able to publish this telegram sent by the Episcopal churches of Toledo, Ohio, and Taylor, Pennsylvania, to President Obregon: 'Millions of Americans feel for you and pray for you while you struggle to unloose the grip of the Roman Catholic Church upon your great country.' "

Masonry, of course, bestowed its own rewards on its faithful servant. The Supreme Grand Commander of the Scottish Rite conferred the Masonic Medal of Merit on Calles, with the words: "The Order over which I have the honor to preside has never before awarded this exalted honor; it has been decreed on account of the extraordinary merit which you have displayed as President of the Republic, solving so many problems in such a short space of time." Calles was therefore a "first," presaging others who would follow. After him, it was utterly impossible for a non-Mason to occupy any government post of any importance, and if Calles was unable to eliminate the Church entirely, at least he would shackle her once and for all to the Masonically controlled state, as had to all intents and purposes happened in the U.S.

One of his opening gambits was the formation of a National Mexican Catholic Church under a "Patriarch," whose role was played by the unpriestly priest and former Mason Joaquin Perez, ably assisted by a Spanish henchman, Fr. Manuel Monge. Covered by police posing as "Knights of the Order of Guadalupe," Perez ousted the parish priest of La Soledad Church in Mexico City and appropriated the premises, only to be violently ejected the next morning by irate parishioners arriving for Mass. At other churches where this was tried, results were the same, and Calles soon saw the folly of tampering with religion at the lower levels, where the basic issues were quickly grasped by rank-and-file believers prepared to deal with them without protocol. Catholics till then lukewarm and wavering soon turned militant.

As resistance mounted, Calles saw the wisdom of imposing restrictions from above as heretofore. The sophisticated methods employed by the Masons of the U.S. to control the Church through a homegrown Americanist hierarchy were not feasible in Mexico, where the vast majority of the population was Catholic. But laws could be passed. He retaliated with the Penal Code of 1926, the abominable *Ley Calles*. To teach religion at all was henceforth illegal, as were all religious vows. Priests had to be Mexican-born and licensed by the government. Their number was limited to the point that in some cases one priest ministered to 50,000 faithful. To make matters worse, the vicious prescriptions of the Constitution of 1917, which till then had been indifferently applied, if not altogether disregarded, were mercilessly enforced. Strangling in torment in the coils of the Serpent, the Catholics of Mexico broke into open rebellion.

+

As one man, there arose the Cristeros. They were not a political party, for not only had this means already been tried to no avail, but now it was proscribed by law. What they were was surprisingly well-organized Catholic guerrillas, who took their name from their battle cry, *"Viva Cristo Rey!* Long live Christ the King!" United on the only issue that mattered, they sprang originally from the Jaime Balmes Student Philosophical

Society, a group formed to counteract the foreign-funded YMCA, which was everywhere threatening the faith of Catholic youth. Reconstituted as the *Liga de Estudiantes Catolicos* (League of Catholic Students), they had functioned for a time as a sort of student auxiliary to the old National Catholic Party.

When the spiritual development of the members was made a priority under the inspired direction of the Jesuit Fr. Carlos de Heredia, the resistance became more supernaturally motivated. Another Jesuit, the French Savoyard Fr. Bernard Bergoend, continued the discipline and subsequently forged the group into the ACJM, *Asociación Católica de la Juventud Mexicana*. In those days it was hoped that the Constitution might be softened and religious liberty restored by peaceful means, but when the ACJM centers were looted under the very eyes of the police, and members found themselves under the necessity of defending churches and clergy from physical violence, battle was joined. Far from neutral, Rome knighted two of its leaders, Pedro Cisneros and Miguel Palomar y Vizcarra, into the Order of St. Gregory for their defense of the Faith. In the meantime, solidly behind their men, the women had banded together as the *Damas Católicas.*

Eventually, a brilliant young lawyer from Guadalajara, Anacleto Gonzalez Flores, active in the ACJM since 1916, founded a broader-based organization called the *Unión Popular*, heading at the same time a special posse known only as "U." When he succeeded in gathering all the various resistance organizations under the *Liga Nacional de la Libertad Religiosa*, the Cristeros proper burst into full flower. Taking his cue from the Book of Machabees, Flores vowed, "Although all nations obey King Antiochus, so as to depart from the service of the law of our fathers and consent to his commandments, I and my sons and my brethren will obey the law of our fathers" (1 Mac. 2:19).

The *Liga* had not neglected to ask counsel of its Bishops on the legitimacy of the armed defense it now contemplated, and these prelates, standing squarely on the Church's traditional doctrine, replied that force was indeed lawful when all other means had been tried and had failed. Although beyond this statement they disclaimed all official connection with the *Liga,* Calles nonetheless expelled eight of them from the country. The most acute problem of the *Liga,* which fought on in the shadow of what episcopacy was left, was a chronic shortage of ammunition, for whereas Calles obtained all he needed from the

U.S., shipments to the Cristeros from any direction were contraband.

In desperation, women pooled their resources to purchase whatever they could find in small quantities, shipping it to the fighters in fertilizer bags, potato sacks or soap boxes. One lucky transaction made with a garrison commander of a government ordnance department, who was being pressed for gambling debts, netted the ladies 20,000 rounds. But there was ammunition in other forms. After the promulgation of the Ley *Calles*, civil disobedience became a way of life for the embattled Catholics. Flores and his followers declared an economic boycott, which significantly reduced the value of the peso, and had it been implemented nationwide, the regime would certainly have been brought to its knees.

On July 31, 1926, the Feast of St. Ignatius, the Mexican prelates took the offensive by ordering the immediate cessation of all public worship. The Blessed Sacrament was removed from the tabernacles; no one could be married or buried; there were no Masses in churches; and normal Catholic life came to a standstill. When Calles responded by expelling nearly all the hierarchy, in November Pius XI lodged a formal protest in the encyclical *Iniquis afflictis.* Remaining open to all possible compromises, the Vatican Secretary of State Cardinal Gasparri was prepared to fill the empty Mexican sees with "non-political" churchmen to placate the government, but the Cristeros did not slacken.

They had acquired maturity, and they demanded an end to secularism in their Catholic country. Their goal was nothing less than a new order, structured uncompromisingly on Christian charity in the spirit of *Quas primas.* Flores summed up their position with, "The martyr is a necessity!" And there were many, both sung and unsung. Bishop Kelley, who as head of the U.S. Catholic Extension Society traveled throughout Mexico at the time, testifies to a "mystery" at work everywhere: "I had seen the love of the people for their pastors. I had talked with men whom I knew had great influence with the President. It was not the people. It was not the educated laity. It was not the President. What I had seen and felt was only a small part of the Mystery. Woe to any President of Mexico who does not think to act with that Mystery!"

One of the Mystery's best-known victims was the heroic Jesuit priest Bl. Miguel Agustin Pro, who carried on an underground apostolate in Mexico not unlike the "hunted priests" in England under Queen Elizabeth, particularly his spiritual forebear, Robert Southwell. Using a variety of disguises, the imaginative young Father risked his life daily despite serious illness to bring the Sacraments to a spiritually starving population. Catechizing, giving retreats in the very jaws of the enemy, providing for the widows and orphans of slain Cristeros, he even headed a sort of speakers' bureau to send lecturers to instruct and encourage the people. Only heaven knows the full extent of his contribution to the inner force of the resistance, but the Mystery was well-aware of its supernatural efficacy. In 1927, he was captured and accused of complicity in an attempt on the life of Calles' political partner, General Obregon.

Without descending to subterfuge, the establishment newspaper *El Universal* reported baldly, "We sought to capture him because he was one of the most zealous propagandists." Bl. Fr. Pro had eluded them for a long time, and there was not the slightest chance of his release. Suspecting that the attempt on his life was actually the work of Calles, Obregon ordered an investigation, but it was never allowed to take place. The martyr's biographer, Fr. Antoine Dragon, S.J., relates that nonetheless, "The matter was soon cleared up. It transpired that, in the evening of November 22, Calles had resolved to put Fr. Pro to death. He sent for General Cruz and ordered him to execute at once the four prisoners taken six days before." Besides Fr. Pro, these four were his brother Humberto and two other Cristeros.

"Cruz suggested that it might be better to save legal appearances. 'I don't want formalities,' retorted Calles. 'I want the thing done!' ...The truth is that President Calles executed Fr. Pro because the latter thwarted his designs against the Church. The man who thought himself all-powerful and stood as the personal enemy of Christ was exasperated at being checkmated by the personal friend of Christ." Led without warning into the yard at police headquarters, Fr. Pro was shot without trial the morning of November 23. To a guard who begged forgiveness on the way, he said, "I not only forgive you, but I will pray for you. I thank you for the great favor you are doing me today." His last words, pronounced with arms extended in the form of the Cross, were those of countless other Cristero martyrs: *"Viva Cristo Rey!"* His companions followed suit.

+

The martyrs' funeral turned into an overpowering demonstration of the Faith. Ironically enough, to Calles, intent on deriving maximum propaganda from the example being made of Fr. Pro, the Church is indebted for a wealth of photographs of the martyrdom. There is even a close-up of the sergeant putting the final bullet through the priest's head. Very soon, however, all were abruptly removed from circulation, for the demand for the pictures on the part of the faithful exceeded every expectation, and the propaganda was backfiring dramatically.

Fr. Pro had known for a long time that he would be killed. The year before, he had written, "The Catholics are making a stand. Reprisals will be terrible, especially in Mexico City. The first to suffer will be those who had a hand in religious matters.... I have had mine up to the elbow!... God grant that I be among the first—or, from another standpoint, among the last—at all events, among those to confess Christ! In that case, prepare to send your petitions when I am in heaven!"

Needless to say, petitions to him began immediately, in some cases answered by miracles, which continue to be reported now that he is beatified and his remains are suitably enshrined for veneration in one of the finest churches in Mexico City. It is well to bear in mind Fr. Pro's promise of help, for the battle for Amerindia is far from over. The last has not been heard of the Serpent's victims, some of whom, alas, are to be more pitied than praised. Years later, when Fr. de Heredia seized an unexpected opportunity to ask Plutarco Calles pointblank why he had killed Fr. Pro, the answer was, "They attacked and attacked till the BEAST rose and struck! I had to defend my hide and the presidential chair."

The Cristeros were never more than an underground movement, with little hope of destroying the tyrant, but under the threat they posed, the government was increasingly unable to function. Far from intimidating them, Fr. Pro's execution had only strengthened their cause, attracting ever more adherents. The situation had become so dangerous that the U.S. Secretary of State sent a warning to the harassed Calles. Flores had been captured seven months before Fr. Pro. Severely tortured, he gave no information, and like Fr. Pro was shot without trial. General Enrique Gorostieta, the able former West Pointer who succeeded Flores, was killed two years later. Still the Cristeros fought on, wave after wave of government troops thrown against them to no avail. Hundreds of priests, religious and laity were tortured and killed, but the movement did not abate.

Despair faced Calles, a consummate politician who could sway congresses, but dared not antagonize "the beast" headquartered next door over the border. Even in the face of the strongest popular pressure, he would not allow the smallest anti-Church article to be modified. Meanwhile, among the State Department papers filed on the Potomac in 1929 was the following item from the U.S. Ambassador to Mexico: "The commercial and financial situation is now at its worst; there is virtually a moratorium as far as the payments of debts are concerned.... It is the general opinion among the better class of Mexicans here that unless the Mexican government is able to exterminate the marauding bands of 'Cristeros' which infest the surrounding country, or come to some agreement with the Church whereby religious services may be resumed, the possibility of a return to normal conditions is very remote."

By phone he told his superiors that the 12,000 Cristeros concentrated in Jalisco and Guanajuato constituted his greatest worry. An oil crisis was building, the tomato crop was not forthcoming, and payments on foreign debts were in default. Something had to be done. As we have noted, along with their guns, the Cristeros were armed with supernatural weapons, not the least of which was the Holy Rosary, with which they were carrying on a major offensive. It had become clear to the Serpent's henchmen that to eliminate troops of this kind, some comparable supernatural power would have to be enlisted against them. The godless forces, driven to extremity, knew it could only be found in Rome.

The ambassador quoted above was Dwight Morrow, an able diplomat. The day after Fr. Pro's murder, he happened to set out with Calles in the company of the comedian Will Rogers and others on a six-day inspection tour of some new dams in conjunction with the oil problems. In this venue, when Morrow was solicited to open discussions with the Vatican regarding the religious turbulence, his reaction was, "No one but a madman would endeavor to settle the question of principle between the Church and Mexico!" Almost everybody knew the Serpent and the Woman were irreconcilable. No, the only hope lay in negotiating with the Pope over the heads of the Cristeros. Some practical compromise not entangled in principles would have to be worked out without their concurrence.

Thus it was that, on the heels of an understanding about the oil, a *modus vivendi* was contrived by the Ambassador and Fr. John Burke, a USan priest acting for the Apostolic Delegate to the U.S., with assistance in the later stages from Fr. Edmund Walsh, Vice-President of Georgetown University in Washington, D.C. Ambassador Morrow never saw the Cristeros as anything but a species of religiously motivated Mexican bandits. He is hardly to be blamed, for there was no one to disabuse him. His only acquaintance with the Faith was gleaned from the Americanist Catholic establishment back home, whose primary religious motivation ever since 1776 had been to avoid difficulties with the government. Bloodshed was unthinkable. Having heartily subscribed to separation of Church and state from the days of Bishop Carroll in the face of papal condemnations, the secularized clergy with whom Morrow came in contact could hardly have urged the cause of dissidents who proved so fanatically un-American.

The late Hamish Frasier pronounced the promulgation of the Feast of Christ the King as the greatest "non-event" of the century, elaborately ignored as it was by democratic governments the world over. By the same token, Catholics promoting the cause of Christ the King became non-persons. Whereas the Mexicans proved worthy of arousing persecution unto blood in this hemisphere, the same cannot be said of their brothers and sisters in the United States. Suffering no persecution themselves as a result of their accommodations to democracy, they offered little or no help to the Church in Mexico, whose plight in fact hardly reached their ears. The few zealous souls trying to raise money met with discouragement, rather than support, from the hierarchy. The true story of the Cristeros, like the true story of Franco's struggle in Spain or Dr. Salazar's in Portugal, has yet to find its way into the textbooks of politically correct parochial schools, which to begin with had been crafted to operate in tandem with a secular, publicly funded educational system.

But to get back to our story, a ready factotum for the contemplated compromise was found in Pascual Diaz, Jesuit Bishop of Tabasco, who for a long time had been trying to "broaden" the *Liga's* base to include non-Catholics by holding out prospects of funds from the U.S. Wishing above all to dispel the image of a holy war being projected by the Cristeros, he believed that they should begin by eliminating the cry *"Viva Cristo Rey!"* He failed to dilute the exclusively Catholic membership of the uncompromising group, but he succeeded in diverting financial aid from them. One American millionaire who was disposed to help was persuaded that it would be cruel to encourage a movement which was portrayed to him as doomed from the start. Foretelling a time when "men possessing great wealth will look on with indifference, while the Church is oppressed, virtue is persecuted, and evil triumphs," Our Lady of Good Fortune of Quito (Ecuador) may well have had the U.S. in mind, for beyond a few pious expressions of sympathy, no help worth mentioning ever arrived from that direction. As Our Lady said to Mother Mariana,"They will not use their wealth to fight evil and reconstruct the Faith." The new leader, Luis Bustos, quickly recognized that the USan giant was "determined to support the red radicals more strongly, and never the white radicals."

Not unnaturally, the *Liga* had initially turned for help to its own Mexican hierarchy, who had funds in the U.S. and Canada and had permission from Rome to sell their sacred vessels for cash. But they too declined to subsidize a movement considered too political for Church aid, but too Catholic for help from other sources. Nor did funds materialize from South America, whose governments feared military involvement. Some Catholics still hoping for U.S. aid formed a *Union Nacional*, in line with Bishop Diaz's suggestions, but like the old Catholic Party and all such hybrids, it produced nothing and only weakened the real militants. After Bishop Diaz was appointed official intermediary between the *Liga* and the episcopate, even Rome began withdrawing its moral support.

+

Although the Church never went so far as to condemn the Cristeros, as it did the Action Française, on February 2, 1926 Pius XI in an apostolic letter forbade both clergy and Catholic organizations to participate in politics. Roman policy having been conciliatory from the beginning, it was no surprise therefore when on June 21, 1929, the proposed *modus vivendi* was concluded. Its terms were devastatingly simple: No laws changed, but they would not be enforced in a manner hostile to the Church, and, in return, public worship would be resumed. The *Liga* battled on fiercely while the negotiations were in progress. When finally it was forced to disband, it was solely on direct orders from the Vicar of the *Cristo Rey* for whom they had fought and died.

The agreement was signed with an interim President, Portes Gil, who the following month exulted at a Masonic banquet, "Today, dear Brother Masons, the clergy have wholly acknowledged the State and have declared without subterfuge that they submit themselves unconditionally to the laws." On the same occasion, he declared, "In Mexico, the State and Masonry in late years have been one and the same thing, two entities who go forward prepared, for the men who have held political power in late years have known how to fortify themselves with the revolutionary principles of Masonry." Quite predictably, Bishop Pascual Diaz, S.J., who had rendered so indispensable a service in consummating this state of affairs, became Archbishop of Mexico.

Again quite predictably, the Mexican government did not keep its word. In *Acerba animi* three years later, Pius XI complained publicly "that not only were all Bishops not recalled from exile, but that others were expelled without even the semblance of legality. In several dioceses, neither churches, seminaries, Bishops' residences, nor other sacred edifices were restored. Notwithstanding explicit promises, priests and laymen who had steadfastly defended the Faith were abandoned to the cruel vengeance of their adversaries." His Holiness was not exaggerating. The Cristeros, far from turning to banditry as their enemies had predicted of them, returned peacefully to their homes and their work, only to be mercilessly exterminated.

All over the country, the anticlericals systematically hunted them down under cover of a nationwide army road-building program. Priests disappeared, along with the most important leaders, despite the fact that the Pope had been prevailed upon to sign the Modus only on condition that they be accorded full amnesty. "Furthermore, as soon as the suspension of public worship had been revoked, increased violence was noticed in the campaign of the press against the clergy, the Church and God himself." The Pope went on to deplore the ratio of one priest to 33,000 faithful in Michoacan, one to 60,000 in Chiapas (ancient bishopric of Fr. Las Casas), and one to 100,000 in Vera Cruz, pointing out that Rome had signed the agreement only as a lesser evil, fearing the disastrous effects which prolonging the suspension of the Sacraments was bound to have on the faithful.

So, of what use the blood of martyrs? Although the Serpent kept Mexico in its coils, the country enjoyed relative peace and stability for many years after they laid down their lives, but today Mexico's woe seems to have spread the world over. In 1970, the year the Traditional Mass of the Latin Rite disappeared to all intents and purposes from Catholic altars, the World Congress of Freemasonry chose to meet in Mexico, where it hailed at long last "the destruction of Papal Rome, regularly anticipated by Italian Masons and which Masons of all countries are inspired to achieve in order to destroy Catholicism."

Six years later, on the anniversary of the USan Bicentennial, the Brother Gomez quoted previously in our tale would tell his counterparts in the U.S.: "Although the 'Black Myth' is still believed by many of the ignorant and uneducated or fanatic, many of the clergy, especially in the hierarchy, have come to believe that Freemasons are not really devils, and since the Fraternity does not fight the Church or the legal authorities, the Bull of Excommunication does not apply to all Masons indiscriminately. You have seen this in the rapprochement with the Church here in the United States. We read of Archbishops and high officials of the Knights of Columbus attending Grand Lodge functions. I saw it in the Grand Lodge of California last year. We see them joining with us in community projects.

"In fact we are considered by them, along with the Protestant churches, the Eastern Orthodoxies and the Anglicans, as 'separated brethren.' Even in Spain, which was always 'more Catholic than the Pope,' and where our brethren have been underground since the rise to power of General Francisco Franco, the Grand Lodge of Spain is in the process of reorganizing itself with the approval of the new government and the consent of the Church.... The Prefect of the Congregation for the Doctrine of the Faith, Cardinal Seper, in a document dated July 19, 1974, admitted for the first time since 1738 the existence of Freemasonry exempt from the Bull of Excommunication, and, for that reason, to belong to the Masons is not, in itself, a cause for excommunication."

Is the Battle for Amerindia already lost? The year 1979 opened on two unprecedented visits to the heart of Amerindia in

Mexico. One was that of the powerful USan President, who apparently deemed it opportune to discuss in person, rather than through intermediaries, the perennial question of oil and other matters of paramount interest. He had arrived on the heels of the first visitor, who was none other than the new Pope of Rome, John Paul II, who was greeted with the respectful title of "Mister" on the part of Mexico's President, with riotous acclamations on the part of the thronging faithful, and with a mild earthquake on the part of nature. The Mexican Bishops assembled in Puebla for the occasion were informed by His Holiness that their Lord "unequivocally rejects recourse to violence," but if they betrayed any surprise at this unusual interpretation of Our Lord's teaching, it passed unrecorded.

This might lead us to believe that Amerindia's battle is only beginning, for the situation is exactly what Christ the King promised Catholics everywhere: "You shall lament and weep, but the world shall rejoice"; yea, even as the Lodges are doing. Had Our Lord not added, "You shall be made sorrowful, but your sorrow shall be turned into joy ... and your heart shall rejoice: and your joy no man shall take from you" (John 16:20, 22), things might be unbearable. Meanwhile, the Woman clothed with the sun who is Empress of the Americas bides her time quietly on Tepeyac Hill at the heart of Amerindia, whence Bl. Juan Diego heard her say, "Am I not your Mother?... Are you not cradled in my arms?" Can a people with so many advocates in heaven not be destined for fiercer battle to come?

PART TWO

The Sides of the North

Chapter V

TERROR OF DEMONS

Among the countless prophecies of the discovery of America was one which the Italian Renaissance poet Luigi Pulci set into his work *Il Morgante Maggiore.* Its content would command no particular interest, were it not for the fact that with singular perspicacity, the author placed it in the mouth of the devil, who declared, "Men shall descry another hemisphere." The development Satan feared most began to unfold as soon as the white men landed, for after the conversion of Papantzin and her brother Montezuma and the re-establishment of the Heavenly Queen's permanent shrine on Tepeyac Hill at the heart of the Aztec Empire, his half of the globe began suffering violence. With Catholic Spain overrunning what till then he had considered his exclusive preserve, there is reason to believe that he withdrew to his strongest position, to recoup his forces as far away from Mexico as he could get, on the east coast of what is now Canada and the United States.

Ages ago he had boasted, "I will sit ... in the sides of the north" (Is. 14:13), and even in America that proved to be his preferred seat of command. His tenure on these northern sides had been maintained by terror, having succeeded in reducing their inhabitants to the most degraded savagery, as compared with those on the other side of the continent. It was with good reason that Our Lord had told Ven. Mary de Agreda to concentrate her efforts on the Amerindians of the west rather than on those of the east, for, as He informed her, the latter were for the most part entirely subservient to the devil, who had convinced them that the white man had come only to destroy them. The first explorers spoke in hushed tones of the Isle of Demons off the coast of Labrador, which appeared in early Portuguese maps as the Isla Tormenta near Belle Isle. In the mountains, griffins were said to lurk.

Even the sober Yankee historian Francis Parkman was constrained to mention two islands which were allegedly "given over to the fiends, from whence they derived their names.... An old map pictures their occupants at length—devils rampant, with wings, horns and tail. The passing voyager heard the din of their infernal orgies, and woe to the sailor or the fisherman who ventured alone into the haunted woods." He quotes the French cosmographer André Thévet, who reported, "I myself have heard it, not from one, but from a great number of the sailors and pilots with whom I have made many voyages, that when they passed this way, they heard in the air on the tops and about the masts, a great clamor of men's voices, confused and inarticulate, such as you may hear from the crowd at a fair or market-place; whereupon they well knew that the Isle of Demons was not far off." Parkman adds that Thévet himself, "when among the Indians, had seen them so tormented by these infernal persecutors, that they would fall into his arms for relief; on which, repeating a passage of the Gospel of St. John, he had driven the imps of darkness to a steady exodus."

Even on this side of the continent, however, the Serpent's rule had been challenged before. Iceland and Greenland are known to have been under the jurisdiction of the Archbishop of Hamburg as early as 831, and Pope St. Gregory appointed St. Ansgar as Apostolic Delegate there four years later. The fabled voyages of the seventy-year-old St. Brendan, Abbot of Clonfort, which are related in the Irish *imrama,* are thought to have taken place much earlier, perhaps in the fifth century. He probably visited the Faroe Islands, the Azores and Iceland, where three hundred years later the Vikings told of finding Irish monks. This is not unlikely, for in the late seventh and eighth centuries Culdees and others resisting alignment with Rome brought another wave of Irish to America, to be joined by still more fleeing Viking raids on the Faroes. Pursued by the Norsemen, some may even have reached the continental shores.

In *The Work of the Catholic Church in the United States of America,* the Italian Carmelite Fr. Alonso Zarrati writes that there are "constant references in Nordic sagas to actual voyages, like that to Vinland attributed to Bishop John, or the notation affixed to Martin Behaim's map of 1492, according to which seven Portuguese bishops in the ninth century, fleeing from the Moors, repaired to a western island called Antilia, where they founded seven cities.... Testimonies such as those of Adam, canon of Bremen (1067), and Ari Thorgilsson (died 1148) may not be lightly dismissed, nor those of Nicholas, Abbot of Thingeyre (died 1159) or the surviving sagas of three intrepid Vikings—that of the Irish merchant Thorfinn Karlscfni (1305-35), which has come down to us in twenty-eight manuscripts; that of King Olaf; and the third, either by Eric the Red or his son Leif....

"These Viking sagas, togethcr with the commission given by the martyr-saint King Olaf of Norway (1015-1030) to missionaries to preach the Catholic faith from Norway to Greenland, would seem to indicate that Europe came into contact first with the northernmost part of the American continent." There was also "the letter of Nicholas V, dated September 22, 1448, directed to the Icelandic bishops of Skalholt and Holar, in which the Pope urged them to undertake the spiritual care of the Greenlanders, who had repeatedly asked him for it; the appointment made by Innocent VIII (1484-1492) of the Benedictine Mattio to the bishopric of Gardar; the rescript (1492) in which Alexander VI congratulated Mattio on his good work and exempted him from the payment of some tributary obligation; and also the fact that these voyages figure in pre-Columbian maps.

"A rare and tangible relic of one such expedition has come to light. On a wide, flat millstone found by a Swedish farmer between Alexandria and Kensington, Minnesota, is this Viking inscription: 'Hail Virgin Mary, save us from hell, year 1362.'" These visitors, who according to the stone were eight

Gotlanders and twenty-two Norwegians from Vinland, were therefore Catholics. In an unpublished study entitled "Concerning the Carvings on the Braxton and Yarmouth Stones," Julius Frasch Harmon concluded that an expedition under the patronage of Sts. Simon and Jude "sailed up the Mississippi after rounding Florida and putting in at Yarmouth (Nova Scotia). It reached Braxton County, West Virginia. It also reached the immediate vicinity of Kensington, Minnesota." Deciphering the number 361 from the runes on the lower line of one of the Yarmouth stones, Harmon read, "The 361st day of the Scandinavian year would be the feast of another Apostle, St. Thomas." If this is correct, the "invaders" would have attached significance to this date with very good reason.

Equally fascinating is the information supplied by Msgr. Peter de Roo in *America before Columbus*, who also tells of early missionaries to Canada. The Cross, for instance, had been well-known among the aborigines of Nova Scotia. The Franciscan Recollect Christian Leclerq, who evangelized Gaspesia in New Brunswick in the seventeenth century, tells of finding that the Cross had been venerated for generations among the Miramichi Indians on Holy Cross River. They "undertook nothing without the intervention of the Cross. When traveling on the water, they had one fastened to each end of their slender bark canoes as a protection against shipwreck, and their chief used it constantly as a cane and had it set upon the most honorable place of his cabin." Beyond these vestiges, however, the Faith left no permanent institutions of any kind.

The early preachers, who dotted both continents with Christian artifacts, had apparently been unable to produce the same lasting effects which St. Peter had left behind him in Rome. Our first Pope had been immediately followed by many helpers, who kept his doctrine alive after his death, whereas in America, alas, each new flock was in every instance abandoned to its own devices, and the Serpent was not idle. No doubt the authorities in Europe, soon entangled in the Crusades, needed all available resources to defend Christendom from the Mohammedan fox at its vitals, and there were no extra forces to deploy on remote frontiers. Inevitably, Catholicism, deprived of hierarchical support, was extinguished on all "the sides of the north."

The Christian missionaries who came to America after the Crusades were probably no more zealous than their forebears, but for various reasons they enjoyed greater encouragement and material assistance from national monarchs grown very powerful in the interim. They recognized themselves as the instruments God intended to use in dislodging Satan from his ancient stronghold and releasing thousands of souls from his tyranny. The sentiments Columbus expressed to Ferdinand and Isabella were those of all Christendom: "Let Christ rejoice upon earth as He does in heaven, to witness the coming salvation of so many people heretofore given over to perdition!"

The zeal of the Crusades was easily diverted to Amerindia, for in those days men were not accounted automatically saved who followed the religion of their choice. "This undertaking," maintained Columbus, "has no other purpose but the increase and glory of the Christian religion." He arrived initially at the northern sides at the base of a long coastline stretching from the Isle of Demons southward to the Devil's Triangle near Bermuda, landing on the island of San Salvador, near the rim of ancient submerged Atlantis, ... the devil's old domain, where in due time Christian heresy would find its first foothold in the western hemisphere, and the United States of America, political incarnation of the satanic "non serviam" would rise in defiance of Catholic Christendom.

The Serpent's brilliant illusion of an entirely New Order of the Ages, flourishing independently of God and His Church in full natural perfection, would begin materializing after a formal Declaration of Independence in 1776. In record time, despite every reasonable argument to the contrary, swamps were drained and a capital city arose at a most improbable and unhealthy location near the outer washes of old Atlantis. Today, overlooking the giant stone phallus which is the Washington Monument, the U.S. Capitol stands on an elevation once used by Powhatan's powerful Amerindian confederation for its religious rites, at the horned head of a great triangle of official shrines and buildings. In 1803, long before these artifacts were completed, the Masonic Irish poet Thomas Moore, well aware of the source of their inspiration, was already singing:

> This embryonic Capital where fancy sees
> Squares in morasses, obelisks in trees!

Inasmuch as religious freedom is a dogma of the *Novus Ordo Seclorum*, Christian saints and holydays are rigorously excluded from its official calendar, where Thanksgiving Day figures as the sole religious holiday. Devoid of Christian roots, this feast carefully addresses itself to no god in particular, although for a while it was conveniently ascribed to the god of the Puritans, who hoped it might displace Christmas. Among the plentiful documents left by the Plymouth colonists who are supposed to have instituted it, only two scanty paragraphs can be found which might have been referring to it, and these convey no religious overtones. Attended by ninety Amerindians and some fifty colonists, the party seems to have been little more than the natives' annual three-day harvest celebration so often excoriated by the Jesuit missionaries. Orgy may be too strong a word to apply to it, but the account says so much food and liquor was consumed at this joint ecumenical *Te Deum* that everyone had to go on half rations to get through the winter. If thanks to God were offered, they were not mentioned.

The Serpent was evidently still in control of the territory at the time, and according to a story in the *Wall Street Journal* for Hallowe'en 1979, even now devils roam the sides. A fiend known as the Jersey Devil has remained so easily identifiable that in 1939 he was proclaimed New Jersey's "official state demon." The *Journal* reported that for the last 244 years he had been "said to prowl the Pine Barrens, a dank 1500-square miles of wilderness infested with rattlesnakes and black widow spiders and incongruously wedged between Camden's boarded-up slums and the seashore's sunny boardwalks.... In 1859, *Atlantic* magazine called the area 'a region aboriginal in savagery.' A turn-of-the-century journalist saw the place as 'a dark, sylvan, medieval realm of witches, wizards, conjurers and monsters,' " where the devil "is said to have rattled Joseph Bonaparte, Napoleon's brother, on a New Jersey hunting trip.... Sightings of the demon have been legion," and apparently continue unabated today.

Under the circumstances, it is easy to see why the early Calvinist missionary Jonas Micaelis had despaired of Christianizing the neighborhood. Writing from New Amsterdam to a Dutch friend in 1628, he reported, "I find the Indians in this land completely savage and barbaric, alien to every decency and civility, as stupid as garden fence posts and given to every vice and bestiality, diabolical people who serve

87

no other than the demon. They possess so much witchcraft, divination, magic and perverse tricks that they cannot be held in check even with chains or with padlocks. Moreover they are thieves and traitors. As for their cruelties, they are worse than inhuman, worse than barbarians and Africans. It is difficult to perceive how such a people can be led to a true awareness of God." Obviously, neither Calvinism nor any other "reformed" religion was equal to such a task, so that before long their divines confined their efforts almost exclusively to tending their own flocks.

When it came to "barbarians and Africans" and the devil himself, only the one, holy, Catholic and apostolic Church founded by Jesus Christ possessed the necessary God-given hope and fortitude to confront the terrors of the northern sides. Not that Catholic missionaries were unaware of the extraordinary difficulties involved. A decade after Micaelis' ministry in those parts, the French Jesuit superior Fr. Jerome Lalemant wrote from his isolated mission in future upstate New York, "Considering from near as well as from afar this country of the Hurons and other neighboring peoples, it has always seemed to me one of the principal fortresses and, as it were, a *donjon* of the devils"—the veritable castle-keep of the satanic adversary. It was this stronghold of the nether world that the Catholics, not of Spain, nor of England, but of France, were divinely appointed to search and destroy. It is not incongruous that France, a preeminently intellectual nation and teacher of others, was entrusted by Providence with the arduous task, against monstrous odds, of turning Amerindia's head toward Christ—in the same direction as her heart.

Not yet suspecting the role Catholic France was to play in God's dispensation of the apostolate, the Spaniards were still preoccupied with colonizing and governing their vast possessions, which literally stretched from sea to shining sea. Each in his own sphere, united in the faith, Spanish seculars and ecclesiastics labored together to give, as Lope de la Vega put it,

Al Rey infinitas tierras,
A Dios infinitas almas.
"For the king, countless lands;
for God, countless souls!"

Although it was on San Salvador at the base of the
northern sides that Columbus had first landed, on the confines
of what he well knew was ancient Atlantis, the Atlantic coast had
hardly been penetrated, let alone explored. The entire northern
continent, from the borders of Nueva Mexico to Newfoundland,
containing the greater portion of the future United States and
Canada, comprised the one great province of Florida. It had
been only partially explored by de Soto, Ponce de Leon and a
few others, like Lucas de Ayllon, who in 1525 probably
established a settlement called San Miguel at the site of what
would eventually be Jamestown in Virginia, or like Esteban
Gomez who explored New York and New England at about the
same time. It was de Leon, anchored off the Florida peninsula
near Tampa Bay in 1521 at a period in history when altars were
already being pulled down in Europe, who was responsible for
the first Mass offered on U.S. soil, at least in post-Columbian
times. An episcopal jurisdiction for Florida was very likely
established a mere six years later, when the Emperor Charles V
appointed the Franciscan Friar Juan Perez as its Bishop, but
unfortunately the appointee died in 1528 on his way to Mexico.
On such data rests the claim that the Catholic Church is actually
the oldest institution in the United States. As Leo XIII noted in
his encyclical *Longinqua oceani* to the American bishops in
1895, "When America was as yet but a newborn babe, uttering
its first feeble cries, the Church took it to her bosom and
motherly embrace."

Curiously enough, it was in the small peninsular remnant
of greater Florida which now subsists as one of the United
States, that the history of Canada begins. The whole continent
being at the time the sole preserve of Spain, according to the
decree of Pope Alexander VI, it is understandable that the first
Frenchmen who presumed to colonize there were no God-
fearing Catholics, but Huguenots or worse. Like the Dutchman
Hugo Grotius, father of international law in the babelian
tradition, these were eager to defy the papal authority on
principle in temporal matters. In order to justify themselves and
lend their ventures better moral color, these same forces
propagated and probably invented the now nearly universally
accepted smear of that Borgia Pope, whose famous Line of
Demarcation constituted so intransigent an obstacle to their
plans for world domination apart from the Church. Profoundly
revered by all who knew him and elected unanimously to the

throne of Peter, Alexander VI, like Columbus, was never once accused during his lifetime of the flagrant simony, nepotism, immorality, incest and other calumnious accusations of which he was convicted without trial after his death by the enemies of Christ's Church.

But that is another story. Under their powerful leader Admiral Coligny, the French Huguenots had long yearned to establish in America what they termed "an asylum for the religiously persecuted." Enjoying the secret support of Jean Calvin (the Jew Jean Chauvin) and the Geneva heretics, not to mention encouragement from many French Catholics who looked forward to getting them out of the country, they disregarded the Papal Bull as early as 1555 and tried to entrench themselves in Brazil near Rio de Janeiro under the leadership of that erratic Knight of Malta Nicolas Durand de Villegagnon. This effort failing, they made a second attempt in 1562 on the Carolina coast near Hilton Head in the great Spanish Florida, this time under the able Jean Ribaut. This too ended in failure, but two years later yet another attempt under René de Laudonnière succeeded in establishing Fort Caroline at the mouth of the St. John River, not far from the present city of St. Augustine.

Meanwhile, however, Philip II of Spain had awarded a patent to his best sea captain, the God-fearing Don Pedro Menendez de Aviles, to organize the entire Florida territory into a proper government, a task which demanded the prompt dislodgement of the illegal heretic settlers. Thus, about the time Ribaut left Dieppe to relieve de Laudonnière— whose position was precarious despite the ready aid he received from the English pirate John Hawkins—Menendez left Cadiz with a company of some 2600 persons from all walks of life, to create the nucleus of a permanent working colony. Except for one ship and three hundred soldiers paid for by the Crown, all the personnel were maintained at the expense of Menendez, who believed "the conversion of the Indians chiefly depended on three things: doctrine, discipline and harmony. The Fathers would supply the doctrine; he would see to the discipline," and both would guarantee the harmony. Accompanying them or joining them later were eleven Franciscans, one priest of the Order of Mercy, a secular priest and eight Jesuits. The superior of these last, Fr. Pedro Martinez, was the first of his Order to set foot in America and was clubbed to death and probably eaten by the Indians in 1566.

Don Pedro founded the city of St. Augustine on September 6, 1565, and took formal possession of his new domain in the very teeth of the returning Ribaut, who was even then approaching the harbor to give battle. Falling to their knees as one man on the decks of their ships, the Spaniards implored the help of Our Lady of Utrera, for not a breath of air was stirring, and they were trapped. According to the historian Mendoza, "Forthwith one would have said that Our Lady herself came down upon the vessel, for after blowing the Spanish ships to safety behind a bar, the breeze grew into a hurricane which subsequently dismantled those of their enemies." Before these could recover, Menendez proceeded overland to exterminate the illicit Fort Caroline, which at the very least would have provided a convenient base of operations for the growing number of French buccaneers like Jacques de Sorie, who ten years earlier had sacked and burned Havana and killed thirty-four prisoners in cold blood.

Menendez spared the women and the children under fifteen, whom nonetheless, as he later wrote his king, "it gives me great pain to see in the company of my men, by reason of their wicked sect." Yet, "I feared that Our Lord would chastise me if I dealt cruelly with them, for eight or ten children were born here." He refused an offer of 50,000 ducats for the ransom of the men, remarking that "although he was poor, he would not do that weakness; when he wanted to be liberal and merciful, he would be so without self- interest." Not executed were twelve Breton sailors who had been shanghaied by the Huguenots, along with four Catholic carpenters and caulkers. Escaped stragglers captured later received no mercy, nor did Ribaut and his rescue party when they arrived on the scene to bargain for free passage. Taken by tens behind the sand dunes, they were asked whether they were Catholics or Lutherans, but quickly dispatched on Ribaut's assertion that all were of the reformed religion. Two teenagers, a drummer, a fifer and a trumpeter were the only ones spared.

"We held their fort," Don Pedro reported to the King, "having taken and put to death those who were in it, for having erected it there without the leave of Your Majesty, and because they were planting their wicked Lutheran sect, seeing that I came by Your Majesty's command to bring the Gospel to these parts, to enlighten the natives thereof with that which is told and believed by the Holy Mother Church of Rome for the salvation of their souls; that therefore I should not give them passage, but on the contrary should pursue them by sea and by land until I had their lives." Inasmuch as Protestant historians have not neglected to make the most of the incident, painting the Huguenots as martyrs put to death by a heartless cold-blooded killer in black and silver lace, the inquiring student may be surprised to learn that Menendez was an intimate of St. Francis Borgia and a gentleman noted for his probity and zeal.

As royal *adelanto,* he was responsible for the entire American continent from Mexico to Labrador, regent for Christ the King under the King of Spain. Legally under his jurisdiction was all the present territorial United States and Canada. In his letters to Philip II, it is clear he intended to launch out from St. Augustine and establish a major fort on Chesapeake Bay (by him originally named St. Mary's), from which to work northward and consolidate the Spanish claims to the northern fisheries around Newfoundland. Had he accomplished his designs, American history would have been radically different, and the Catholic faith the religion of the land, for he was particularly determined that heresy should never take root there.

When his men first encountered the Huguenots in American coastal waters, Menendez sent the following volley in reply to Ribaut's shout for identification: "I am Pedro Menendez, General of the Fleet of the King of Spain, Don Philip the Second, who have come to this country to hang and behead all Lutherans whom I shall find by land or sea, according to instructions from my King, so precise that I have power to pardon none; and these commands I shall fulfill, as you will see. At daybreak, I shall board your ships, and if I find there any Catholic, he shall be well treated, but every heretic shall die." Such was the politically correct response in those days, when the monarch himself could be quoted as saying, "Better a ruined kingdom, true to itself and its king, than one left unharmed to the profit of the devil and the heretics." Speaking for the aristocracy, the Duke of Alva remarked, "A prince can do nothing more shameful or more hurtful to himself than to permit his people to live according to their consciences!"

Frankly admiring Ribaut's extraordinary qualities as a soldier and organizer, Menendez wrote Philip that he considered this man's death "great good fortune.... He would do more in one year than another in ten, for he was the most experienced sailor and naval commander known, and of great skill in this navigation of the Indies and the coast of Florida. He was, besides, greatly liked in England, in which kingdom his reputation was such that he was appointed Captain-General of the whole English fleet against the French Catholics in the war between England and France some years ago." As we shall see, these early encounters set the pattern for the unappeasable warfare which inevitably developed between the old Latin Catholic civilization and the new WASP culture hatched in the policy of the upstart English Tudors. His Most Catholic Majesty the French King Charles IX, under pressure of his conniving mother, Catherine de Medici, and the troublesome Huguenot nobility she manipulated for her own political ends, made token demands on Spain for reparation for the massacre of his subjects in Florida, but he could have neither desired nor expected redress in a case where Spain was so clearly in the right.

Sending regrets, Philip placed the blame on Coligny for authorizing so illegal an enterprise in the first place, but the Huguenots made every bid for sympathy. In 1567, while Menendez was in Spain, Dominique de Gourges, a French adventurer who decided on his own responsibility to avenge his nation, is said to have fallen on the Spanish fort of San Mateo and put to death without discrimination all he found there. Paraphrasing the inscription Menendez had set over those hanged at Fort Caroline, which read "I do this not as to Frenchmen, but to Lutherans," de Gourges is said to have set over the Spanish victims the inscription: "Not as Spaniards, but as traitors, robbers, murderers." De Gourges' "revenge" probably never happened, but the story illustrates very well the basic difference in motivation between the two parties. Most likely fabricated propaganda, de Gourges' exploit receives no mention in either the Spanish archives or the Menendez family papers, but only in French sources. Ignored by the French king, it was publicized only by the Huguenots to fan the fires of dissent. Juan Lopez de Velasco, cosmographer for the Council of the Indies, in fact, states that San Mateo was voluntarily abandoned in 1570, three years after the alleged event.

In the meantime, at home in Spain, Menendez received the Apostolic Benediction from St. Pius V and returned to duty in Florida. The holy Pontiff's letter read, "For We hear such an account of your person, and so full and satisfactory a report of your virtue and nobility, that We believe without hesitation that you will not only faithfully, diligently and carefully perform the orders and instructions given you by so Catholic a king, but also that by your discretion and habit, will do all to effect the increase of our holy Catholic faith and gain more souls to God. I am well aware, as you know, that it is necessary to govern these Indians with good sense and discretion; that those who are weak in faith, from being newly converted, be confirmed and strengthened; and idolaters be converted and receive the faith of Christ, that the former may praise God, knowing the benefit of His divine mercy, and the latter, still infidels, may by the example and model of those now out of blindness, be brought to a knowledge of the truth. But nothing is more important in the conversion of these Indians and idolaters than to endeavor by all means to prevent scandal being given by the vices and immoralities of such as go to those western parts. This is the key of this holy work, in which is the whole essence of your charge."

Alas, the Indians of Great Florida were not like the Aztecs, who in the distant past had been enlightened by earlier apostles of the faith and lately favored with heavenly prophecies and apparitions. These were the Serpent's own well-trained shock troops, who operated at the very center of his American *donjon*, and excelled in liquidating missionaries. As Our Lord had predicted to Ven. Mary de Agreda, they for the most part flatly rejected the Gospel message. Entirely content with their lot, they would tell the padres, "The devil is the best thing in the world. We adore him. He makes men brave!" Nothing daunted, however, Menendez founded Fort St. Philip in the Carolinas, and from there dispatched missionary expeditions as far north as Virginia, where a log chapel had existed as early as 1570.

Eight Jesuits from St. Augustine, under their Vice-Provincial Fr. Juan Bautista Segura, followed the Potomac River to a village called Ajacan, which some authorities locate on the Rappahannock River. Betrayed by one of their Indian converts, they were butchered by the natives. Menendez led a punitive expedition which apprehended eight of the murderers and hanged them from the yardarm of his ship, but with the exception of the Timuquans and Apalaches, few eastern tribes were won to the Faith. Although other Spanish missionaries were martyred in what is now Georgia, by and large their apostolate flourished only in the vicinity of St. Augustine. Thanks to the doughty Don Pedro, however, French Protestantism made even less headway. The Huguenots never succeeded in establishing the political hegemony they desired in America, and although they survived in numbers, it was only as useful adjuncts to English Masonry.

In 1574, at the height of his career, Menendez was called home to lead the great Spanish Armada that Philip II was already mustering against England and Flanders, but he died suddenly that same year. Even without the unforeseen disaster to the Armada in 1588, his death would have proven a heavy blow to the Faith, for Great Florida seems to have perished with him. Not that his tenure was fruitless, for the first school on what was to be U.S. soil was the one established at St. Augustine by the Franciscan Minims he brought from Spain. In 1586, St. Augustine was sacked and burned by another of Queen Elizabeth's pirates, Sir Francis Drake, only to be rebuilt by the Spaniards with help from Havana. For many years, it struggled on as the sole viable European settlement in the future United States, but it would appear that on the east coast the Serpent had definitely won the first round.

+

It may seem incongruous to begin a study of French Canada with so much Spanish history, but it will serve to illustrate the contradictions which from the outset plagued French colonial policy. Preceded and ever accompanied by her bitterest internal enemies, Catholic France found herself inexorably maneuvered against Spain, the one other powerful nation who shared her zeal for souls and normally should have been her strongest ally against the machinations of the Serpent. Add to this the savagery of the eastern Indians, the northern demons and the pirates and buccaneers underwritten by the English crown, and some idea can be formed of the difficulties France faced. Spain also had her problems, arising mostly from the inevitable conflict of interest between her padres and her conquistadores, but she began her colonization a good half-century ahead of her future rival, with the papal blessing and as a monarchy whose people were solidly knit in faith and purpose under a strong paternalistic government.

France on the other hand arrived in America years later, as a nation already deeply divided religiously and forced to bring her household enemies with her. Able to cooperate with her heretics well enough on the natural plane of national self interest, she found her missionary efforts hampered at every turn by anti-Catholics ably aided by practicing Catholics vowed to the new humanism. With Rousseau's "noble savage" already conceived and ready to spring from ambush, intellectuals like Montaigne, Ronsard, Boileau and La Fontaine did not scruple to recommend that the Indians be spared Christianity and left to their own natural "innocence."

Worst of all, France entered America, as it were, by the back door, and that was not until the reign of the liberal King Francis I. Although Alexander VI's Bull restricted political sovereignty in the new world to Spain and Portugal, exploration was not forbidden to other nations, especially those seeking trade routes to the Orient. Among these was Giovanni da Verrazano, a Florentine in the French merchant marine, who in 1524 sailed the French flag into New York Bay, the Hudson River and Narragansett Bay, heading as far north as Newfoundland and as far south as Cape Hatteras. It was he who described to King Francis what is now Rhode Island as a land "as delightful and as large as the island of Rhodes." In 1533, when the French king prevailed upon the new Medici Pope Clement VII to modify the terms of his predecessor's Bull of Demarcation by interpreting them as applicable only to territories already discovered, Verrazano's voyages added up to a powerful claim for France.

Not that they were that nation's earliest. There was a persistent tradition, duly noted by the historian Parkman, that America had been discovered (yet again!) in 1488, four years before Columbus: "Cousin, a navigator of Dieppe, being at sea off the African coast, was forced westward, it is said, by winds and currents to within sight of an unknown shore, where he presently descried the mouth of a great river. On board his ship was one Pinzon, whose conduct became so mutinous that on his return to Dieppe, Cousin made complaint to the magistracy, who thereupon dismissed the offender from the maritime service of the town. Pinzon went to Spain, became known to Columbus and told him the discovery," being that same Pinzon who accompanied the great Navigator on his famous voyage in 1492. Proof has yet to be found, but it is known that Normans,

Bretons and Basques had inaugurated at a very early date, probably before 1497, a flourishing fishing trade in Newfoundland, which by 1517 was supplying much of Europe during Lent. In a footnote in *Pioneers of France in the New World,* Parkman opines, "The name of Cape Breton found on the earliest maps is a memorial of these early French voyages."

In 1534, on the heels of the mitigation of the Bull, the pious master mariner of St. Malo, Jacques Cartier, who had already sailed to the New World with Cabot, was dispatched to the northern sides by the French king to seek for the elusive Northwest Passage to the Orient and lay claim to the burgeoning New France. There he "found the capes and bays of Newfoundland already named by his countrymen who had preceded him. In 1565 Charles IX of France informed the Spanish ambassador that the coast of North America had been discovered more than a hundred years before and is therefore called *Terre aux Bretons.*" Also noted is that Sebastian Cabot, sailing to Labrador for the English, had named the place *Baccalaos,* the native name for codfish, which also happens to be the Basque word.

Cartier made three voyages, all with a special blessing from his bishop after the entire crew had gone to Confession and heard Mass at the Cathedral of St. Malo. The first trip was little more than a grand reconnaissance of the Bay of St. Lawrence and the discovery of the Island of the Assumption (Anticosti), and unlike most explorers of his day, Cartier was rigorously truthful about what he found there. In his *Première Relation,* he wrote of Labrador, "I am inclined to regard this land as the one God gave to Cain!" Nevertheless he had gained entry into the Sides, and on July 7 Mass had been celebrated there for the first time on the Gaspé Peninsula. By way of the St. Lawrence River and the Great Lakes, the French would eventually open up a field of apostolate vaster than all Europe, reaching to the Dakotas and down the Mississippi to the Gulf of Mexico.

Believing he now had the key to the ardently desired Northwest Passage, Cartier returned the next year, naming the Bay of St. Lawrence on that saint's feastday. Proceeding to the Rock of Quebec, where the little Indian village of Stadaconé was situated, he went on to another village called Hochelaga, whose site is now roughly occupied by McGill University in Montreal. Ever intent on finding the passage to China, he found himself hopelessly blocked by the turbulent rapids known as La Chine, a name applied to them in derision a hundred years later by the Sieur de la Salle, who lived on an estate nearby. As it was, Cartier's third voyage assumed an entirely different character from the two previous ones, for on his second return to France he had been accompanied by some Hurons, whose wily chieftain, Donnacona, in order to make sure he saw home again, filled Francis I's royal ears as he had Cartier's with tales of fabulous riches to be found up the Ottawa River in a "kingdom of Saguenay." This mythical land proved as elusive to the French as had the "seven cities of Cibola" to the Spanish. Relying on a notarized (!) statement from the chief, Francis was convinced the gold, rubies and spices of Saguenay would restore his faltering fortunes. Determined to establish a permanent base of operations in Canada, the "cluster of tents" called *kanata* in the native dialect, in 1540 he appointed Cartier Captain-General of the project. "We have resolved," averred His Majesty, "to send him again to the lands of Canada and Hochelaga, which form the extremity of Asia towards the west." Unfortunately, in command over Cartier he placed Jean François de la Roque, Sieur de Roberval, a member of the high nobility, who was only too eager to head the expedition as Viceroy and Lieutenant General of New France. This was a prime example of the contradictions inherent in the French overseas program, for the Sieur de Roberval was not only a protégé of the king's sister Marguerite d'Angoulême, Queen of Navarre, but a Calvinist, whereas Cartier was a staunch Catholic—as with certain reservations was the King.

Pope Paul III, unlike his more accommodating predecessor Clement VII, did not look upon the venture with a kindly eye to begin with, but he especially disliked seeing it entrusted to a heretic. As Samuel Eliot Morison was quick to point out, the supreme irony was that the new commissions "put conversion of the heathen on a par with discovering Saguenay," giving the expedition a distinctly missionary flavor, all the while committing a Calvinist politically to spreading the Catholic faith! Needless to say, such a two-headed expedition drew so few volunteers that Roberval was forced to load his boats with chained convicts in order to fill the required quota of colonial personnel. Among them was an eighteen-year-old girl by the name of Manon Lescaut, who refused to be parted from her convict fiancé and emerged from history three centuries later as the heroine of the opera by Massenet which bears her name.

One wonders what kind of Catholic example these prospective colonists must have given potential Indian converts. As it turned out, Roberval was so late in reaching his destination with this contingent that Cartier had by that time already laid out a settlement on Cap Rouge, where he had collected to take back to the King several huge baskets of quartz "diamonds" and fool's gold which he naively mistook for the real thing. Today "Canadian diamonds" rank alongside wooden nickels and gold bricks in current jargon as synonyms for egregious fakes, but as soon as Roberval's ships hove into sight, Cartier immediately took off with his loot and headed home without further notice, leaving his Calvinist commander to face the winter alone. That Cartier was never censured for his defection, either by the Crown or any of its subjects is testimony to the tenor of the times. He died a respected citizen of St. Malo not long after, a victim of the plague. As for Roberval and his settlers, they were forced by the rigors of their new habitat to abandon the colony in 1543, putting an end once and for all to French dreams of Saguenay. Indeed, with the accession of Henri II, France for a time lost all interest in developing her overseas potential. Roberval, whose cousin Diane de Poitiers became the new King's mistress, found other areas in which to exercise his talents and was killed in a religious riot in Paris in 1561.

Some insight into his character may be gleaned from an incident involving the notorious Isle of Demons, which figures as No. 67 among the *nouvelles* of the *Heptameron,* a popular collection of tales from the pen of Francis I's sister, the aforementioned Queen Marguerite of Navarre. Among the highborn passengers on Roberval's ship as it entered the Gulf of St. Lawrence was Marguerite de la Roque, a young relative of his who was accompanied on the voyage by her old Norman nurse. On discovering that Marguerite had a lover aboard, Roberval felt he owed it to his Calvinist principles to maroon both her and the old woman, who was found guilty of covering up the affair. Left on the dreaded Isle with four heavy matchlock guns for defense, the women were immediately joined by the intrepid lover, who, as the romance would have it, had signed on in the first place only to be with his lady love. Jumping overboard, he swam the distance from ship to shore, somehow managing to bring along two more guns and extra ammunition.

The three were left to the mercy of the elements and the demons of the Isle, who, according to the Queen's account, relayed by Parkman, "beset them day and night, raging around their hut with a confused and hungry clamoring, striving to force the frail barrier. The lovers had repented of their sin, though not abandoned it, and heaven was on their side. The saints vouchsafed their aid, and the offended Virgin relenting, held before them her protecting shield. In the form of beasts and other shapes abominably and utterly hideous, the brood of hell, howling in baffled fury, tore at the branches of the sylvan dwelling, but a celestial hand was ever interposed, and there was a viewless barrier which they might not pass. Marguerite became pregnant. Here was a double prize, two souls in one, mother and child. The fiends grew frantic, but all in vain. She stood undaunted amid these horrors, but her lover, dismayed and heartbroken, sickened and died. Her child soon followed; then the old Norman nurse found her unhallowed rest in that accursed soil, and Marguerite was left alone.

"Neither her reason nor her courage failed. When the demons assailed her, she shot at them with her gun, but they answered with hellish merriment, and thenceforth she placed her trust in Heaven alone. There were foes around her of the upper, no less than of the nether, world. Of these the bears were the most redoubtable; yet, being vulnerable to mortal weapons, she killed three of them, all," says the story, "as white as an egg." When hard-pressed by the demons, she quelled their fury by reading the New Testament out loud to them, and two-and-a-half years later, the indomitable Marguerite, emaciated and in rags, was sighted by a fishing vessel and returned to France, where she became a schoolteacher. She related her tale to Roberval's former pilot Alfonce, who passed it on to Marguerite of Navarre. This highborn promoter of feminism, free love and the new humanism thought it well to include it in her *Heptameron*, as proof of St. Paul's dictum that God chooses the weak things of this world to confound the mighty!

+

Amerindia's giant heart was won to Christ by the Spaniards, a people of prodigious power and vitality, who accomplished wonders beyond telling under the maternal inspiration of Our Lady of Guadalupe, but it turned out to be the French who were called to do the rest, under the paternal inspiration of her glorious spouse St. Joseph. If Mexico be rightly called the Heart of Amerindia, lying as a heart should at the geographical center of gravity, then it is to the north that its Head should be looked for. As head of the Holy Family, where Our Lady is the heart, her spouse St. Joseph, virginal father of her Divine Son, would therefore officiate as the head of Amerindia, where the Great Lake now called Michigan was originally named in his honor as a major landmark of his preserve. If the Jersey devil is still at large, we may be sure it is only by permission of St. Joseph, whom the Church designates precisely as "Terror of Demons." Even Satan, who must abide by the rules, had been constrained by organic necessity to establish his own high command in the north, exacting there bloody sacrifices consonant with the locale; for whereas in Mexico his worshipers were required to tear out living hearts from their victims, up north he apparently inspired them to rip living scalps from their heads.

St. Joseph had been proclaimed "Patron of New France" by the French of Quebec as early as 1624, but perhaps because he is the "hidden saint," he did not fully disclose his stewardship of Canada until the opening of the twentieth century. Acting in a capacity similar to Juan Diego's in regard to Our Lady, in 1904 the humble Holy Cross Brother André Bessette raised funds out of nowhere to build a little wooden chapel to St. Joseph on the great volcanic height which Jacques Cartier had named Mont Royal, and which now overlooks modern Montreal. Having appropriated the eminence for his Oratory, St. Joseph soon made his presence felt, for pilgrims to the spot began witnessing a stream of miraculous cures and conversions received through the hands of Br. André, and before long the little chapel was bursting at the seams with supplicants, its walls festooned with *ex votos* and discarded crutches from grateful beneficiaries.

Somehow the Amerindian natives who had greeted Cartier at the same spot nearly four hundred years earlier seem to have expected miracles to take place there, for Cartier tells us that when he arrived they not only crowded around him excitedly, but to his consternation brought him their sick and crippled. "One would think that God had come down there to cure them!" In desperation, to satisfy their entreaties, he distributed some little tin Agnus Dei medals to their children and

101

read the *"In principio..."* from St. John's Gospel, making the Sign of the Cross over their heads and "praying God to give them knowledge of our holy Faith and of the Passion of Our Lord," which he read them from Chapters 18 and 19. However much the Indians understood, they gave the bewildered Cartier every evidence of "marvelous joy."

To those besieging him with similar requests, Br. André would insist in his turn, "I am only St. Joseph's little dog," but by 1924, without worldly means or influence of any kind, he had managed to lay the cornerstone of the towering Basilica to St. Joseph which now dominates the area. Alerted to the threat to their rule, the demons of the Sides tormented him relentlessly in their efforts to impede construction, but they were no match for the little laybrother's unqualified confidence in the power of St. Joseph. Maltreated physically by the devils like the Curé d'Ars, he was also accused of insanity and hideously slandered, but his apostleship prospered. In 1937, when he died and was laid to rest in the Basilica, nearly a million people arrived to pay their respects and submit their petitions. Shortly before his death, he is said to have confided to a friend that Canada's patron was not entirely pleased with the building and that it would never actually see completion. According to a guidebook, in 1966 there was effected "a rearrangement of the sanctuary according to the new liturgy," which of course included the customary displacement of the Blessed Sacrament from Its traditional position on the high altar and celebration of the so-called "new Mass." Pilgrimages have dwindled steadily ever since, but the primitive chapel remains intact. Br. André's simple living quarters under the tiny belfry can still be visited, where he continues to reign in spirit in the shadow of St. Joseph, and all who "Go to Joseph" at the Basilica for help in their difficulties may take home blessed oil. St. Joseph's statue, blessed by St. Pius X for the Oratory, was pontifically crowned in 1955.

Before permitting special veneration to himself on Mont Royal, St. Joseph had been chivalrously promoting devotion to his Immaculate wife for some 300 years. Of all the Marian shrines of the North, none is more justly famous than the one at Cap de la Madeleine at Trois Rivières, at the confluence of three rivers midway between Montreal and Quebec. This region had been consecrated to the Immaculate Conception as early as 1643 by Jesuit missionaries, and at least three canonized saints, Fr.

Jean de Brébeuf, Antoine Daniel and Gabriel Lallement, labored there, distributing rosaries which continue to turn up for archaeologists examining Indian gravesites. The Cap also became the site of miracles, not the least of which occurred in 1897. In answer to a multitude of rosaries prayed by determined parishioners, the Saint Lawrence River froze over during the spring thaw after an exceptionally mild winter, permitting stones newly cut for the construction of their new church to be hauled from the opposite bank. In return for the favor, the parish priest had promised to spare the old chapel previously erected on the spot and convert it to a shrine to Our Lady, which soon became a place of international pilgrimage and a major center for propagation of the rosary. During the first stirrings of St. Joseph's Oratory in 1904, St. Pius X authorized the crowning of the image of Notre Dame du Cap, who is venerated today as the national patroness of French Canada.

In 1960, Br. André's cause was introduced in Rome, and he has since been beatified. Through his intercession and that of Bl. Juan Diego, we may therefore believe that Mary and Joseph together, the one from Tepeyac Hill at the heart of America and the other from Mont Royal at its head, are holding the North American continent in a protective, parental embrace. Who is more qualified to preserve America from the vengeance of the Serpent than St. Joseph, who not only saved the Infant Lord from Herod, but to whom heaven vouchsafes a singular power over the demons who afflict us? "Those that sought to kill the child" (Matt. 2:20) at the beginning of His earthly life were many and active, and their numbers can only increase as America relapses into barbarism.

With the erection of St. Joseph's Oratory on Amerindia's northern height, a command post was been planted from which "the seed of the Woman" can launch its divinely decreed warfare against "the seed of the Serpent" (Gen. 3:15) with telling effect. They have at their disposal a *donjon* of their own, replete with all the weapons wielded so successfully by the great Patron himself: silence, prayer, poverty, work, suffering, and, if need be, flight from the Enemy, with Christ in one's arms. When useless argument and sterile recourse to polls are finally abandoned in favor of this kind of heavy artillery, the northern sides will be converted to the Faith, as their Catholic discoverers intended. *"Ite ad Joseph!"* Go to Joseph, for as the liturgy says, God "hath made him lord of His household and prince over all His possessions." The exercise of St. Joseph's power from Mont Royal has yet to be invoked to full purpose. Cardinal Tisserant believed that his Oratory was in fact not restricted to America, but meant to be "the world's capital of devotion to St. Joseph." If America was capable of cradling world democracy under the influence of the devil, is she not capable of cradling the reign of Christ the King under the influence of the Holy Terror of Demons?

Chapter VI

THE WASP'S NEST

As the dimensions of Catholic France's efforts to carry the Faith to North America cannot be adequately conveyed without speaking of Spain, it is even less possible to avoid speaking of England, the little island kingdom once known as Our Lady's dower, but since become rather a lair of the Serpent. If French Canada began on Spanish soil, it bade fair to end on English, for Canada soon became one more battleground in the irreconcilable conflict between Latin Catholic civilization and the new Wasp culture (White, Anglo-Saxon Protestant) hatched by the upstart Tudor nobility which engulfed Europe. It was not Germany, and certainly not the Low Countries, which proved to be the headquarters of the Great Revolt, but poor little England, one of its first victims. In England, after the ascendancy of that malevolent political genius William Cecil over the puppet Queen Elizabeth, the dismantling of Christendom fell into the hands of well-organized professional wreckers—masterminds like Sir Francis Bacon, who forged modern speculative Masonry for that very purpose.

Revealing itself to be of Talmudic inspiration by its own internal evidence, Masonry was a close relative of Protestantism, which, as William Thomas Walsh so ably demonstrated in his biography of Philip II, was little more than a semi-regression into Judaism. Without openly denying Christ, these two forces achieved their common end in one Catholic nation after the other by attacking the Church He founded, questioning her authority and sacramental system. Many Jews who by reason of the European Inquisitions found it difficult to masquerade convincingly as Catholics for any length of time, fared easily enough under cover of Protestantism. The Marrano historian Cabrera states as common knowledge that most of the Christian heresiarchs and many heretics of his day were in fact Jews. In Jewish Life in the Middle Ages, Abrahams also says that the first leaders of the Protestant sect were everywhere actually called *semi-Judaei*, men of Jewish descent being as prevalent among them as they had been among the Gnostics in the earlier centuries, and, we might add, among the Communists in the later. Cecil's own origins are suspicious. His name was spelled variously as Sissill, Cecill, Sissille, etc., and his coat of arms bore a disturbing resemblance to that of the prominent Jewish family of Toledo, whose most famous son turned out to be Queen Victoria's political mentor, Benjamin Disraeli.

Prime targets were necessarily Spain and France, where Cecil and his friends underwrote, with the able help of a growing body of international usurers like the moneychanger-become-financier Sir Thomas Gresham, any subversive movement within their jurisdictions which might further their objectives. The Serpent's progress was slow in Spain, where a vigilant Inquisition still protected the faith of its citizens, but France, alas, had till then felt no need of such an institution and soon became infected with heresy at her highest levels of government. In the bloody civil wars which ensued, Spain aided the Catholic party of the Guises, whereas England supported Admiral Coligny and the Calvinist dissenters. Ribaut, the organizer of the aforementioned Huguenot colony in Spanish Florida, had actually begun his enterprise after conferring with interested parties in London. Thus, long before England had succeeded in anchoring a permanent colony of her own in North America, she was already at work laying the foundations of an anti-Catholic presence there.

In the circumstances, Catholics soon found themselves torn between loyalty to their Faith and their natural patriotism, national pride more often than not winning out over religious fervor and catapulting them into dangerous compromises with their spiritual enemies. Cecil had agents everywhere. One named Borghese was the Spanish ambassador's secretary; Sir Thomas Sackville served in Rome. Whereas some moved among seminarians and students of the expatriate colleges in Douai and Rheims, or at Louvain, others ordained for the purpose succeeded in infiltrating the Jesuit Order. A priest named John Cecil, educated at the English college in Valladolid, even insinuated himself into the confidence of the shrewd Fr. Robert Persons, Superior of the underground English mission. Other spies worked among the Spanish friars. In France, the task was relatively easy, for there the English ambassador Throckmorton met regularly with the Huguenot leadership and their secret sympathizers.

The earliest whirrings of the Wasp against the Lily of New France were quiet enough. Perhaps they were first heard in the arcane study of Dr. John Dee, the Welsh occultist so close to Queen Elizabeth and her masters, as he enumerated briefly on his new global map the territorial claims of England in North America. These were not insubstantial, especially in view of the growing disregard of Alexander VI's Bull on the part of supposedly Catholic monarchs like Francis I, who once told a Spanish legate that "the sun shone for him as for others, and he would very much like to see Adam's will to learn how he divided up the world!" This *bon mot* became a byword everywhere but in Spain and Portugal, the two nations which happened to be the sole beneficiaries of the papal allocation. Juridically unassailable as long as kings recognized the Pope as temporal head of Christendom, the Bull was attacked obliquely after Alexander's death by calumniating its author, who had the further misfortune of being a Spaniard. His alleged malfeasances have been seriously controverted by excellent authorities, like Msgr. de Roo, Roscoe, Rohrbacher, Capefigue,

Msgr. Justin Fevre, Leonetti and others, but to no avail. The falsehoods are now so securely entrenched in secondary historical sources that even pious Catholics believe and perpetuate them.

When John Dee set himself to making a case for England, he did not scruple to appropriate the fabled discoveries of the Irish Abbot St. Brendan and his sailor-monks around the Canary Islands, to which he added the weightier explorations of the naturalized Venetian John Cabot and his three sons, commissioned by the first Tudor king Henry VII in 1495. Seeking to reach China by the north as Columbus had sought India by the south, Cabot, styled *uno como Colón* by the irate Spanish ambassador, landed on Belle Isle off Cape Dégrat on northern Newfoundland. The seas being open to all, exploration was not limited by the Bull, but in open defiance of its strictures, the Cabots were empowered by the English king, in terms closely patterned on previous legitimate Portuguese charters, to govern whatever lands they discovered as his lieutenants, provided only they paid the Crown a fifth of their gains.

According to the chronicles of the Wasp propagandist Richard Hakluyt, Dee also produced in evidence the discoveries of the Oxford friar who, "being an astronomer, went in company with others to the most northern islands of the world" in 1360. His exploit, recorded in a lost volume titled *Inventio Fortunata* by one Nicholas of Lynn, was known to Columbus, according to the latter's son and Bishop Las Casas. Perhaps because the Tudors were Welsh like himself, Dee also advanced the largely nebulous pre-Colombian claim of the semi-legendary Welsh prince Mardoch ap Owen, who is supposed to have established a Cymric colony on the Atlantic shore as far back as 1170, leaving the Welsh language behind him among certain blue-eyed "Indians," who are said to have eventually moved to the Far West.

Both at home and in the great European universities, where heresy was already rampant, Dee's opinions carried enormous weight, not only because of his personal connections with many of the rulers of this world, but by reason of his standing as a "polymath," proficient in every branch of mathematics, astronomy and astrology. As a student at Louvain, where he made friends with the great Flemish cartographer Gerard Mercator, he was called "Doctor" without ever acquiring more than a Master's degree. One of the original

Fellows of Trinity College, created by Henry VIII, he traveled everywhere and created a sensation at the University of Paris. His private library at Mortlake on the Thames was consulted by new-breed intellectuals of every description, among whom was Queen Elizabeth herself. On one occasion, his residence was sacked by a mob of irate citizens who had become outraged at his pursuit of the black arts.

A professed practitioner of sorcery and alchemy despite his Anglican Orders, even in his college days he was regarded by fellow students as a disciple of the devil. He continued to be held in deep suspicion by many, and his refusal to perform exorcisms as Warden of Manchester College did not pass unnoticed. (It may be of more than passing interest that the best biography of Dee is supposed to be one written by Benjamin Disraeli's father Isaac d'Israeli, under the title *The Occult Philosopher.* A volume not easily found, it merited some 20 pages in Volume II of the 1842 Paris edition of *Amenities of Literature.*) Well-acquainted with William Cecil, John Dee first found favor with Edward VI. During Mary Tudor's reign, he was accused of attempting to kill her by poison and magic, and although he was cleared of charges of treason against this Catholic queen, he continued to be examined for heresy.

With Elizabeth's accession, he was immediately absorbed into the royal service, beginning by making astrological calculations to determine the proper time for her coronation. He also instructed her in the art of cipher, of which he was an acknowledged master. He made no secret of possessing a crystal and conjuring spirits, with the able assistance of the necromancer Edward Kelley, a convicted forger whose cropped ears were habitually concealed under a long cap. For a time, Dee and Kelley were known to hold wives in common, allegedly at the behest of the spirits they served. Apparently Dee's unsavory habits did not prevent his being entrusted with political missions by Elizabeth's handlers, for he proved himself particularly useful to the spy-master Francis Walsingham and Elizabeth's secret husband, the Earl of Leicester, legitimate father of Sir Francis Bacon and the Earl of Essex.

In John Dee, Judaic Protestantism appropriated to its own use the secret tools of the Old Religion of godless naturalism, for in him Herod and Pilate once more became friends, not for the destruction of Christ, but this time for the destruction of His Mystical Body. As we shall see, except for one equivocal exception in Maryland, the Faith played no part whatever in British colonization, toward which the English nation as a whole, still Catholic at heart in those days, was totally apathetic. In the *Dedicatory Epistle to his Divers Voyages,* Richard Hakluyt wrote in 1582, "I marvel not a little, that since the first discovery of America, which is now full fourscore and ten years, after so great conquests and plantings of the Spaniards and Portuguese there, that we of England could never have the grace to set fast footing in such fertile and temperate places as are left as yet unpossessed of them."

Clearly England was not motivated to discovery and conquest by Christian zeal, not even for the reformed religion. Another kind of zeal, however, kindled a steady flame in a small active minority of adepts, who like Dee were closely allied with the Illuminati of Spain and Germany. Slowly but surely, England would be propelled westward despite itself, as the visible, political spearhead of what was a well-organized undercover operation. To decipher its hidden agenda, one need only read the prolific utopian literature of the day, which poured as if by magic from international media based primarily in Holland, where so many Sephardic Jews had relocated after their expulsion from Spain. There is even some evidence that Sir Francis Bacon, author of the *New Atlantis,* had himself settled in Amsterdam after faking his death in England, living to the ripe old age of 104 under the name of William Franklin.

Inasmuch as the *Utopia* attributed to St. Thomas More was not published in England, but in the Low Countries under the aegis of the humanist Erasmus, there is reason to wonder whether More ever really produced so uncharacteristic a work. If he did, was it in jest, as a lampoon on rationalism? All the utopias of that era purported to delineate a self-governing society where man perfects himself according to the dictates of his own natural reason. The underlying heresy is evident, for apart from lack of dependence on God, no allowance is made for original sin and fallen human nature, which, when left to itself, inevitably inclines to evil. In accordance with the tenets of Judaeo-Masonry, in which this kind of world is conceived, the theological virtues of revealed religion—faith, hope and charity—are replaced by the democratic virtues of liberty, equality and fraternity. By practicing these, mankind forges itself into one great brotherhood, which declares itself the sole source of the political authority which the Son of God told Pilate is derived from God alone.

The futuristic vision preached in the *New Atlantis* being identical nearly word for word with John Heyden's *The Land of the Rosicrucians,* the dreamers hoped to see Bacon's ideal community of Bensalem materialize at last on those northern Sides of America not yet won to the Faith and still out of reach of the Church. Of such stuff was conceived the United States of America, a fiercely predatory nation whose novel political structure, largely adapted from yet another *Utopia* by the adept John Harrington, rests upon three anti-trinitarian governing branches—executive, legislative and judicial—whose interlocking checks and balances automatically promote universal harmony and justice without recourse to Divine Providence. When George Washington, first wielder of that nation's executive authority, assured the Mohammedan Barbary pirates of Tripoli in a projected treaty that he had no quarrel with them on religious grounds, inasmuch as "the government of the United States is not in any sense founded on the Christian Religion," it was clear that its Masonic framers would never have taken part in the Crusades, let alone the Battle of Lepanto. Not because of any partiality to Islam, but because religion was supposedly irrelevant in Utopia and not worth fighting about.

+

Or so it would appear. In the *New Atlantis,* the visitors to Bensalem make the acquaintance of a mysterious personage named Jacobin. "He was a Jew and circumcised," runs the narrative, there being "some stirps of Jews yet remaining among them, whom they leave to their religion ... of a far differing disposition from the Jews in other parts. For whereas they hate the name of Christ and have a secret inbred rancor against the people among whom they live, these contrariwise give unto our Savior many high attributes, and love the nation of Bensalem extremely. Surely this man of whom I speak would ever acknowledge that Christ was born of a virgin and that he was more than a man; and he would tell how God made him ruler of the seraphims which guard his throne; and they call him also the Milken Way and the Elijah of the Messiah and many other high names which, though they be inferior to his divine majesty, yet they are far from the language of other Jews." This man believed that the laws of Bensalem had been ordained by Moses in a secret cabala and that "when the Messiah should come and sit at his throne at Jerusalem, the king of Bensalem should sit at his feet, whereas other kings should keep a great distance...."

On their arrival, the visitors were informed of an Order known as the House of Salomon or the College of the Six Days' Work, whose similarity to Masonry is more than passing. The Father of the Order, lately returned from Spain in Bacon's story, deigns to enlighten them (in Spanish) on its secret workings, whose purpose is "the knowledge of causes, the secret motions of things; and the enlarging of the bounds of human empire, to the effecting of all things possible." As summarized by William Thomas Walsh in his biography of Philip II, the sage reveals that "the Order has many caves, some three miles deep, for the concealment of its experiments in science, alchemy (the producing of new artificial metals) and medicine. It also has high towers on three different levels, the Upper, Lower and Middle regions; and they use them for observation, conservation, refrigeration and so on. The members of the Order control medicine, science, astrology and a large variety of natural commodities and riches; and music in which even quarter-tones appear." They also carry on what amounts to experimentation in weather control, aerodynamics, locomotion, optics, health foods, toxicology, agriculture, weaponry, not to mention artificial resuscitation and genetics.

The Father tells of dissecting animals "that thereby we may take light of what may be wrought upon the body of a man.... By art likewise we make them greater or taller than their kind is, and otherwise dwarf them and stay their growth; we make them more fruitful and bearing than their kind is, and contrariwise barren and not generative, " even producing new species. To sustain this gigantic inquiry into the hidden forces of nature, twelve "Merchants of Light" are designated who "sail into foreign countries under the names of other nations (for our own we conceal) who bring us books and abstracts and patterns of experiments of all other parts." Also appointed are Depredators, Mystery-men, Pioneers or Miners, Compilers, Dowry-men or Benefactors, Lamps, Inoculators and most important of all, the Interpreters of Nature," all further assisted by "novices and apprentices ... a great number of servants and attendants, men and women.

"And this we do also: we have consultations, which of the inventions and experiences which we have discovered shall be published and which not; and take an oath of secrecy, for the concealing of those we think fit to keep secret; though some of those we do reveal sometimes to the State and some not." We who are living in a highly technological society four centuries after this fable was penned are in an excellent position to judge how much of it has come true. Modern technology, so carefully controlled behind the scenes, was therefore not only an integral factor of the resurging pagan empire, but an indispensable means of absorbing the entire world into its orbit. The Industrial Revolution did not just happen to begin in England, or come to flower across the Atlantic. From its inception it was conceived as a worldwide project. Not to be overlooked is the ominous last sentence of Bacon's unconcluded opusculum. He says the Atlanteans "give great largesses, where they come, upon all occasions." Who was it who tempted Christ the King in the desert with "all the kingdoms of the world?"

John Dee moved constantly throughout England and Europe, promoting the glorious project of which Bacon wrote. He even reached Cracow, seat of Copernicus and his revolutionary theory of the heavens, which was actually nothing more than a rehash of the error of Aristarchus, but very useful to the Brotherhood. Dee was even invited to Russia, but refused to travel so far. He saw the Emperor Rudolph briefly in Prague, but that worthy, despite his weakness for the black arts, was still too Catholic to conspire directly against the Papacy. Dee is credited with coining the name "British Empire," not only long before such an entity existed, but at a time when English sea power was far inferior to that of most European nations. He set himself to remedying this deficiency by turning his prodigious talents to navigation. He searched in vain for a quick method of calculating longitude, but he was an accomplished map maker and abreast of every successful new device. Not the least of his inventions was a means of getting news ahead of everyone else by using a succession of mirrors positioned at strategic locations.

Advisor to all the great English navigators of the day, he was also special consultant to the Muscovy Company, which had been formed by the new financiers to market English woolens to the inhabitants of the cold North. A main objective was Newfoundland, where Henry Tudor had made a beginning with the Cabots' exploratory voyages. As instigator of numerous searches for northern passages to the Orient by which England could circumvent the southern routes controlled by the Catholic powers, Dee believed it feasible to sail over the North Pole. In 1576, he personally instructed the pilots of Martin Frobisher's ships in the use of several newly invented instruments, among them the cross-staff or balestila, which he had recently brought from Holland to calculate celestial altitudes. The maps used by Frobisher, which actually led to the discovery of the northern outlet to the Pacific via Baffin Bay, were Dee's inspiration.

His close associates also bear mention. Besides Sir Thomas Gresham and those two notorious persecutors of Catholics Sir Francis Walsingham and Sir William Cecil, were three blood relatives from Dartmouth, who formed the working nucleus of his imperial enterprise: Sir Humphrey Gilbert and his half-brother Sir Walter Raleigh, and John Davis. To this group may be added the afore-quoted propagandist Richard Hakluyt, whom Walsingham appointed to the English embassy in Paris in 1583, and whom only old age prevented from playing Rector to the heretic English colony founded at Jamestown in Spanish Florida on the heels of the Huguenot attempt. Having popularized the glories of discovery in nearly a thousand pages of the *Voyages* for which he is famous, Hakluyt became a staple of secondary school curricula.

At Raleigh's request, he also wrote for Queen Elizabeth a *Discourse concerning Western Planting,* and although it was not published until three hundred years later, it had enormous influence in the state of Maine in the USA! Among the seven basic objectives the work proposed, was a quick solution to England's acute unemployment problem, caused by the new Tudor nobility, who reduced thousands of honest farmers to beggary overnight by preempting their lands to pasture sheep for the increasingly lucrative new woolen trade. So why not ship the dispossessed off to America? Besides the extension of the Reformed Religion, other purposes for colonization were economic independence for England, whose only share so far in the wealth of America was the booty procured by Elizabeth's pirates; the development of the crucial Northern Passage; and the acquisition of overseas bases in view of open warfare with Spain.

Hakluyt assured the Queen that despite Alexander VI's Bull, the Spanish claim to mainland America was invalid, not only because of Prince Mardoch, but because "Cabot discovered this long tract of firm land two years before Columbus ever saw any part of the continent thereof." It would be a pity, said he, "and incur great danger and inconvenience in suffering Papists ... to enrich themselves under our noses, to be better able to supplant or overrun us.... This enterprise may stay the Spanish King from flowing over all the face of that waste firm of America, if we seat and plant there in time.... How easy a matter may it be to this realm, swarming at this day with valiant youths rusting and hurtful by lack of employment ... to be lords of all those seas and to spoil Philip's Indian navy and to deprive him of the yearly passage of his treasure into Europe, and consequently to abate the pride of Spain and of the supporter of the great Antichrist of Rome, and to pull him down in equality with his neighbor princes."

Much of what Hakluyt proposed would have been expected from the administration of Sir Humphrey Gilbert, for it was to him and to Francis Bacon before him that the devil's *donjon* had been entrusted by Elizabeth. Her grant to Gilbert in 1578 was in fact the first English proprietary charter, whose terms constituted a precedent for later English allocations abroad. Guaranteeing colonists the same rights they enjoyed in England, the charter also imposed the same laws and religion of the mother country. Conspicuous by its absence is any mention of converting the natives to Christianity, reformed or otherwise. The only stipulation regarding religion was that the colony's laws must never be "against the true Christian faith or religion now professed in the Church of England." Sir Humphrey himself, who firmly believed that Quetzalcóatl was none other than the fabled Prince Mardoch, was a zealous anti-Catholic, who had implemented the English Plantation in Ulster, Ireland, and was responsible for crushing the Munster rebellion with unconscionable cruelty. Like most of his ilk, he also dabbled in alchemy.

Granted permission by his charter to take possession of any land between Labrador and Florida not yet claimed by a Christian government, he made two trips to America. Neither yielded any tangible results, but on August 5, 1583, he took possession of Newfoundland and raised there—certainly not the Cross of Christ the King—but a wooden post bearing the arms of England. The Wasp had a nest on the Sides of the North at last, and it is more than curious that three years previously Gilbert had made an oral gift to John Dee of all the land above the 50th latitude, which happens to comprise nearly the whole of Canada. What Dee may have bestowed on Gilbert in exchange is not known, but some high tors in Greenland were once known as Dee's Pinnacles, and Narragansett Bay was once called Dee's River. Gilbert made smaller grants to pay off investors, but strangely enough the source from which he expected the most revenue was the large body of English Catholic recusants, who wanted no part of the new religion, and whom he hoped to lure away from England with a promise of religious toleration in an overseas ecumenical colony.

He found two Catholics, Sir George Peckham and Sir Thomas Gerard, who agreed to collaborate with him in this project, for which a dangerous precedent had been set forty years earlier by Catholic France's Cartier-Roberval experiment. That mixed settlement had failed miserably, but the gambit was a good one, and the Wasp would play it again and again until the Masonic dogma of freedom of conscience was imposed over all North America. Oftentimes, it would be proclaimed most loudly by Catholics, who hoped to sidestep open persecution by availing themselves of ecumenism's paralyzing shelter. Thus Gilbert planned to remove to the New World any possible instigators of the Catholic counterrevolution which constantly threatened Elizabeth's precarious rule at home over a population still preponderately Catholic in instinct.

His hopes were premature, however, for Catholics still found exile even less attractive than paying fines or risking prison and the gallows in expectation of a Catholic restoration, which actually occurred during Mary Tudor's brief reign. Another deterrent was the Spanish ambassador, who wished to keep as many Catholics as possible in England to facilitate the invasion his master Philip II was planning. No doubt divining the true nature of the Gilbert Plan, he warned that any Englishmen settling anywhere near Florida could expect to have their throats cut, as had already happened to Ribaut and his Huguenots. We are told that on his last voyage Sir Humphrey took with him a copy of Sir Thomas More's *Utopia*, which accompanied him to Davy Jones' locker when he was lost at sea. His patent was subsequently transferred to Sir Walter Raleigh, and his end duly recorded by Hakluyt. One Thomas

Churchyard celebrated his exploits in a long poem, commending him as a hero who wished to save America from the cruel Spaniards.

+

In *The Northern Voyages,* the Yankee historian Samuel Eliot Morison says Gilbert "regarded a colony not as a place to exploit the natives and get rich, but as a social experiment to cure unemployment at home and realize the Utopian dream outlined in the last book which he is known to have read," referring to St. Thomas' *Utopia.* "Long did he entertain these ideas, never did he give them up, and after his death they were in part attained"— wrote George Calvert, better known as Lord Baltimore, whose career exhibits numerous contradictions which hardly support the popular versions taught in parochial and public schools throughout the U.S. The zealous, enlightened and fearless Catholic convert who, in his newfound fervor, wrested permission from his bigoted heretic sovereign James I to found a sanctuary where persecuted Papists could practice their faith in peace and tranquility simply refuses to stand out clearly from the existing documents.

We are sorely tempted to believe that this idealized Calvert was fabricated to bring Catholics in line with the prevailing utopian schemes which from the beginning underlay the English colonization of America. As in the case of the Cecils and others who seemed to spring full-blown out of nowhere to wield positions of power in an England lost to the Faith, the origins of George Calvert are lost in obscurity. Possibly of Flemish extraction, as his name would imply, he is said to have come from an old Yorkshire family, but nothing certain is known beyond the fact that his father Leonard lived there in the days of Elizabeth. Whoever they were, they were well-to-do, for George studied on the Continent, where he presumably formed his close friendship with William Cecil's son Robert, for whom he named his first son.

The historian William Hand Browne says, in *George Calvert and Cecilius Calvert,* that "he became Cecil's secretary, and was appointed by the king Clerk of the Crown and of Assize in County Clare, Ireland, an office of importance resembling that of an attorney-general. This was the first link connecting Calvert with Ireland, in which kingdom he was afterward to hold considerable estates and a place on the roll of nobility." His reports dwelt "especially on the harmful influence of the Jesuits; a point worth noting, as we shall see later that his son and successor entertained a strong dislike and suspicion of that order." Employed in important diplomatic missions besides, Calvert was knighted in 1617 and succeeded the Cecils as England's Secretary of State. According to the French ambassador Tillières, the control of all public affairs thenceforth rested with Calvert and his adjunct, Lord Buckingham. In addition to a key treasury post, he had a seat for Oxford in Parliament in 1624. Three years earlier, he had been rewarded for his innumerable services to the ruling powers by a 2300-acre estate in Ireland.

When King James died, Calvert continued in favor with his successor Charles I, allowing him to begin turning his attention to his main interest in life: establishing an English colony on the Sides of the North, where Sir Humphrey Gilbert had failed. He had been a member of the second Virginia Company and of the New England Company, and in 1620, he had purchased a plantation in Newfoundland called Avalon. This name, which perhaps dates from Sir Francis Bacon's previous tenure, is one drawn from Arthurian romance, with its democratic Round Table representing an ocean isle of terrestrial happiness, where all sit as equals. Rosicrucians say it is an occult synonym for Atlantis and figures in cipher as Prospero's island in the Bacon-Shakespeare play *The Tempest.* Eventually Avalon was set up by royal charter as a palatinate province including the entire southeastern peninsula from Placentia Bay to Trinity Bay, over which Calvert ruled as a virtual potentate who lay down laws framed with the advice and consent of its freemen.

With this second Wasp's nest anchored in the upper north, the Lily of France was closely threatened. During Calvert's incumbency, hostilities quickly developed between the French and the English, and he himself relates with some pride how he seized six French ships under the command of Admiral de la Rade. The armed vessels sent out against him should be of special interest to American Catholics, for they were no other than the well-known Ark and the Dove, which, in 1634, would bring the first contingent of English Catholics to America. By that time, the ships had seen considerable military action in those northern waters, for as Calvert wrote his king, "I came to build, set and sow, but am fallen to fighting with Frenchmen, who have here disquieted me and many others of his Majesty's subjects by fishing in this land." The irony was apparently entirely unintentional.

A few years after all this transpired, presumably between visits to his new colony, George Calvert, the illustrious and devoted agent of the expanding heretic Empire, is said to have, suddenly and without warning, proclaimed himself a convert to the Church of Rome! God's grace can act in mysterious and wonderful ways, but facts in support of this unexpected reversal have so far proved impossible to establish. The exact date of his conversion has never been fixed with any certainty, but it is said to have been the work of the volatile Fr. Tobie Matthew, S.J., intimate friend of Sir Francis Bacon and well-known to Robert Cecil. A son of the Anglican Archbishop of York, Sir Tobie was himself a convert, who in 1617 had been ordained to the Catholic priesthood by no less a personage than Cardinal St. Robert Bellarmine. Strangely enough, this event did not prevent Fr. Matthew from being knighted nine years later, in a land where it was against the law even to attend Holy Mass.

According to the *Aspinwall Papers,* Sir Tobie took Calvert to the North of England to be received secretly into the Church in February of 1625, yet on the 16th of that same month, wonder of wonders, Calvert, despite his change of religion, was elevated to the Irish peerage as Baron Baltimore of County Longford! King James' death occurred not long after this, but Calvert was retained by the new King Charles I in the Privy Council. He had already resigned the Secretaryship, not for religious reasons as generally inferred, but in order to devote his full time to the Avalon project. This was to be a utopian ecumenical colony like Gilbert's, designed for commercial profit. Unlike the one founded by the Pilgrims in New England at about the same time, Avalon made no pretense of offering a refuge for the religiously persecuted. Baltimore provided both Protestant and Catholic pastors for the settlers.

John Pendleton Kennedy, a severe critic of Baltimore and a one-time President of the Maryland Historical Society, notes that Baltimore had for a long time been "a member of a company concerned with the colonization of Virginia.... One of the Committee of Council for the plantations, he had ample opportunities to become acquainted with the character of these enterprises which very few possessed. There is indeed abundant evidence that these schemes of colonization were a favorite speculation of his. He was engaged in them from the date of his early manhood until the close of his life." Furthermore, as Proprietary and absolute lord of Avalon, "he possessed the patronage and avowedsons of all churches and chapels, and ... [caused] them to be consecrated according to the ecclesiastical laws of England." If he was a Protestant in those days, this should cause no surprise; but was he?

Kennedy believed his conversion was a myth and that he had always been Catholic, for "there is proof extant to show that he had always been attached to the Church of Rome, or at least from an early period in his life." Uncovering no record that Baltimore was ever a Protestant, Kennedy wonders whether he was not rather "one of those who did not choose to make any very public exhibition of his faith." As it is, the sole authority for Calvert's alleged conversion is Fuller's *Worthies of England,* on which all other references to it rest. All Baltimore's children, furthermore, passed for Catholics, most of them already grown at the time of their father's supposed change of religion. Is it logical to assume they too were converted at the same time he was? If Kennedy's conclusions prove correct, then Baltimore would appear to have been merely one of those many indifferent Catholics in political life whose religious principles rarely present any serious obstacle to their advancement in this world.

Among other discrepancies which have been pointed out, George Calvert could never have retained the king's favor had he really left the Church of England for Rome, for James I was no religious fence-straddler, but a militant Protestant, who prided himself on his knowledge of theology. Kennedy notes,"There were several Catholic noblemen who enjoyed the confidence and friendship of James," who harbored no resentment "against such Catholics as had been bred and nurtured in that Faith .... But he was noted for the avowal of particular hostility against such as had been converts from the Protestant Church. In a memorable speech at Whitehall, James in fact singled these out as "apostates" and vowed, "I can love the person of a papist, being otherwise a good man and honestly bred, never having known any other religion, but the person of an apostate I hate!"

These anomalies have been conveniently dismissed by Americanist historians bent on portraying Baltimore as a zealous apostle of the Faith, but never have they been refuted or explained by any one of them. The contradiction remains: Why was it expedient for Calvert to proclaim himself Catholic at so great risk to his career if he had always been one? And if he did in fact convert, why was this no hindrance to his aspirations? What were George Calvert's true affiliations? The only known contemporary portrait of the first Lord Baltimore is one by King James' court painter Mytens. Strangely enough, it is, or at least was, in the possession of the Earls of Verulam, heirs of Francis Bacon, founder of modern English Masonry. Like many prominent Catholics of the period, is it possible that the Calverts had double allegiances which would be openly avowed only by their descendants?

Who, exactly, was the "Calvert" listed in the annals of Masonry among the seven founders of the Grand Lodge of London in 1717? In the *Weekly Journal or British Gazeteer* for April 11, 1730, the following item occurs: "A few days since, their Graces the Dukes of Richmond and Montagu, accompanied by several gentlemen who were all Free and Accepted Masons, according to ancient custom, formed a lodge at the top of a hill near the Duke of Richmond's seat at Goodwood in Sussex and made the Right Hon. the Lord Baltimore a Free and Accepted Mason." This would have been Charles, fifth Lord Baltimore, Protestant son of the apostate fourth Lord, Benedict Leonard. The first Papal Bull forbidding Catholics to join the Masons was promulgated in 1738. Might not Catholic Calverts have been affiliated long before that date and already promoting the Masonic ecumenical agenda in good conscience?

The colony at Avalon did not prosper, and Baltimore was granted a new but very similar charter for a huge tract farther south on the Atlantic coast around Chesapeake Bay. Charles I wished it to be called "Marianna," but Baltimore opted for "Crescentia." They finally compromised on Mary-Land, in honor of the king's wife Henriette Marie, daughter of the French King Henri IV. If the state of Maryland was named for Our Lady, as some Catholics believe, history is silent on the subject. George Calvert having died in 1632 before the charter passed the Great Seal, the grant was conferred on his eldest son Cecil, second Lord Baltimore. Choosing to direct affairs from England, where he could keep an eye on the deliberations of Parliament, Cecil appointed his younger brother Leonard Governor of Maryland. On that soil was supposedly born under

Catholic auspices the principle of freedom of religion for all men, which was later incorporated into the Constitution of the United States and eventually into the pronouncements of the Church's Second Vatican Council.

The historian Sebastian Streeter, however, has this to say: "The assertion has long passed uncontradicted that toleration was promised to the colonists in the first conditions of plantation; that the rights of conscience were recognized in a law passed by the first Assembly held in the colony; and that the principal officers from the year 1636 or 1637, bound themselves not to molest, on account of his religion, anyone professing to believe in Jesus Christ. I can find no authority for any of these statements." He maintains that no such act was passed "until fifteen years after the first settlement, at which time a Protestant had been appointed Governor, ... a majority of the Burgesses were of the same faith, and ... for the first time a clause involving a promise not to molest any person professing to believe in Jesus Christ and 'particularly a Roman Catholic' was inserted by the direction of Lord Baltimore in the official oath."

Before that, says he, only practical toleration could have existed. He would accord the honor of toleration to neither Catholic nor Protestant. Under the circumstances, Lord Baltimore simply had no other choice, and the laws "were drawn up in deference to the progressive doctrines and increasing political strength of the Independents in England, as well as to meet the wants of the mixed population." It was, in other words, plain civil necessity without religious character and "an unavoidable consequence of the provisions of the charter, the peculiar position of the Proprietary and the mixed religious opinions of the people."

Whatever the truth of the matter, it is of record that the Baltimores accorded Catholics no special privileges in what the U.S. Church likes to think of as a Catholic colony. Religious discussions were strictly forbidden to all, and the second Lord's dislike of the Jesuits, who hoped to convert souls there, is well-documented. In defiance of the Bull *In caena Domini,* in which the Pope asserts full jurisdiction over ecclesiastics, Baltimore insisted that the Fathers be subject to the common law like everyone else. He refused them the right to own property, nor would he contribute to their support, even going so far as to petition Rome for their removal in favor of a secular clergy. Maryland became the only state in the Union where no land could be owned by a religious body without the consent of the legislature. Even so, the Crown soon suspended the charter as unsafe in Catholic hands. When it was eventually restored to the Baltimores, it was to Charles, that fifth Lord Baltimore who openly joined the Masons in 1730.

J. P. Kennedy likewise emphatically denies that "in the planting of either Avalon or Maryland Lord Baltimore was moved by a special desire to provide asylum for persecuted Catholics, as many have alleged." And as we have seen, he furthermore found "no reason to believe that he was a very ardent or zealous follower of his faith." Be that as it may, by that time many English Catholics were worn out by nearly a century of specious compromises, which always worsened their situation with both God and man. Succumbing once more to compromise, they hoped to find respite from their enemies in the Rosicrucian exile offered them so opportunely in the new Atlantis. Thus the colony designed to rid England of unemployed farmers and troublesome Catholics, which Sir Humphrey Gilbert first envisioned in Newfoundland, become a permanent reality a half- century later, not in Catholic Canada as first planned by John Dee and Francis Bacon, but in what had been Spanish Florida.

Small wonder that among those arriving on the Ark and the Dove was Richard Gerard, son of the Thomas Gerard who had taken so active a part in Sir Humphrey's expedition. Today, an obelisk to the memory of Maryland's first Governor, Leonard Calvert, marks the spot where Maryland's colonists, both Protestant and Catholic, joined in common brotherhood to collaborate in establishing the *Novus Ordo Seclorum*, which would shake the Christian world to its very roots.

Chapter VII

PLANTING THE LILY

Hovering at a safe distance from the Lily of France before risking open confrontation, the Wasp had nonetheless loosed its barb into the side of America, and it stuck fast. The Lily had struck roots by then, but flowered slowly, amid many thorns. By "Wasp" must be understood, not the English nation any more than any other, but the power of the Serpent wherever it ruled in the trappings of legalized "white supremacy" Protestantism. Nor is the designation "Lily" as applied to France meant to imply that the French nation was holy and above reproach merely by virtue of her political representation of the Catholic cause. God and the devil were at work in both camps, each wielding chosen instruments poised for mortal confrontation. To this day, the history of Canada is the story of that confrontation.

France's fratricidal wars of religion ended at last at the close of the 16th century, when the Huguenot Henri of Navarre, father of Charles I's Queen, renounced Protestantism and ascended the French throne as Henri IV, with the cynical remark that, after all, "Paris is worth a Mass!" The Spaniards, allies of the Guises and the Catholic League, pulled out from their bases in Brittany and returned home, their monarch Philip II requesting no remuneration for their services beyond the satisfaction of having helped to confirm the Faith as France's state religion. Less than ten years later, the religiously indifferent but politically astute Henri promulgated the Edict of Nantes, which granted the Huguenots equal political rights with Catholics and a limited freedom of worship.

In the relative peace bought at this exorbitant price, Catholic France could at least begin to turn her attention once more to her colonies, after the long disastrous lull during which almost the only Frenchmen in the New World were Norman and Breton fishermen, doggedly plying their trade in the rich fishing grounds off Newfoundland. During Lent, when the demand for fish was high, two ships per day set out from French ports to these waters. The good Don Pedro Menendez accused the settlements there of despotic rule over the fisheries, and his grievance was not without foundation, for their motives were purely economic, in no wise apostolic, and wholly unregulated by higher authority. The problem worsened when many fishermen abandoned their nets for the more lucrative fur trade and, penetrating the interior, began antagonizing the indignant Indians.

What gold became to the Spaniards, furs became to the French, and the same tragic conflict of interest which had developed between the padres and the conquistadores soon became evident between the French missionaries and the fur traders. In New France as in Mexico, the Serpent adroitly exploited the situation, pitting seculars against ecclesiastics to the serious detriment of both, with the Indians caught in between. Many moons had passed since the devout Jacques Cartier had raised the Cross on Gaspé Peninsula, while a crowd of curious but friendly redmen looked on. "After It was raised," he wrote later, "we all fell on our knees, adoring It in their presence, with hands folded; and looking up and pointing to heaven, we conveyed to them by signs that It was the means of our

Redemption, at which they greatly marveled, as they turned to gaze at that Cross."

Despite several attempts, the 1600's had dawned on no permanent French (or, for that matter, no English) colony on the Sides. The fiasco under Roberval was succeeded by another settlement of convicts under the Marquis de la Roche, Lieutenant General by royal appointment, but this too ended in disaster, and had this policy continued, the new settlements would have turned out to be, like many of the English ones, little more than human landfills for unwanted citizenry. Only with the appearance of Samuel de Champlain does the real action begin. To judge supernaturally, he was the visible instrument provided by God to extend overseas the great spiritual renewal which became manifest almost immediately at home in France, once she rose purified and triumphant over her internal enemies. So much blood, tears and suffering in such a cause could not go unrewarded, and Champlain was one of many proofs.

From this point on, the story of Canada, like that of Mexico, reads with difficulty as anything but ecclesiastical history. Interpreted in purely secular terms, the events make no sense, lacking both meaning and cohesion. Plain facts drove the USan historian Bancroft to one conclusion: "It was neither commercial profit nor the ambition of kings that brought French power into the heart of our continent, but rather religion." Rightly called "the Father of New France," Champlain was a man gifted with extraordinary natural talents, coupled with great piety, who entertained the highest notions of the mysterious interplay of Church and State in human society. He would tell Marie de Medici, widow of the assassinated Henri IV and regent for the young King Louis XIII, "I have always desired to make the Lily flourish in New France with the Roman Apostolic Religion."

This was quite simply his vocation, for which he was duly endowed and prepared by Divine Providence. An experienced soldier who had fought under d'Aumont against the Huguenots, the young Champlain wanted to be an explorer. With this end in view, he accepted a Pilot-Generalship in the Spanish navy. Commanding one of Don Francisco Colombo's vessels heading for the West Indies to defend Puerto Rico against English attack, he proceeded on to Mexico, where he was one of the first to conceive a feasible plan for a canal across

Panama, a project originally envisioned by Columbus and later broached to Philip II, who forbade further mention of it under pain of death! In preparation for a career as a colonizer, for two years he studied firsthand the incomparable Spanish colonial system, ever remaining its admirer and emulator.

With his first reconnaissance of Canada in 1603, at the invitation of the pious and dedicated Admiral de Chastres, Champlain was fired with the hope of planting a colony— not of traders, but a permanent Catholic community living its own organic life—at the foot of the "Gibraltar of the North," the 350-foot cliff jutting above the St. Lawrence River, now known as the Rock of Quebec. With this object in view, the next year he attached himself as a surveyor and explorer to Pierre de Monts, an upright Calvinist on whom Henri IV had conferred vice-regal powers for the government of Acadia, a vast expanse, then not only comprising Nova Scotia, but stretching roughly from Montreal to Philadelphia. Like Roberval before him, the Protestant de Monts was officially pledged to spreading the Catholic faith, and therefore began his tenure amid the usual mass of contradictions. A monopoly of the fur trade abrogating all previous claims forming the basis of his charter, indignant protests from the dispossessed were heard; yet the fur trade was the only bond of unity in the motley assortment of ruffians, convicts, volunteers, idealists, priests, Protestant ministers and younger sons of aristocrats and commoners alike who made up the personnel.

Even before they arrived, quarrels had broken out on shipboard. "I have seen our curé and the minister," said Champlain, "fall to with their fists on questions of faith. I cannot say which had the more pluck, or which hit harder, but I know that the minister sometimes complained to the Sieur de Monts that he had been beaten. This was their way of settling points of controversy. I leave you to judge whether it was a pleasant thing to see." It would be a long time before the spirit of the treaties which concluded the wars of religion permeated the grass roots at any depth. In his *Histoire du Canada,* the Franciscan Brother Sagard tells with horror how, "After their destination was reached, a priest and a minister happening to die at the same time, the crew buried them together in the same grave, to see whether they would lie peaceably together."

Such is ecumenism. Heresy, checked too late and compromised with in the mother country, rendered impossible any French expeditions with a single apostolic objective like those of the Spanish. It was clear that Acadia would never see spectacular conversions in the millions, like those worked by Our Lady of Guadalupe among the natives of Mexico. As we shall see, St. Joseph had been handed very rocky soil to work, requiring many hard-won graces on the part of chosen souls. De Monts' enterprise had been put together by merchants for profit, which meant that the missionary-minded Catholics had to fit themselves into the pattern as best they could. During the next four years, despite endless bickering and the problems created by the rigors of the climate, Champlain pursued his explorations not only up the St. Lawrence, but along the New England coast, where he entered Plymouth Harbor and named it Port St. Louis a good fifteen years ahead of the so-called Pilgrim Fathers.

De Monts' charter was eventually rescinded, but not before settlements of a kind had been successfully planted, one on the island of Sainte Croix and another at Port Royal, the present site of Annapolis in Nova Scotia. Port Royal, which belonged to the Baron de Poutrincourt by prior grant from de Monts, soon contributed an interesting vignette to Church history: On Pentecost Sunday in 1611, two Jesuits arrived there, Fr. Pierre Biard, a theology professor from Lyons, and Fr. Enemond Masse. Their welcome from Poutrincourt was chilly, for this worthy was what today would be called a liberal Catholic, of the national party which sided with the Huguenots against Spain and the Catholic League, and had put Henri IV on the throne. Although intent on spreading the Faith, he nonetheless had his own ideas on how to go about it. Like Lord Baltimore, he much preferred to deal with an accommodating secular clergy, rather than with the Jesuits, a Spanish order wholly committed to the supranational authority of the Papacy and enjoying the political independence laid down for religious by the Pope.

Poutrincourt had not dared refuse Fr. Biard, who was sent on direct orders from the French court, but he had contrived to have him left behind at the port of embarkation for an entire year without being able to secure passage. The Father's next attempt was foiled by the Huguenot merchants underwriting the sailing, who suddenly refused to risk money in any venture involving Jesuits. Had it not been for an intrepid lady by the name of Antoinette de Pons, Marquise de Guercheville, lady-in-waiting to the Queen, the two priests might never have seen Canada. A young widow renowned for wit and beauty, she had attracted the attentions of Henri IV, who had hopes of making her his next mistress. Her virtue matching her good looks, however, she refused him with a quip that made history: "Sire, my rank is perhaps not high enough to allow me to be your wife, but my heart is too high to allow me to be your mistress."

With that she repaired to her chateau, where the king followed her, begging lodging. Unable to refuse a royal request for hospitality, with supreme graciousness she invited him into comfortable quarters, with orders to her servants to afford him every convenience, but at the same time, she called for her coach to take her to a friend's house for the night. To the astonished monarch's remonstrance, she replied, "Sire, where a king is, he should be sole master; but for my part, I like to preserve some little authority wherever I may be." Such was the mettle of the lady who, in her mature years, got the first Jesuits into Canada. With the help of two other ladies of the court, one of them the Queen, Mme. de Guercheville raised a subscription and bought out the merchants' interest, which she handed over to the Jesuit Fathers. Out of the surplus, these were able to lend 730 livres to the other associates of the venture and advance 1,225 more to complete the outfitting of the ship, thus becoming entire masters of the situation. Their only remaining problem was restraining the zeal of the lady in question, who declared herself patroness of the American missions.

Arriving at Port Royal at last, they had to struggle with the Micmac language spoken by the natives, which had no abstract terms in which to convey the mysteries of the Faith; and of course with Poutrincourt, who, in a desperate attempt to keep Church and state separate in his preserve, put Fr. Biard in his place with, "Show me my path to heaven, and I'll show you yours on earth!" Except for the Baptism of a dying Indian girl given up as worthless by her relatives, there was little spiritual fruit in such adverse circumstances. Mme. de Guercheville, however, was not idle. The following year she not only bought out all of de Monts' remaining claims to Acadia, but she secured from the new King Louis XIII a grant to herself for all the territory from the St. Lawrence to Spanish Florida! A third Jesuit, Brother Gilbert du Thet, arrived as her administrator. Thus, momentarily, the Jesuits were in complete charge of the

"Northern Paraguay," which many devout souls hoped to see established in North America like the one in South America.

The northern *donjon* of the demons of the Sides was now seriously threatened. All possibility of a theocracy for Catholics like that of the Puritans in New England must be quashed at all costs. As soon as the Wasp recovered from his surprise, there was a cruel, retaliatory sting on his part from an unexpected direction. Far to the south, in 1607, the English had succeeded at last in founding the Jamestown colony in Virginia, whose Governor, Sir Thomas Dale, was a zealous champion of Wasp rights. According to Francis Parkman, he ruled a settlement drawn "from tavern, gaming-house and brothel ... ruined gentlemen, prodigal sons, disreputable retainers, debauched tradesmen," which was visited one day in 1613 by an illicit trading vessel commanded by the Thomas Argall, known to history as the kidnapper of Pocahontas and the perpetrator of other crafty projects. Governor Dale lost no time in commissioning him to expel the French from Canada, all North America being then claimed by England in virtue of the Cabot explorations.

His first prey was St. Sauveur, a small mission established by the Jesuits on Frenchman's Bay in tents donated by Mme. de Guercheville. Its defenders were easily overpowered, and Brother du Thet was among those killed. John Gilmary Shea judges that such "an unprovoked attack by men pretending to be Christians on a mission station established for the conversion of the heathen, followed by bloodshed and indiscriminate plunder, has no parallel in history. Virginia shares the infamy by endorsing Argall's action, as does England by refusing reparation." But that is not the end of the tale. "Argall put Fr. Masse and fourteen Frenchmen in a small craft and turned them adrift; Fathers Biard and Quentin were carried to Virginia, then ruled by a code of blood, where Sir Thomas Dale threatened to hang all the prisoners. Finally resolving to extirpate the French settlements, he sent Argall back with a considerable force. The English vessels carried the missionaries and many of the French prisoners, who were glad to escape from the soil of Virginia. Argall completed the destruction of St. Sauveur, then demolished the post on Sainte Croix Island and that at Port Royal, where Biencourt [Poutrincourt's son, left in charge there] showed his hatred of the missionaries."

Poutrincourt and the English chroniclers later maintained that Fr. Biard actually guided Argall to his quarry out of revenge, but an anonymous Englishman wrote that the real traitor was Biencourt, who had offered to transfer his allegiance to King James if he could be allowed to retain Port Royal under English protection. Whatever the truth was, Acadia nearly perished in its beginnings. Fr. Masse and those set adrift were eventually rescued by fishermen, who took them back to France; Fr. Biard and Fr. Quentin returned home by way of the Azores and England. Thus ended the first Jesuit mission to Canada. Not an auspicious beginning, but in due time the Jesuits would be to New France what the Franciscans were to New Spain, and would, like them, strew its soil with saints. As for Thomas Argall, he became Deputy-Governor of Virginia, grew immensely rich and was knighted in 1623. Thus, writes Parkman, "In an obscure stroke of lawless violence began the strife of France and England, Protestantism and Rome, which for a century and a half shook the struggling communities of North America and closed at last in the memorable triumph [of the Wasp] on the plains of Abraham." But that is getting much too far ahead of our story.

+

These tribulations provoked the Lily into refulgent bloom. Six years before the destruction of Poutrincourt's little kingdom at Port Royal, Pierre de Monts had organized yet another expedition of three ships. One of these, the *Don de Dieu* ("God's Gift") was commanded by Samuel Champlain, now under orders to establish his long-desired city at Cape Diamond, where the Rock of Quebec once overlooked the wily Chief Donnacona's village of Stadaconé. After a tussle with some recalcitrant Basque traders, he sailed up the St. Lawrence, and on July 3, 1608, founded the future capital of New France. He left to posterity a pencil sketch of its first wooden buildings. Inaugurating his residence by foiling a plot to assassinate him, three years later he planted roses in his garden and sallied farther up the river to lay out the rough lines of future Montreal, near the ancient Hochelaga of the Amerindians. When the Comte de Soissons became Lieutenant-General of New France, the vice-regal powers were transferred to Champlain, and from that time forth, as Parkman put it, "in Champlain alone was the life of New France."

He was now prepared for a physical confrontation with the Serpent's primordial allies, the five confederate Indian nations known collectively as "the Iroquois." Noted for their cruelty and cannibalism, these tribes inhabited fortified towns throughout what is now New York state, from which they systematically terrorized their hapless neighbors.With sure supernatural instinct, Champlain quickly detected, and inevitably aroused to fury, this savage force. Some have blamed him for provoking it deliberately, but history proves it always aligned itself automatically against Christ's friends. The first encounter occurred at Ticonderoga. "I looked at them," Champlain writes, "and they looked at me. When I saw them getting ready to shoot their arrows at us, I leveled my *arquebuse* [heavy matchlock gun], which I had loaded with four balls, and aimed straight at one of the chiefs. The shot brought down two and wounded another. On this, our Indians set up such a howl that one would not have heard a thunderclap, and all the while the arrows flew thick on both sides. The Iroquois were greatly astonished and frightened to see two of their men killed so quickly, in spite of their arrow-proof armor. As I was re-loading, one of my companions fired a shot from the woods, which so increased their astonishment that, seeing their chiefs dead, they abandoned the field and fled into the depth of the forest."

After a second crushing Indian defeat on the St. Lawrence, there was peace for a while, but it could not last long. Champlain soon saw the strategic importance of creating a buffer state of neutral or friendly natives between his feeble new settlements and the Iroquois, as well as the Wasps to the south. The latter were not only the English, but also Henry Hudson's Dutch, now on Manhattan Island and advancing ever northward up the river. (The Netherlanders, incidentally, have more than once been accused of teaching the fine art of scalping to the Amerindians, who before the advent of the white man may indeed have been ignorant of the technique.) Champlain therefore employed his prodigious diplomatic talents in concluding an alliance of mutual assistance with the thousands of Hurons, Montagnais, Algonquins and other tribes, who gladly accepted the offer of his leadership and superior weaponry, even if they availed themselves only sporadically of the eternal salvation proffered by his Catholic missionaries.

In contrast to the Wasp, the Lily never disdained the Amerindians as political entities, nor as human beings. Far from remaining aloof from their internal affairs, she often umpired their quarrels, to their grateful satisfaction, a salutary policy largely owed to Champlain, who had witnessed its good effects in the Spanish West Indies. Thus there came into being along with Quebec and its three subsidiary trading stations at Montreal, Trois Rivières and Tadoussac, a configuration around the Great Lakes known vaguely as Huronia, which became a prime field of apostolate. After a decade of gubernatorial duties, which included regular yearly trips to France, explorations into the interior, searches for the back door to China, battles with Iroquois on the one hand and Huguenots on the other, not to mention authoring a shelf of books, Champlain exclaimed, "I felt an apostle being born in me!" He could not abandon the poor Amerindians of the Sides, who, unlike their more civilized counterparts in the West, "lived like brute beasts, without faith, without law, without religion, without God."

He sought help in France from a new monastery of Franciscan Recollects of strict observance, recently founded in his hometown of Brouage. With the enthusiastic support of the French hierarchy, several of these Recollects boarded the St. Stephen with Champlain in 1615 "to go plant the standard of Jesus Christ in those parts, being determined to live or die for His Holy Name." The pledge was soon fulfilled. Fr. Nicholas Viel du Cotentin met martyrdom when his prospective converts threw him into the rapids beyond Montreal, a spot since called Sault-au-Recollect. Leaving two of their number to minister in Quebec at the modest monastery of Our Lady of the Angels, Fr. d'Olbeau headed for the Saguenay and the Montagnais, while Fr. Joseph Le Caron, former Chaplain to the Duke of Orleans, started up the Ottawa to discover Lake Huron. In Le Caron, the Indians were to find the champion that those of Mexico found in Las Casas. He worked indefatigably, preparing their conversion by reforming their savage ways and teaching them to read and write. With the support of the Governor and Fr. Sagard, Canada's earliest historian, he addressed both in letter and in person many complaints to the royal authorities regarding the objectionable behavior of the traders towards his charges.

On one occasion, addressing sixty Huron chieftains, Champlain told them, "Here are our Fathers. It is neither hunger nor want that brings them to this country. They don't come to see you for the sake of your goods, nor for your pelts. If as you say you love the French, then love these Fathers. They will show you the way to Heaven." More Recollects arrived, and even the Nipissings were reached, an Algonquin tribe so infested with demons and the black arts that they became known as "the Sorcerers." The field was too vast, however, being greater than all of Europe. In 1626, five Jesuits, accompanied by twenty farm laborers came to help, among them the Fr. Masse, who had been captured by Argall, plus Fr. Charles Lalement and St. Jean de Brébeuf. But missionaries, alas, were not enough. No matter how many there were, their best efforts remained fruitless without the solid example of the Faith lived in daily life, which only a fervent Catholic laity could give. The comportment of the traders and their affiliates was scandalous, and worse yet was the influence exerted on the Indians by the open rivalry between Catholics and Protestants, who both professed themselves Christians.

Champlain was no Lord Baltimore, motivated by expediency; Champlain was the colonial governor who coined the maxim, "The salvation of a single soul is worth more than the conquest of an empire." The corporation financing the colony was unfortunately headed by two Huguenots, Emery and William de Caen, who were realizing a forty percent profit per annum and in one year harvested 22,000 beaver skins. Although Protestantism was proscribed, they assembled the Huguenot sailors for prayer services and had the effrontery to force the Catholics to join in. Champlain was indignant, and a compromise was reached. "A bad bargain," he admitted, "but we made the best of it we could." What he had in mind for New France was not profiteers, but self-sufficient people close to the soil, producing "the necessities of life, food, clothing, lodging, and exporting its natural products to France and the Antilles." He was impatient with the floating population he had to deal with, who not only had no wives, no farms and no permanent ties to the country, but who escaped starvation only by dint of constant supplies from abroad, with the Huguenots further endangering their survival by selling brandy and firearms to the Indians.

The merchants discouraged population centers, arguing that "if the country becomes populated, their power would diminish, not being able to do as they pleased there, and they would be deprived of the greater portion of the pelts, which they could secure only from the hands of the inhabitants, and would soon after be driven away by the very ones they had set up there at great expense." As it was, the twenty farm workers brought by the Jesuits had to be sent home, and the corporation very nearly forced Champlain's resignation. Determined, nonetheless, that Quebec should become the center from which Christian civilization would progressively penetrate North America, he labored to attract the nomadic Amerindians into settled villages, where they could be taught the agricultural arts and freed from the winter famines which so often drove them to cannibalism. One such was established at nearby Sillery, but most Indians proved incapable of sedentary life. Otherwise receptive and friendly, particularly the Hurons, they told Champlain, "Bring wives and children, so that we can see how you live and farm your land. We'll learn more that way in one year than in twenty listening to you talk."

Under the French, the Indian was a free citizen with rights equal to the Frenchman, and as much intermarriage as possible was encouraged within the Mystical Body: "Our boys shall marry your girls, and we shall be one people," urged the Governor. Some years later, Louis XIV would offer 150 livres to each Indian girl who married a Frenchman. Had it not been for the takeover by the Wasp, with his near psychotic racial prejudice, Indians would hardly be found on reservations in Canada today, or in poor little villages like Caughnawaga, which survives somehow under a gigantic skyway outside Montreal, and where St. Kateri Tekakwitha lies buried among her people. The transcendent Christian mission demands help from the laity, handmaid of the priest and "a helper like himself," as Eve was to Adam and Our Lady to Our Lord. They must supply not only material support, but a projection of the supernatural life as it is lived at all levels of society. Champlain excelled at giving good example. Twenty-two years after his death, Amerindians for miles around still spoke admiringly of his perfect continence, a virtue which aroused their curiosity about the Faith as did no other, because it was so rare among them. Champlain had married late in life a gentle young bride, whose father, he discovered to his consternation, was a secret Huguenot. He

135

easily converted her, and she lived with him about four years in Quebec, beloved of all, as she catechized squaws and children. They themselves were childless, and with her husband's permission she returned to France, where after his death she founded an Ursuline convent at Meaux.

+

At the end of New France's first twenty years, its French inhabitants numbered barely a hundred. A lesser man than the Governor would have given up in discouragement. In all, there were five families, only two of whom farmed the land, those of a widow and her son-in-law. Their presence was due entirely to a Parisian apothecary, Louis Hébert, who had moved from Acadia at Champlain's express invitation. This saintly "Abraham of New France," as he came to be known, pursued a lone apostolate of the laity, which was hampered at every turn by the company agents. Allowing him to work his farm only on his off-hours, they furthermore required him to sell its produce exclusively to them at prices determined by them. His fervor matched the Governor's, however, and he would declare on his deathbed, "I die happy, for it has pleased Our Lord that converted savages die before me. I crossed the seas to come to their rescue."

With the rise to power of Cardinal Richelieu, a political genius as systematically defamed in Wasp annals as was ever Philip II or the Mary called "Bloody," the spiritual climate of New France changed dramatically. Following a crushing defeat of the resurgent Huguenots at La Rochelle, Richelieu turned his attention with the sure instinct of the Catholic statesman to the French foothold across the Atlantic. He terminated the mismanagement of the Caen brothers by peremptorily annulling their privileges and forming a new organization composed of one hundred "associates," which he called the Company of New France. He headed it personally and included Champlain in the membership. Delineating its main lines, Parkman wrote, "Maréchal Deffiat and other men of rank, besides many merchants and burghers of condition, were members. The whole of New France, from Florida to the Arctic Circle, and from Newfoundland to the sources of the St. Lawrence and its tributary waters, was conferred on them forever, with the attributes of sovereign power.

"A perpetual monopoly of the fur trade was granted them, with a monopoly of all other commerce," except for the whale and cod fisheries still open to all, "within the limits of their government for fifteen years. The trade of the colony was declared free for the same period from all duties and imposts. Nobles, officers and ecclesiastics, members of the Company, might engage in commercial pursuits without derogation from the privileges of their order; and, as evidence of his good will, the King gave them two ships of war, armed and equipped.On their part, the Company were bound to convey to New France during the next year, 1628, two or three hundred men of all trades, and, before the year 1643, to increase the number to four thousand persons of both sexes; to lodge and support them for three years; and, this time expired, to give them cleared lands for their maintenance. Every settler must be a Frenchman and a Catholic; and for every new settlement at least three ecclesiastics must be provided.

"Thus was New France to be forever free from the taint of heresy. The stain of her infancy was to be wiped away. Against the foreigner and the Huguenot the door was closed and barred." Champlain tells us, "The intention of most of the Company's interested parties had no other design but to contribute to the conversion of those poor savages," who would be held and considered as natural Frenchmen with all the rights of citizens. The astute Parkman is quick to point out the disadvantages of this heroic policy, so contrary to the worldly prudence of the Wasp, whose colonies soon teemed with population by dint of admitting anyone at all who would come for any reason. France, on the other hand, "shut out those who wished to come and admitted only those who did not—the favored class who clung to the old faith and had no motive or disposition to leave their homes." In other words, the Wasp shrewdly harnessed all man's lower appetites and ambitions to its enterprises, whereas Catholic France, the eldest daughter of the Church, appealed almost exclusively to his higher instincts. So much wiser in their generation are the children of this world than the children of light!

It is nevertheless interesting that the Wasp betrayed increasing apprehension at these developments. Once again his retaliatory sting was felt. It was loosed this time not from colonial Virginia, but from mother England, and in fact from France herself. Sir William Alexander, who had been granted a rival claim to Acadia by the Scottish crown and who had been attempting to colonize it for the British, was authorized by Charles I to head an expedition underwritten by London merchants to seize all French holdings on the now- hotly contested Sides of the North. A privateer working for English interests from the French port of Dieppe, one Gervaise Kerkt (anglicized in history books as Jarvis Kirk), outfitted three ships for the project, each commanded by one of his sons, David, Lewis and Thomas. Numbered in their crews were many Huguenots bent on vengeance, who had been lately expelled from Canada by the new Catholic regime. One of them, the skillful navigator Jacques Michel, served as Vice-Admiral. A brilliant stratagem of Champlain staved off the inevitable for nearly a year, but by then it was all over, the enemy having little more to do than intercept the French ships bringing provisions to the helpless little colony. The starving town being incapable of defense, many of its inhabitants fled to the woods to join their Indian friends.

After incredible hardships, Champlain and a ragged little band of sixteen finally capitulated and were forced to watch Lewis Kerkt plant the Cross of St. George at the spot where 130 years later another Wasp commander, General Wolfe, would it plant it definitively. This was Champlain's severest trial, the only one over which he was ever seen to weep. On the whole, the Kerkts treated their prisoners with courtesy, with the exception of the Jesuits. The real issue is glimpsed in an anecdote recorded by Champlain in the foreign service archives: Apparently Lewis Kerkt took two silver chalices from the Fathers, and Fr. Masse warned him, "Do not profane them, for they are sacred!" "Profane them?" retorted Kerkt. "Since you tell me that, I'll keep them, which I wouldn't have done otherwise. I take them because you believe in them, for I will have no idolatry!" Vice-Admiral Michel died as a result of a fit of frenzy brought on by a verbal encounter with the mild-mannered giant St. Jean de Brébeuf. At Michel's funeral, Champlain, who had once tried to befriend him, remarked laconically, "I do not doubt that his soul is in perdition." Brébeuf's Indian friends were more demonstrative. They dug up Michel's body and hanged him posthumously.

A few families, Hébert's among them, elected to remain in Quebec despite the English occupation, confident that neither God nor France would abandon them. And indeed the Company continued to send help. Meanwhile, Champlain and fifty others, among them all the missionaries, had been taken prisoner, incarcerated below deck and returned to Europe. The Indians, who at first welcomed the conquerors as is their wont, soon saw their mistake, learning the basic difference between the Lily and the Wasp the hard way. Their importunate visits at all hours, which the French had tolerated in an effort to convert them, being now met with oaths and blows, they soon shunned Quebec entirely and betook themselves to their old haunts. Champlain reached France by way of London, where the French ambassador assured him that Canada's restoration to the French crown was a foregone conclusion, inasmuch as this was a stipulation of the Convention of Suza lately signed by the two powers.

This meant that the Kerkts had been committing acts of war, even as peace was being declared, and Champlain was not entirely convinced. He deemed it wise to approach Richelieu and the Associates in person, and diplomatic pressure was applied. Finally, with the treaty of St. Germain-en-Laye in 1632, New France and Acadia were relinquished by the Wasp, with the exception of one province. How King Charles could have been brought so easily to give up prizes so well in hand for England was a puzzlement to all who were not privy to the real reason, which he revealed in a letter to his ambassador in Paris: He feared that if he did not comply, the French crown would retain the half still owing of his Queen Henriette Marie's dowry, and he was desperate for money. There may have been another more potent reason emanating from a higher cause, for on his return to France, Champlain had promised Notre Dame de Recouvrance (Our Lady of Recovery) a chapel in Quebec if ever he returned there as Governor. He kept his promise, and when he died there three years later on Christmas Day 1635, he was buried in it.

On his return, he had been riotously welcomed by an armed escort, amid rolling drums and cannonades, with two hundred colonists marching behind him. St. Jean de Brébeuf and Fr. Masse shared the honors with him, for Richelieu had replaced the Recollects by officially entrusting New France to the Jesuits. No doubt the able Cardinal felt that a religious order organized on military lines was best suited to the hostile conditions then pertaining. Champlain seconded the decision by choosing the Jesuit Fr. Paul Le Jeune as his spiritual director, under whose guidance he continued to grow in virtue, making exceptionally giant strides in the last years of his life.

"A stranger visiting the fort of Quebec," writes Parkman, "would have been astonished at its air of conventual decorum. Black Jesuits and scarfed officers mingled at Champlain's table. There was little conversation, but in its place the lives of the saints were read aloud as in a monastic rectory. Prayers, Masses and Confessions followed one another with an edifying regularity, and the bell of the adjacent chapel, built by Champlain, rang morning, noon and night" at the Angelus. "Godless soldiers caught the infection and whipped themselves in penance for their sins. Debauched artisans outdid each other in the fury of their contrition. Quebec was become a mission. Indians gathered thither as of old, but not from the baneful lure of brandy, gifts, kind words and politic blandishments.... Trade, policy and military power leaned on the missions as their main support, the grand instrument of their extension.... France aimed to subdue, not by the sword, but by the Cross." Is that the way to run a country? It must be, for as long as these conditions prevailed, the fruits were only too evident, and the Serpent began whipping the Wasp to fury.

Chapter VIII

CANADIAN DIAMONDS

We have said that the true story of Canada is hagio-history, and indeed, after the consolidation of the government of New France under the inspired Champlain, some extraordinary developments began taking place within the weft of the political chronicle. When the good Jacques Cartier collected those baskets of quartz crystals on Cap Rouge to take home to his King, he was convinced he had found an inexhaustible trove of diamonds. His simplicity provided Europe with a good laugh, but as it turned out, he had in fact discovered a diamond mine.

These gems would not, however, be of mineral composition, but rather of that supernatural "immortal diamond" celebrated by the Jesuit poet Fr. Gerard Manley Hopkins. No doubt to the unspeakable indignation of the demons of the Sides, their *donjon* bade fair to become one vast reliquary, for Canada was destined to produce a wealth of saints.

The Church was in sore need of shock troops in that region, for as time went on the beleaguered satanic empire would increasingly concentrate its defenses in North America, whence it would direct its onslaughts against the territories it had lost to the Faith. By May 16, 1974, the Franciscan Minim known as the Portavoz of Mexico would report that Our Lord told her, "My enemies ripped Mexico from the womb of its mother country, Spain! And consequently they have introduced themselves in all the American countries, having their satanic seat in the states of the north. These events cannot be concealed from the face of the world, because history is the witness of what happens at all times."

St. Jean de Brébeuf, already mentioned in connection with Champlain, was martyred by the Mohawk Iroquois in 1649. Half of his skull may be viewed now in Quebec in the chapel of the Jesuit Fathers on rue Dauphine, the other half at the nearby Hotel-Dieu hospital, with most of the remainder of his body at the Jesuit College. Since his day, the number of Canadian saints whose mortal remains grace the soil of the Sides, whether known to us or only to God, have been joined by many others, some of them from very far away in space and time. For over three centuries, there has been a shrine to St. Joseph's mother-in-law, St. Anne, on the St. Lawrence at Beaupré, about twenty miles from Quebec, where her arm is exposed for the veneration of the faithful, and many miracles have taken place through her intercession.

At the time of the French Revolution literally hundreds of other first-class relics of saints of the universal Church were brought to Canada for safekeeping and have remained there ever since. Such a collection could hardly be found anywhere outside the Eternal City itself. One need only enter the chapel of the old diocesan seminary next to the Cathedral in Quebec to venerate relics of the Apostles and hundreds of other major saints, patiently awaiting the conclusion of the battle for Amerindia. Who knows but some of the earliest relics are those of missionaries who actually evangelized America in apostolic times and returned to lend their presence to the completion of the work?

The world, alas, has little more use for these Canadian diamonds than it had for Jacques Cartier's. Even Mother Church was singularly slow in calling attention to them. The Jesuit martyrs of Canada were not canonized until 1930, and like Juan Diego and Fr. Pro of Mexico, only recently has Bl. Kateri Tekakwitha been beatified. Perhaps their time has not yet come, for whatever saints are, they are not dead. "The kingdom of heaven is like to leaven, which a woman took and hid in three measures of meal, until the whole was leavened" (Matt. 13:33), and leaven is all the more potent for working unseen over a period of time. Suddenly, on June 22, 1980, after more than three hundred years, three seventeenth-century Canadian diamonds were beatified by John Paul II in the thick of the chaos created by the Second Vatican Council. They were François de Montmorency Laval, the first Bishop of New France; Mother Marie de l'Incarnation, foundress of the Ursulines in Quebec; and one native Amerindian, the young virgin Kateri.

From 1632 on, following the recommendation of their founder, St. Ignatius, the Jesuits in America had been sending to Europe regular reports of their progress in the missions, commonly known as the Jesuit Relations. On these fed avidly the great spiritual renewal in France, which had been set in motion by the saints of the Counter-reformation. Père Le Jeune said people were writing the missionaries "with such ardor and in such numbers, from so many different places, that it's merely a question as to who will be the first to scorn the fury of the sea and the savagery of the land. If we opened the door to their desires, a whole town could be formed of nuns, and there would be ten teachers for every schoolgirl." Only dedicated laypeople were lacking. He asks, "When will the French peasants become Canadians, so that the Canadian savages may become Christians? When will those French ladies fettered by vanity soften at the thought of those little savage girls and boys who pray God one day and fly off into the woods the next, for fear their parents may be forced into sedentary life?"

Soon everyone wanted a share in the evangelization of the New World, and suddenly God made His particular will known. One day in 1636, at La Flèche in Anjou, a tax collector renowned for his piety and austerity of life, by the name of Jerome le Royer de la Dauversière, heard in prayer a voice commanding him to found an order of nursing sisters to staff a hospital dedicated to St. Joseph in the Canadian wilds on the island of Montreal. The father of six children, disposing of only a modest income and having no talent whatever for public relations, Dauversière was understandably at a loss, but equally determined to obey. At the same time, a young priest called Jean-Jacques Olier, future founder of the Sulpicians, happened to be praying at St. Germain des Près in Paris, where he was told interiorly that he would found a society of priests who would be sent to serve the Faith at Montreal.

No less extraordinary is that both these future apostles, each unknown to the other, were at the time of their call miraculously invested with all the necessary knowledge of the distant territory in question, down to specifics of size, shape, topography and climate. Champlain, of course, had already pointed out the island as an ideal site for a city, situated as it is at the confluence of the St. Lawrence and Ottawa Rivers. Setting out for Paris to look for help, Dauversière was favored there at the Cathedral of Notre Dame with a vision of the Holy Family, who confirmed him in his vocation. Soon after, at the chateau of Meudon near St. Cloud, he made the acquaintance of Fr. Olier. The historian Faillon relates: "Impelled by a kind of inspiration, they recognized each other at once, even to the depth of their hearts; greeted each other by name, as we read of St. Paul the Hermit and St. Anthony, and of St. Dominic and St. Francis; and ran to embrace each other like two friends who had met after after a long separation."

Forthwith commending their work to God at a Mass said by Fr. Olier, they planned three religious communities for Montreal: a society of secular priests to minister to the colonists and convert the Indians, and two congregations of nuns to care for the sick and teach the children. In their own words, these would "plant the banner of Christ in an abode of desolation and a haunt of demons," establishing their post within the very fangs of the Iroquois. For this purpose, the two friends formed with some wealthy acquaintances the Society of Notre Dame de Montreal, which acquired the necessary title to the land from the President of the old Hundred Associates of Quebec. According to all norms of worldly prudence, the scheme was insane, and was in fact immediately dubbed *"la folle entreprise."* Displaying none of the ordinary motives for founding a colony, the members of the new Society, unlike the aforesaid Hundred, agreed to draw no personal profit whatever from the project, but only to raise money and recruit personnel to start a settlement whose sole purpose was to provide the indispensable base for the three religious communities in question. It would also serve as a useful link between Quebec and the lonely outposts established years previously by the Recollects and now manned by the Jesuits.

Heaven soon designated a zealous lay apostle by the name of Paul Chomedey de Maisonneuve to head the expedition. An experienced soldier who had commanded a regiment in Holland at the tender age of thirteen and wished to consecrate his sword to the Church, he would be the colony's Governor, independent of the establishment in Quebec and accountable only to the King. A seminary and a school would wait on the successful implantation of the enterprise, but the hospital was deemed a present necessity in so wild and brutal an environment. Its foundress appeared providentially in the person of the Marquise de Buillon, and its administrator would be Jeanne Mance, a chosen soul, who, although not yet a religious at the age of thirty-four, had made a vow of chastity when she was seven. Her hour now come, her spiritual director, the enlightened Fr. St. Jure, assured her that her vocation lay across the Atlantic. When she met Dauversière, the same supernatural recognition took place between them as he had experienced with Fr. Olier.

In 1641, the latter met in Notre Dame Cathedral with the sponsors of the future city, in order to consecrate it to the Holy Family, naming it Ville-Marie de Montreal. The seminary was consecrated to Our Lord, the hospital to St. Joseph, and the school to Our Lady. At the opportune time eleven years later, a teaching nun was provided for the school in the person of St. Marguerite Bourgeoys from Troyes. With forty men and four women, Maisonneuve set sail, despite much opposition from sober heads in France, and even more on arrival in Canada, where the Governor of Quebec, de Montmagny, naturally apprehensive of a rival governor in his preserve, would have been happier to see Maisonneuve's small but disciplined militia garrisoned for the protection of Quebec, rather than deployed out in the wilds.

On May 18, 1642, the new city was established at the foot of St. Joseph's Mont Royal. At the first Mass said there, the Jesuit chaplain Fr. Vimont prophesied truly to those assembled there, "You are a grain of mustard seed that shall rise and grow till its branches overshadow the earth. You are few, but your work is the work of God. His smile is upon you, and your children shall fill the land." The new settlers then caught fireflies and, tethering them with thread, festooned the altar, where the Blessed Sacrament was exposed. Today Montreal, the old Ville-Marie, is the second-largest French city in the world. It was not for nothing that St. Joseph had been officially proclaimed patron of the country in Quebec's first parish back in 1624. When at the first Christmas in Montreal the St. Lawrence threatened to overflow its banks and destroy the whole endeavor, Maisonneuve vowed to carry a huge cross and plant it at the summit of Mont Royal if the calamity was averted. It was, and he kept his promise. The "Mountain Cross," into which relics were later inserted, thenceforth became a place of pilgrimage, where Mass was often celebrated. Sometimes novenas were made during nine entire days under armed guard, for fear of the Iroquois, who eventually succeeded in tearing down the Cross, but St. Marguerite Bourgeoys had it set up again, and today a luminous metal one continues to proclaim the Faith at the great Oratory erected by Bl. Brother André.

The statutes founding Montreal read, "The purpose of the Associates of Montreal is to work exclusively for God's glory. Through the divine goodness, the Associates hope to see shortly a new church which will imitate the purity and charity of the primitive one." Fervor there was, similar indeed to that of the early Christians. Sr. Morin of the Hôtel Dieu wrote in 1654, "Nowhere were locks or keys considered necessary, for houses, chests and cellars were left open, and there was never any reason to regret this seeming imprudence. The well-to-do settlers shared their goods with the poorer ones, not even waiting to be asked for aid, but giving freely and generously." The unusual lay character so evident in the evangelization of Canada is, along with that of Vietnam, a salient example of the extraordinary new development which took place in the missionary Church of the seventeenth century, when, for the first time in the modern era, nuns and laywomen were sent into the mission field, along with laymen like Dauversière and Maisonneuve.

The colonists must nonetheless have profited immensely from frequent and close association with religious, and with Jesuits in particular, several of whom would be canonized. It was from Montreal that St. Isaac Jogues, with a premonition of his final martyrdom, wrote a friend, *"Ibo et non redibo"* (I am leaving and shall not return). His companion, the Oblate St. René Goupil, had already suffered four years previously in 1642, the very year Montreal was founded. He was struck down for making the Sign of the Cross over an Indian child, whose grandfather commanded a young brave, "Go, kill that French dog. The Dutch have told us that the Sign he just made is useless. I fear something worse. I fear it may bring us misfortune." During the three years following St. Isaac's death, sometime between 1646 and 1649, a like grace was conferred on St. Jean Lalande, St. Reni Goupil, St. Antoine Chabanel, St. Charles Garnier, St. Jean de Brebeuf, St. Gabriel Lalemant, St. Noël Chabanel and others known and unknown, some of them Indian converts. Such were the seeds of the Faith in the Sides of the North. The remains of at least three, Fr. Jogues, Br. Goupil and Br. Lalande, do not enjoy the repose of reliquaries, but remain hidden in the soil of Ossernanon on the Mohawk near modern Auriesville, N.Y., where a shrine has become a place of pilgrimage.

+

The supernatural character of these vocations is evident from the fact that so many educated intellectuals like St. Isaac were called, who were totally unfitted by nature or inclination for life at near brute level which had to be endured if they were to subsist in such a mission field. Even the vicious destruction of the Huron missions by the Iroquois did nothing to discourage vocations, but only served to increase their number. In the *Jesuit Relation* for 1636, that gentle hulk Brébeuf, as outstanding an organizer as he was a man of prayer, gave "Important Advice for Those Whom It Shall Please God to Call to New France, especially to the Country of the Hurons," in which he painted an all-too-realistic picture of what was to be expected. After dwelling on the rigors of travel by foot and canoe, pestilential fleas and the malice of savages who "may set fire to your house or cleave open your head in some lonely spot," he warns aspirants, "You are entirely responsible for the sterility or fecundity of the earth under penalty of your life. You are the cause of droughts; if you cannot make it rain, the Indians talk most casually about doing away with you."

These were the friendly tribes, however, for "I will pass over the dangers that threaten from our enemies....Here we have nothing, it seems, to incite us towards good. We are among peoples who are astonished when you speak to them of God and who often have nothing but horrible blasphemies on their lips. You are frequently forced to deprive yourself of the Holy Sacrifice of the Mass.... I pass over the slight opportunity for recollection you have among these barbarians, who almost never leave you and who do not know what it is to speak in a low tone of voice. Most of all I hesitate to speak of the danger there is of losing your soul in the midst of their impurities, should your heart not be sufficiently anchored in God so as to resist this poison."

On the other hand, he concludes with a reassurance for the fervent apostle, which is equally suited to twenty-first century America, as it steadily regresses into its former barbarism: "Ah! Whoever you are to whom God gives such feelings and such light, come, come, my dear brother! It is workers like you that we need here; it is to souls like yours that God has appointed the conquest of so many others whom the devil still holds in his power. Anticipate no difficulties. You will have none, since your whole consolation is to see yourself crucified with the Son of God!... As for the dangers of the soul, to speak frankly, there are none for him who brings the fear and love of God to the country of the Hurons. On the contrary, I find unparalleled opportunities for acquiring perfection.... Can we plant the seeds of the Faith in others without profiting by them ourselves?" St. Jean's own life is proof of his preaching, for he rose to mystical heights, favored by many visions, and by 1630 he humbly acknowledged to his superior that he had lost all inclination to venial sin. No one suffered more then he from the demons of the Sides, who persecuted him without respite, frequently appearing to him in terrifying forms. His special tormentor was the demon of infidelity, who was so often able to persuade hard-won converts to forsake the Faith.

His martyrdom, which took place before the eyes of Fr. Lalemant, is described in *The Work of the Catholic Church in the USA* by Fr. Alphonse Zaratti, who writes, "First his hands were cut off and then red-hot hatchets placed under his armpits and on his shoulders. Because he challenged his torturers, his mouth was smashed with a stone and a burning brand thrust down his throat. Then the Indians tore off his living skin, and by way of ironic blasphemy, baptized him three times with boiling water. Lastly they tore out his heart, which an Indian chief proceeded to devour. But for all their cruelty, they were conquered by his indomitable resistance. Thus they fought to drink his blood so that they might imbibe his superhuman courage." May he impart it to us! Francis Parkman, Wasp that he was, called Brébeuf "the Ajax of the missions." Fr. Lalemant's martyrdom followed in like manner three hours later. Fr. Paul Le Jeune, a converted Huguenot, declared, "Nature is not endowed with the sacred breath to kindle such ardors. These flames spring from a fire wholly divine."

Breathing the same air, the Montrealais thrived spiritually in physical deprivation. In the very teeth of the Iroquois, who besides being armed by the Dutch and English were diabolically inspired to perpetrate the atrocities for which they are famous, Montreal survived. Even after the Iroquois had destroyed the last Huron village in the vicinity, Montreal survived. Its work must indeed have been of God, as was claimed in a little contemporary tract written to refute detractors under the title *TheTrue Motives of the Ladies and Gentlemen of the Society of Notre Dame de Montreal for the Conversion of the Savages of New France.* According to the author, "You say the undertaking of Montreal is an enormous expense, more suitable for a king than for a few private persons too feeble to sustain it, ... besides the perils of navigation and shipwreck which can destroy it.... How could you ever think that, relying on our own strength, we could have presumed to entertain so glorious a design? If God is not in the business of Montreal, if it's a human invention, don't trouble yourselves about it, it won't last!... Till now He has provided the necessary; we don't look for abundance, and we hope His Providence will continue."

Also pointed out is that their venture was in fact an affair of the King's, for Louis XIV had taken their side against the remonstrances of their rivals in Quebec. He reminded its Governor de Lauson, "Inasmuch as my primary consideration in New France is God's glory and the propagation of the Catholic Faith, I expect you to have particular concern for anything that might contribute to it. This is what draws me to bear special affection for the Company of Montreal, which is composed of persons of quality and piety, who have no other interest but the salvation of souls and the preaching of the Gospel." Fr. Vimont wrote, "Would you believe that many of the workmen working in Montreal never entertained any other motive since their departure from France but the glory of God? The mere thought that here they contribute as much as they can to the salvation of souls keeps them working with such high courage that they are never heard to complain." One of those original settlers declared, "Not only shall we make our America French, but we shall make it entirely Christian, and out of a vast wilderness we shall make a sanctuary where the Divine Majesty will find worshipers of every tongue and nation!"

+

What happened? Whatever ills the colonists brought with them from Europe continued to proliferate in Canada on their own. Civil authorities found themselves pitted against the Church; Montreal competed with Quebec; Jansenists contended with Jesuits and Gallicans with Ultramontanes. De Tocqueville spoke truly when he remarked, "The physiognomy of a government can best be judged in its colonies, for there its characteristic traits usually appear larger and more distinct." Continuing to incite the Iroquois, English and Dutch against the French, that father of agitators, the old Serpent, was not slow in exploiting all these internal problems, especially bending to his purposes any indifferent Catholics who might be ready to betray the cause to further their interests. Prominent among the last was Charles de la Tour, who distinguished himself by accepting a baronetcy from the British to consolidate his claim to Acadia. Going so far as to enlist the aid of the Puritans in Boston against his King's representative, he even found it expedient to accompany Governor Winthrop to the Sabbath services!

For a long time the ecclesiastical authority had needed regularizing, and with the establishment of a second, near-autonomous population center at Montreal, the situation became acute. As Canada had no bishop of its own, contention and conflict of interest had free play. The rivalry between the religious orders, Sulpicians, Recollects and Jesuits, with congregations of nuns caught in between, provided endless friction, with no arbiter of sufficient authority to allay it. Although lacking the stature of Champlain, the early governors of Canada were all pious, good men. Montmagny was a Knight of Malta; Charny, son and successor of Lauson, resigned his office to enter the priesthood. His example was followed by d'Ailleboust, whose wife and he had lived as brother and sister. Secular authority, however, no matter how saintly, was not equal to the task.

Until the 1650's, the Church in Canada had to all practical purposes been governed from France by the Archbishop of Rouen, whose de facto jurisdiction the Jesuits and Sulpician superiors had accepted in order to insure the validity of marriages and religious professions among the settlers. Rome did not view this with an approving eye, in view of the ominous growth of Gallicanism, a prototype of Americanism which was gaining ground in the mother country, where even Bossuet, the great Bishop of Meaux, would argue for the Gallican Articles of 1682　promoting separation of Church and state and the subjection of the Pope to general councils. For the good of souls, Rome had so far tacitly supported Rouen's rulings in Canadian matters, but a better solution had to be found quickly, for a huge mission territory dependent on a French prelate whose Gallican propensities were a matter of record might set dangerous precedents.

By 1657, the original Associates who founded and supported Montreal found themselves so reduced in numbers that they relinquished the colony to Fr. Olier's Sulpicians, now flourishing at their headquarters in Paris. Four of their fathers had been sent to take charge, among them Fr. de Queylus, who became the Archbishop of Rouen's Vicar General in Canada. Clothed with episcopal powers, the zealous Vicar proceeded to exercise his authority in no uncertain terms, not only in Montreal, but also in Quebec, to the great discomfort of the Jesuits. Professed Ultramontanes, as servants of the Pope, these appealed to the new French minister Mazarin, who withdrew his assent to the arrangement, and the Queen-Mother Anne of Austria invited Fr. Le Jeune to nominate a bishop for Canada.

Only a saint was equal to the task, and the man Fr. Le Jeune proposed turned out to be pure Canadian diamond. He was François Xavier de Laval-Montmorency, who was not only descended from one of the greatest families in France,　but whose ancestor was the first after King Clovis to receive the Sacrament of Baptism from the hand of St. Remi. Destined for the Church from earliest childhood, he received the tonsure at the age of nine while still a schoolboy at La Flèche, where he first read the *Jesuit Relations* and made the acquaintance of the martyr Fr. Lalemant and other saintly members of the Society. At thirteen, while still pursuing his studies, he was appointed a canon at Evreux. At twenty-four, renouncing his inheritance and the headship of his family, which had fallen to him after the death of his two older brothers, he espoused the priesthood, assuming responsibility for no less than fifty-five parishes and four subsidiary churches.

At the Hermitage of Caen, he formed a friendship with St. Jean Eudes and briefly considered going to Vietnam with Fr. Alexander de Rhodes, but heaven disposed otherwise, and in 1658 Rome appointed him Vicar Apostolic for Canada, with the title of Bishop of Petraea. His consecration was entrusted to no French bishop. According to Faillon, "The Nuncio, to whom the sentiments of the Queen-Mother Anne of Austria were well-known, was determined to consecrate M. de Laval, and even found two bishops to assist him in the ceremony.... The ordination was set for Sunday, December 8, Feast of the Immaculate Conception [which had been proclaimed in the New World by Our Lady of Guadalupe long before she did so at Lourdes]; and in order to forestall any opposition which might mar it, it took place in the morning in great secrecy in the Abbey of St. Germain-des-Près, which at that time was exempt [from French jurisdiction], and in a chapel which the Nuncio had requested of the Prior for a pontifical function, begging him to speak to no one of his design."

Thus it was that Laval, headed for a charge where he would need all the help he could muster from the French king and the greats of this world, entered upon his role completely independent of them, following only the orders of the Holy See, according to the canons of the universal Church. Bl. Marie de l'Incarnation, destined one day to be beatified with him, declared even before she met him, "Say what you like, he was not chosen by men!" It takes one to know one. He himself was wont to remark, "There is only God; everything else is pure nothing!" Nothing less than so supernatural an attitude could fortify him against the problems he would face, for in Quebec, Gallicanism was by that time firmly entrenched, especially among the secular authorities.

Trouble began immediately at Mass, where Governor d'Argenson, as personal representative of the royal authority, was accustomed to occupy a kneeler within the sanctuary. When the new Bishop ordered it removed and placed outside the

Communion rail, there were vigorous protests. At both Mass and Vespers, the Governor was also in the habit of being incensed immediately after the celebrant and the Bishop, but, here again, Bishop Laval insisted that this take place only after the incensing of all the other ministers of the Altar. He furthermore dismissed d'Argenson from his ex officio church wardenship, and at "solemn catechisms" the children were instructed to salute the Bishop before the Governor. When the latter had the temerity to take issue with His Excellency regarding a sentence he had pronounced on a heretic, sword and crozier became locked in mortal combat.

The Jesuits dared invite neither of the two to dinner, either singly or together, for fear of mortally insulting one or the other. On Palm Sunday, there was no procession and no distribution of palms, because the question of precedence could not be resolved. On Corpus Christi, there was more trouble, because d'Argenson would not permit his soldiers to kneel while drawn up in formation before the Blessed Sacrament. "The disputes in question," wrote Parkman, "though of a nature to provoke a smile on irreverent lips, were by no means as puerile as they appear. It is difficult in a modern democratic society to conceive the substantial importance of the signs and symbols of dignity and authority at a time and among a people where they were adjusted with the most scrupulous precision and accepted by all classes as exponents of relative degrees in the social and political scale. Whether the Bishop or the Governor should sit in the higher seat at table thus became a political question, for it defined to the popular understanding the position of the church and state in their relations to the government."

Because Bl. François de Laval was adamant where the rights of God were concerned, the tilting went on for years, disrupting the whole life of the colony. Unfortunately his preeminence was disputed not only by the secular powers, but also by many religious. The Gallican Archbishop of Rouen refused to relinquish what he maintained were his nation's rights to a prelate lately set over Frenchmen by Rome. For a long time, he persisted in supporting his Vicar-General Fr. de Queylus by exacting obedience to him. Many Canadians, unfortunately, adhered to his side, reasoning in good conscience that the authority of a full Archbishop superseded that of a mere Vicar Apostolic who was only a bishop, and a titular bishop of a non-existent Arabian see at that. The religious communities were caught in a dilemma, and Bishop Laval himself was confused when, after setting up the parish of Notre Dame de Quebec, he discovered he had no authority to do so!

He nonetheless undertook official visitations, determined in charity to reconcile the warring elements as effectively as he could. At Montreal, he confirmed a hundred and seven persons, one of them, strangely enough, being Chomedey de Maisonneuve. His most important project, however, was the establishment of a single seminary for Canada, on which he pinned all his hopes for the future. Specially designed to fill the needs of a missionary country, it was affiliated to the French Foreign Missions of Paris, and because the colony was too poor to support regular parishes as in France, priests from the seminary served as movable pastors wherever they were needed. Gathered as a family around their Bishop, they were administrators for all diocesan affairs under his direction, holding all property in common and deriving their support from royal subsidies and tithes levied on the people. On this novel seminary was built the Church of Canada, and the plan worked admirably well.

The Indians were assigned to the Jesuits, Montreal to the Sulpicians, and the Recollects had charge of Acadia. Communities of hospital nuns and teaching sisters were already flourishing under the direction of some Canadian diamonds already mentioned. Jeanne Mance headed the Hôtel-Dieu in Montreal, Bl. Marie de l'Incarnation the Ursulines in Quebec, and St. Marguerite Bourgeoys the Congregation of Notre Dame. The year 1688 saw the opening of a minor seminary where five French and six Huron students were enrolled. Like the renowned Las Casas in the West, Bishop Laval was always the friend of the Amerindians, whose name for him was Hariwawagu, "the Man of the Great Business."

All this had been accomplished by 1674, when his jurisdictional problems finally ended with his appointment as Bishop of the Diocese of Quebec, primatial see of Canada. The second in North America after that of Mexico, Quebec was immediately subject to Rome and not to France, with jurisdiction over all territory discovered by the French. Its expanse was immense. Although in all it contained probably less than four thousand French Catholics, about fifteen hundred of them Indians, it extended literally over the whole of North America, with the exception of Spanish Florida and the Wasp coastal settlements. USan Catholics now tend to forget, if they ever knew, that the majority of their parishes have their roots, not in the U.S. Constitution, but in the charism of Bl. François de Laval. Whoever would know the true history of Chicago, St. Louis, Seattle, Des Moines and other American cities, which began as French Catholic settlements, must read French ecclesiastical annals. During Bishop Laval's tenure, the number of parishes increased from twenty-five to one hundred and two, and religious from thirty-two to about ninety-seven. With him, the Faith stuck fast to the Sides.

And, of course, there was always the interminable quarrel about brandy, whose sale to the Indians had originally been strictly forbidden. The redskin's inability to handle firewater is proverbial, and there are many firsthand contemporary accounts of the havoc it caused in the colonies. Bl. Marie de l'Incarnation speaks of the Bishop "withering away" at the sight of the "murders, rapes, monstrous and unspeakable brutalities" which were committed by drunken Indians. Unfortunately, the brandy traffic greatly facilitated the fur trade, and following the example of the Wasps, the French merchants bent on profit soon appreciated its power to extract pelts from Indian hunters. Although directly or indirectly everyone profited economically, Bishop Laval promptly excommunicated anyone taking part, and even requested the death penalty from the temporal authorities. Argenson's successor, Governor Avaugour, consented to enforce this desperate measure, but soon relented under pressure and granted full license to the liquor dealers. A tremendous upheaval ensued, with the Bishop launching into fresh excommunications and popular fury forcing him to revoke them.

In desperation he left for France, in order to appeal to the King, and during his absence heaven made its own move. Early in 1663, Fr. Lalemant reported, "We beheld blazing serpents which flew through the air borne on wings of fire. We beheld above Quebec a great globe of flame which lit up the whole night and threw out sparks on all sides. This same meteor appeared above Montreal, where it seemed to issue from the bosom of the moon, with a noise as loud as cannon or thunder; and after sailing three leagues through the air, it disappeared behind the mountain whereof this island bears the name." A good Algonquin Christian squaw heard a voice in the middle of the night which said, "Strange things will happen today; the earth will quake!" And that same night Mother Catherine de St. Augustin, a hospital nun of Quebec who is now also beatified, beheld four demons shaking the four corners of Quebec, restrained only by Our Lord from doing worse. She heard them say, "Let us keep shaking and do our best to upset everything!"

The next day a momentous earthquake occurred. Extending as far as New England and New Amsterdam, it is amply substantiated by contemporary accounts and subsequent geological findings. The tremors did not cease entirely until midsummer, leaving the St. Lawrence so filled with mud that the water was undrinkable. Entire hills disappeared, streams were diverted, waterfalls leveled and new springs started. Severe drought followed, then torrential rain. Not the least extraordinary effect of the cataclysm was that in all the sound and fury, not one life was lost. But what a warning! The Wasp was not so fortunate, for two years later, in the wake of the comet, London was visited by the Great Plague and the Great Fire, costing thousands of lives and untold misery.

In Canada, nature quieted down with Laval's triumph at the French court, where Louis XIV decided to take New France in hand personally. The brandy traffic was outlawed, and Avagour was recalled, in whose place the Sieur de Mézy, a devout military official from Caen, was appointed governor on the Bishop's recommendation. The moribund Hundred Associates were dissolved in favor of a Council composed of the Bishop, the Governor and members appointed by them. To centralize dangerously divided authority, de Mézy removed the good Chomedey de Maisonneuve from Montreal and replaced him with a vice-governor subject to the Council. Never a rich man, Maisonneuve spent his remaining years without rancor or bitterness in Paris, pursuing a life of prayer and ever faithful to the vow of chastity he had made in his youth. On her trip to France in 1670, St. Marguerite Bourgeoys happily availed herself of his hospitality.

For the moment, it looked as if the Church might control the state in New France, but this would have been equally dangerous, and the situation was not to last long. The Bishop found himself sadly mistaken in his man the Sieur de Mézy, who seemed to change character completely under the weight of his new office. The brandy trade burst out afresh, and the new Governor's successors proved even more incorrigible than he. Fresh paroxysms set in under the worldly and irascible

Frontenac, who became Governor in 1672. "Nearly all the disorders in New France," argued he, spring from the ambition of the ecclesiastics, who want to join to their spiritual authority an absolute power over things temporal, and who persecute all who do not submit entirely to them!" His special targets being the Jesuits and the Bishop, he aggravated the situation further by taking sides with the Recollects. Bl. Bishop de Laval struggled through one more governorship until 1684, at which time, too ill physically to carry out his duties, he resigned his see. In constant suffering, but free of exterior work, he picked up the heavier spiritual weapons and took on the enemy at closer quarters.

The underlying cause of Bishop de Laval's troubles was, of course, his sanctity. In a letter to her son, Bl. Marie de l'Incarnation confides, "Our prelate is ... very zealous and inflexible. Zealous in promoting the observance of anything he feels will increase God's glory; and inflexible in not giving way to anything contrary.... He gives away everything and lives like the poor .... Nevertheless, where the dignity and authority of his office are concerned, he overlooks no occasion." We have seen how Governor d'Argenson fared with him regarding the honors of the sanctuary.

His bitterest purifications were those he endured in the last twenty years of his life, when he lived as a recluse in his dear seminary. Assisting his successor Bishop de Saint-Vallier only incidentally, he was forced to look on helplessly as the new prelate embarked on the systematic destruction of all he had so painfully achieved. Aiming to pattern the new Canadian see on those of the mother country, Saint-Vallier made the unusual seminary his first target. Although working admirably for the purpose for which it was designed, it was quickly reduced to a mere school for boys and seminarians on the European model, its staff functioning no longer as diocesan administrators in close touch with the people, but only as pedagogues. De Laval suspected this was the devil's work, and when shortly thereafter fire devoured it along with its chapel and rectory, he was sure of it. Hardly rebuilt, minus the chapel, it burned a second time.

Despite all, however, according to Br. Hubert Houssard, who tended His Excellency faithfully to the end, he "never for one moment lost his peace, joy and tranquility, because such accidents were not of a nature capable of attacking his patience and virtue, which were well above that." Brother testified that, until his last illness, his master rose at two in the morning and at three thereafter, to pray in his room, "where it froze hard every night in winter, there being no stove." At four he would go to the church, "his lantern in his hand, to open the doors and ring the bells for his Mass, which was the earliest, for the laborers at four-thirty," remaining in the unheated building to pray until seven. Assiduous in enhancing the canonical offices of the Cathedral by his episcopal presence, he would have himself carried there over the protests of his doctor when he was too weak to walk. As long as he was able, he continued tending the sick with his own hands at the hospital nearby.

Shortly before his death Br. Hubert discovered in his cash box a small penknife worth a few cents and asked him for it. "My child," he was told, "if I still own this knife, I give it to you with all my heart, so as no longer to possess anything on earth and to free myself entirely from the goods of this world." At the last, he could speak only of God, offering his deathbed sufferings "for all the sins of the seminary." Heaven hearing, his pain doubled, "which was excessive from that day till his death" on May 6, 1708, at the age of eighty-five. Not even his enemies doubted his holiness. When his heart was removed for special veneration, bits of bone were taken from his chest, his hair was cut and linen dipped in his blood to satisfy some three thousand requests for relics. Crowds attended the funeral, and immediately began the stream of miracles which have not ceased for those who invoke him. In due time, his body was laid in the seminary chapel, rebuilt once more, in the company of all those other sacred relics so little noted by the world, but so feared by the Enemy.

Chapter IX

MORE DIAMONDS

Jacques Cartier had collected his "Canadian diamonds" by the basketful, and so it is with saints, who are rarely if ever produced in isolation. Being the most active cells in the Mystical Body, they are deeply interrelated and marvelously fruitful. The grace God poured out through His servant François de Laval did not return to Him void. Among his diocesans was the little hospital sister who had seen the four demons shaking the four corners of Quebec, Marie-Catherine de St. Augustin, a lively, pretty, unassuming young woman, nobly born and virtuously reared by saintly grandparents. Favored since early childhood with mystical graces of a high order, at the age of twelve she entered the Augustinian order in Bayeux, France. At sixteen, while still a novice, she volunteered for the Hôtel-Dieu in Quebec, which had been managed by her sisters in religion since 1639. She sailed in 1648, on the same ship which brought the saintly Governor d'Ailleboust to his new assignment.

The opposition stirred by hell against her departure pursued her aboard, for during the voyage an outbreak of pestilence carried off the captain and several others. Near death herself, she was rescued from an infernal dragon by Our Lady, who offered her the choice of dying on the spot with the assurance of going to heaven, or remaining on earth in uncertainty of her salvation. Abandoning herself to God's will, Sr. Catherine soon found herself recovering in Quebec at the height of the Iroquois terror. "From year to year their audacity and insolence grew towards New France," writes Goyau in *Origines Religieuses du Canada.* "The Dutch, their neighbors to the southeast, supplied them with arquebuses.... It seemed that Satan in person rose up, ready to expel from his Canadian kingdom this newcomer called Jesus, by means of the complicity of the pagan Iroquois and the secret assistance of the Dutch Calvinists." Catherine took comfort in these adversities, for long ago her director had assured her that "those who suffer are more likely to be doing God's will." She refers to her new home as "a little paradise."

The true nature of her vocation gradually dawning on her, she writes back to Bayeux, "I offered myself to the Divine Majesty to serve Him as a victim, as often as He pleases." A forerunner of the legion of victim souls demanded by the unparalleled needs of the embattled Church in America in the latter days, Sr. Catherine would enter into the closest kind of encounters with the demons of the Sides. She would paralyze whole battalions of them by literally keeping trapped within her body those who sought to possess her. Making her daily rounds at the hospital, where she served as Treasurer and later as General Administrator, besides nursing the sick, writing letters for them and counseling them—for she had the gift of reading hearts—she betrayed nothing exteriorly of her unusual vocation.

Bl. Marie de l'Incarnation tells us that when she died, "no one in the Community knew there was anything extraordinary about her, not even her Superior. Only His Excellency the Bishop knew, and her director." She wrote her son that the favors Sr. Catherine received from heaven would "fill a volume," but that she was more astounded at her virtue. She tells how the young nun, seriously ill herself, carried out her duties "for over eight years without taking to her bed, without complaining, without failing in obedience or omitting her religious exercises, whether in choir, office or community." Bishop de Laval often confided in Sr. Catherine and regarded her as the guardian angel of his far-flung dioceses: "This was a soul God chose for the purpose of communicating very great and very special graces. Her holiness will be better recognized in heaven than in this life."

She is still virtually unknown, although her cause was opened in Rome in 1980, and she has been beatified. After she died at the age of thirty-six, the Bishop ordered her director Fr. Paul Ragueneau, S.J., to write her biography. Based almost entirely on a journal she was commanded to write under obedience, it contains details increasingly pertinent in these latter days, when heaven seems to be addressing calls to victimhood to the faithful generally. Like St. Teresa of Avila, Bl. Catherine had been shown her place in hell if she proved unfaithful. Favored with mystical Communions, allowed to caress the Infant Jesus, and even nourished with Our Lady's milk, she entered deeply into the Mysteries of the Faith. Presented to the Holy Ghost as spouse by the Blessed Virgin, she saw Him at work "in the form of a huge cloud only waiting to empty itself everywhere. Under this cloud I saw a large number of people on whom the Holy Ghost was pouring Himself out, but very differently. This mist penetrated the first with great ease and sweetness. It ran off the second and fell to earth. As for the third, not only was it lost on them, but when it fell on them it encountered such great resistance that it spattered far away, sometimes more, sometimes less."

She was also shown the many souls in Purgatory saved from damnation by her prayer and suffering. She had need of such consolations, for when she arrived in Canada it was no longer a missionary colony, but had been raised to the full status of a French province, and the demons of the Sides were deploying all their strength to retain the empire which they saw slowly but surely slipping from their grasp. Even as a child, she had experienced Satan's onslaughts, but they had been mere preparation for what she would face in Quebec. St. Jean de Brébeuf suffered his martyrdom a year after her arrival, and, although she had never met him, towards the end of her life he was assigned to her as a special director from heaven. He appeared to her frequently and sometimes brought her Holy Communion. With him she made a pact to save Canada, for "he told me many times that he would take care of the country's affairs."

Her triumphant apostolate began with furious temptations to gluttony, impurity and only-too-understandable yearnings to return to France. The last never left her, and, to counter them, she made in 1654 a solemn vow of perpetual stability to Our Lord, "Who by an all-loving disposition of Your Divine Providence have wished to place me in this country." Hell redoubled its fury, and five years later she offered herself formally as a victim for Canada. Already in 1633, the year of the great earthquake, she had cried out, "My Savior and My All! If [having] demons dwelling in my body is pleasing to You, I am happy to have them stay as long as You please. Provided sin doesn't enter with them, I fear nothing, and I hope You will grant me the grace of loving You for all eternity." At times she was invaded by hordes of devils, who gave her no rest day or night. "I was as if maddened by the violence I did myself so as not to give in to [their] desires."

Although sorcery was far from unknown in Canada, it never got out of hand, held at bay as it was by the Catholic priesthood. On one occasion, however, Sr. Catherine delivered a young possessed woman, whose condition had proved impervious to exorcism after the ministrations of a Huguenot miller who was a secret warlock. These cases were nonetheless rare, and in this one the devils retaliated by launching an epidemic of influenza. It is possible that the young nun had caused many of the embattled demons to flee south to New England, where they could easily have fomented and directed the famous witch trials in Salem, Massachusetts, in 1692. The final verdict, delivered outside the salvific pale of the Church, exonerated fifty-five men and women who confessed to practicing witchcraft and hanged nineteen who pleaded innocent!

Tormented by doubts of the Real Presence, with deep aversion to prayer and Holy Communion, she was on one occasion saved from committing suicide by St. Jean de Brébeuf, who appeared in the nick of time, when, driven by diabolical compulsion, she had seized a knife to dispatch herself. Without her help, Quebec's Basilica, the first cathedral to be constructed on the Sides, would not have been dedicated, nor would the terrible earthquake have passed off harmlessly. To her the impenitent Governor de Mézy owed his deathbed conversion, his eternal sentence commuted to as many years in Purgatory as he had spent days in Canada. In 1662 she had seen Satan holding court, receiving the homages of the devils of Quebec, Beaupré, Trois-Rivières and Montreal, as they boasted of the trouble they were causing. Just prior to the earthquake, she saw St. Michael wielding three arrows for "three kinds of punishment for three kinds of sins habitually committed in this country: impiety, impurity and lack of charity, especially by detraction and dissension."

In *Dieu et Satan,* a modern study of Sr. Catherine, Sr. Ghislaine Boucher, RJM, writes, "Catherine thus interiorized to the maximum the warfare waged against Satan in a new country still partly savage. She bears in herself the very mystery of Christ, Who comes to cast out the prince of this world by dying on the Cross. By her interior agony Catherine drives the devil out of this country, by carrying within herself all the tragedy and suffering of sin." Thus was laid bare the true nature of the political struggle taking place throughout Amerindia. Our young heroine died a warrior, singing the *Te Deum.* She still cures the sick, her body reposing at the Hôtel-Dieu in Quebec.

+

"Pray our Divine Lord to grant me a life as holy and a death as holy as He did this good girl!" exclaimed Bl. Marie de l'Incarnation, another member of Bishop Laval's diocese, whom we have had occasion to quote before. It would seem that Our Lord did so, for her story in its own way is as inspiring as the little hospital sister's. Alike in that both these extraordinary women succeeded in uniting exalted contemplation with unremitting exterior activity, in the stately Marie's case, her mystical gifts could not be concealed from others. Regarded as the "Mother of the Church in Canada," she arrived there ten years before Catherine and lived much longer. Called to divine union in a dream at the age of seven and longing for the religious life, she had nonetheless married in obedience to her parents, only to be left a widow at nineteen with a small son. Her youth was spent in liquidating her husband's debts and managing her sister and brother-in-law's large transport business in Tours, where she displayed exceptional executive talents.

"I passed whole days in a stable which served as a warehouse," she recalled, "and sometimes at midnight I was at dockside overseeing the loading and unloading of merchandise. My ordinary companions were porters, draymen and even fifty or sixty horses which fell to my care. Sometimes I found myself so overloaded with work that I didn't know where to start. I addressed my usual Refuge, telling Him, 'My Love, there is no way for me to do everything, but do it for me, otherwise all will be left undone.' Thus, confiding in His goodness, everything was easy for me. These new problems never distracted me from the close attention I paid to God and which always absorbed me, but rather I felt strengthened in it, because all was done in charity and not for my personal profit."

When her son reached the age of twelve, Marie, under divine inspiration, prevailed upon her sister to take charge of him and allow her to enter the Ursuline convent in Tours. Like St. Jeanne de Chantal, she found this the cruelest renunciation of her life. Reports of the growing boy caused her much anguish, but he wound up an exemplary priest and his mother's confidant. Posterity is indebted to their transatlantic correspondence for much of the early history of Canada. Soon after her profession, she was favored with a mysterious dream in which she beheld herself and an unknown laywoman leaving for a vast, strange country of mists and mountains, where, after myriad difficulties, they were met by an Apostle, who brought them into the presence of Our Lady. Thereafter, she said, "My body was in our convent, but my spirit could not be shut up," and eventually Our Lord explained to her, "It is Canada I let you see. You must go there to make a home for Jesus and Mary." Although cloistered, she would become the first French missionary sister.

The unknown companion turned out to be an intrepid Norman aristocrat by the name of Mme. de la Peltrie, who at the time was dying of fever. She too had married obediently, despite aspirations to the religious life, and was now widowed, but childless. Determined to answer the appeals of Fr. Le Jeune in the Jesuit Relations for teachers for the Indian girls, for whom there were as yet no schools, she obtained a miraculous cure from St. Joseph, in return for her promise to build a house in his honor in Canada. Unfortunately, her father threatened to disinherit her if she did not remarry. Helpless without the necessary fortune, she devised a stratagem worthy of that earlier benefactress of the Canadian missions, Mme. de Guercheville. Exposing her dilemma to M. de Bernières de Louvigni, future light of the famous Hermitage at Caen where Bishop de Laval received his spiritual formation, she entreated him to enter into a sham marriage with her. Bound by a vow of chastity, Bernières was reluctant, but with the salvation of the Amerindians at stake and the encouragement of their spiritual directors, he capitulated—to the intense satisfaction of her father, who died happy before learning of the deception.

Another vow to St. Joseph having obtained the dismissal of a lawsuit on the part of irate relatives with an eye to the lady's property, the new "Mme. de Bernières" proceeded as planned. In Tours, she met the capable Marie, already designated to make the new foundation overseas, who recognized her on sight as the lady in her prophetic dream. In 1639, the two set sail with the Hôtel-Dieu sisters in the company of M. de Bernières and two Ursulines, the entire venture having been confided to St. Joseph by Marie. His hidden hand ever at work in Canadian history, he saved them from shipwreck, Spaniards and an iceberg before they reached Quebec. Marie nursed no illusions, having "had a vision of what would happen to me in Canada. I saw endless crosses, interior abandonment on the part of God and creatures to the point of crucifixion, that I was to enter into a hidden and unknown life.... I cannot express the fright felt in my spirit and whole nature in this vision." Long before Sr. Catherine arrived, she too had offered herself a victim for Canada.

Her gigantic undertaking began in a little two-room house, replaced three years later by a three story convent and school. When this burned down in 1650, the Ursulines found shelter for a time at the Hôtel-Dieu with Bl. Catherine and her Augustinians, but soon all was rebuilt by the dauntless Marie, who found ample challenge for her practical talents. Before long, she gave evidence of a superior intellect as well. Not only was it used to the full in her capacity as educator to both French and Indian girls, but her convent became a cultural and spiritual center for the entire colony. From stark necessity, she found herself writing voluminously for her new field of action, snatching time for it like St. Teresa, amid a merciless round of duties. She wrote hundreds of letters to anyone likely to provide help or influence, as well as training manuals for teachers, textbooks, moral instructions for the young, dictionaries and catechisms in the Indian dialects, containing translations of Christian prayers.

Her autobiographical writings alone would have ensured her a place in history. Written under obedience, they rank with the most elevated spiritual teaching in the Church, prompting the great Bossuet to call her "the Teresa of the New World." Still at her task in 1668 when she was nearing seventy, she wrote her son, by then Dom Claude Martin, in France, "From the beginning of Lent up to the Ascension, I wrote a big book in Algonquin on sacred history and holy things, together with a dictionary and a catechism in Iroquois, which is a treasure. Last year I wrote a big Algonquin dictionary in the French alphabet. I have another in the native alphabet." Her spiritual stature may be gauged from a sample taken from the famous Relations for 1654, where she speaks of the three degrees of poverty of spirit: "My whole soul tended to this sublime virtue, which I saw held the highest place in the sublime life of the Son of God, for I saw all the other virtues enclosed therein, and its object was none other than the pure and naked love which in its simplicity no longer possesses anything but God." She died in 1672 in the odor of sanctity and was beatified on the same day as her holy Bishop François de Laval.

Although Marie's companion Mme. de la Peltrie never became a nun, she remained her faithful friend through fires, famine, earthquake, Iroquois raids and the rigors of winter, ending her days in the Ursuline convent one year before its foundress. Working for a time in Montreal, as well as in Quebec, she had taken part in the historic procession led by Maisonneuve, carrying the huge votive Cross to the summit of Mont Royal. She was on hand in 1653 when yet another Canadian diamond, St. Marguerite Bourgeoys, arrived to undertake the education of girls in Montreal. An experienced young teacher from Troyes, Marguerite had been recruited by Maisonneuve, whom she had immediately recognized from a dream, as was the case with so many of these chosen apostles. Like Mother Marie in Quebec, it was her privilege to form the first "Mothers of Canada," but not from the cloister. Although Bishop de Laval ardently wished to incorporate her into the Ursulines, she doggedly resisted all efforts to enclaustrate her group, even when their building burned down and they were temporarily destitute. At long last, when she was in her eighties, her community of uncloistered teaching sisters was formally established as the Congregation de Notre Dame, which flourishes to this day.

Arriving on board ship with her had been several prospective brides for the settlers, and these would become a special apostolate. In order to populate the country as quickly as possible and to discourage bachelorhood, always a source of social instability where there was no religious motivation, Louis XIV arranged to send poor but honest girls as suitable wives. Known as "the King's daughters," about a thousand came between 1665 and 1673, dowries and transportation provided by the royal bounty. The imputation, sometimes heard today as in the past, that these girls were taken off the streets of Paris is grossly false, but it acquired plausibility because this was accepted practice in the Wasp colonies, and we have seen that the Huguenot Roberval had initially recruited French women by such means. In 1658, Governor d'Argenson, in fact, pronounced a judgment against a merchant of La Rochelle who was "so insolent as to send to this country a girl debauched and actually pregnant, and whom he knew to be in this condition. I sentenced him to return her to La Rochelle at his expense."

In point of fact, each candidate had to have a certificate from her pastor or magistrate in France proving that she was free to marry, and all were accompanied by pious chaperones on the voyage. St. Marguerite herself had once served in this capacity on her return from a recruiting trip, and she recalled, "As they were to be the mothers of future families, I thought it only right that they should be brought together in a safe place, and that, of all others, the Blessed Virgin's house ought to be open to her children. Filled with this thought and scarcely waiting to consult the sisters, I hurried to the shore to meet these girls and take them to our house." Supervising them closely and well aware of the difficult adjustments they would have to make, some being barely sixteen, she taught them catechism and household skills. Every girl had the right to decline a suitor not to her taste, and Mother Bourgeoys interviewed all the young men who applied. Today her small neat handwriting can still be read on some of the marriage contracts which have come down to us. Inasmuch as bonuses for each child born in wedlock were provided by the King, with parents of ten children receiving a yearly pension of three hundred livres and parents of twelve four hundred livres, the population of New France doubled within a decade.

+

Canada's first canonical solitary was a woman, the wealthy Mlle. Jeanne Le Ber of Montreal. Under God, she was the product of both the cloistered contemplative Bl. Marie de l'Incarnation and the active nun St. Marguerite Bourgeoys, for she studied with both communities. Godchild of Jeanne Mance, the saintly foundress of Montreal's hospital sisters, Jeanne withdrew from society completely while still in her teens, confining herself to a room at home for some ten years under temporary vows. Practicing extremes of mortification, she refused to leave it, even when her mother lay dying under the same roof, and again when her brother was brought home mortally wounded from a skirmish with the English and Iroquois.

After so long and successful a test of her singular vocation, Mother Bourgeoys accepted Jeanne as a member of her Congregation, believing that she was called to represent among them "Magdalene who dwelt in a grotto, as St. John the Baptist had in the wilderness." On the eve of the Feast of the Transfiguration in 1695, she was installed in a cell behind the altar of the new chapel which Jeanne had built and endowed for the community from her own fortune, and she never left it. The Sulpician Superior Fr. Dollier de Casson, who performed the appropriate ceremonies, recalled, "I blessed a little room with its little door and grille for Mlle. Le Ber.... After the blessing, which I gave as Vicar General, before the clergy as well as all the Sisters of the Congregation and other people from the outside, I pronounced a brief exhortation to which she listened on her knees, after which I led her to the above-mentioned apartment, in which she locked herself up at once."

Dead to the world, occupied solely in prayer, penance and needlework, she was nonetheless often appealed to in cases of conscience and public calamity. When the English invaded in 1711, a banner of the Virgin embroidered by her bearing the inscription "She is as terrible as an army in battle array. She will help us vanquish our enemies," was credited with destroying their fleet by means of a sudden south wind. This instance and all we know of her heroic hidden life were imparted to her biographer by her spiritual director Fr. de Belmont. He tells us that the last twenty years of her life were bereft of all consolation, endured only by sheer force of will with God's

THE BATTLE FOR AMERINDIA

grace. She died in rags, but the angels are said to have mended her spinning wheel and helped her with her beautiful embroidery, some of which can still be viewed in Montreal.

Never can it be said that the Canadian diamonds were little more than French implants, for Jeanne was a native. So was St. Marguerite d'Youville of Montreal, widowed young like Bl. Marie and Mme. de la Peltrie and left with the care of two sons. Granddaughter of Governor Pierre Boucher of Trois-Rivières, she would found the Sisters of Charity, who were immediately dubbed by her detractors *"les soeurs grises,"* a slang nickname meaning either the gray or the "tipsy" sisters, alluding to the foundress' husband, who died a dissolute drunkard. Not lacking a sense of humor, she chose gray as the color of her new community's habits, and the name stuck. And there was the Montreal-born Bl. André Grasset de Saint-Sauveur, who found himself in Paris during the Terror and was martyred along with three bishops and one hundred eighty-eight priests who refused to take the revolutionary civil oath.

It would be impossible to mention all the Canadian diamonds of French extraction. But what of the savages who were the objects of their labors? Before the close of the 17th century, the Holy Ghost Himself bore witness to the fruitfulness of their efforts by drawing out of the northern forests, from the very donjon of the demons, that miracle of grace Bl. Kateri Tekakwitha, the "Lily of the Mohawks." In her can be seen that savagery is anything but the primitive condition from which all mankind originally sprang, as the Serpent would have us believe, but rather the one to which civilization separated from God inevitably leads. It is the ultimate fall from Adam's original justice. Clutching about him tatters of past glory, the Amerindian of the Sides was a man disfigured, crying to be restored to the divine image in which he had been created, with all its intellectual and volitional adornments. The Spanish and French missionaries understood this perfectly.

In contrast with what might be called the "natural" savages, the urban savages "evolving" today, semi-nude, semi-literate and stifled in conscience, have been scientifically degraded. Clear proof that the latter days are upon the world, they require that final missionary effort which only God can make by His second coming. Tekakwitha was a joyful presage of this apocalyptic event. If Bl. Marie de l'Incarnation is the New World Teresa of Avila, then Kateri must be its Thérèse of

Lisieux, its Little Wildflower. Like Thérèse, Kateri died at twenty-four, with as little display of spectacular talents or mystical states, yet she has inspired over fifty biographies in ten languages. Her life was extraordinary beyond all telling, in that it was extraordinarily Indian. She is truly the "noble savage" the French philosophes expected to find here ready-made, but which only God's grace working through the French missionaries could produce.

It would seem she was the supernatural seed of St. Isaac Jogues, St. René Goupil and St. Jean Lalande, for it was near Auriesville, N.Y., on soil watered by their blood ten years before that she first saw the light, in 1656. Her mother was a Christian Algonquin, piously reared by a French family in Trois-Rivières, who had been captured by the Mohawks and married to one of their warriors. Although she must have imparted Catholic teaching to the little girl and her brother, she dared not bring them up openly in the Faith for fear of reprisals, the Mohawks being among the last to tolerate the French or their religion. When Tekakwitha was four, smallpox carried off her family, and she was adopted by her uncle, Chief Big Wolf, an ardent hater of Christians, and two aunts. Left badly scarred by the disease, with eyesight so weak and her constitution so delicate that she had to remain indoors much of the day doing only household chores, the girl was left much to herself and drawn to divine contemplation. She must nevertheless have been capable and resolute, for at the age of eight, when, according to Indian custom, children received their appropriate adult names, she was called Te-ka-kwitha, or "she who drives all before her." A good translation might be Valiant Woman, for such was the Mohawk ideal for her sex.

After 1666, the year of the dedication of Bishop de Laval's Basilica, the Mohawks finally accepted the presence of the Jesuit "Blackrobes," but they were despised by Big Wolf, who contemptuously relegated their entertainment to Tekakwitha whenever they made a visit. Nonetheless, converts were made, and from these the girl managed to learn something of her mother's religion. When she became of marriageable age, she shocked the whole village by refusing any suitor her aunts proposed. This was incomprehensible, for celibacy was unknown among the tribes, and Tekakwitha was proving to be a lily of purity in a culture which had no place for that virtue, which the missionaries found the hardest of all to implant. After her decision, unremitting persecution from her nearest and dearest became her daily bread.

One day, however, while she was confined to quarters with an injured foot, and the villagers were away on their seasonal hunting trip, Fr. Jacques de Lamberville managed to see her alone for a period of time. He received her as a catechumen, and on Easter Sunday 1677, when she was twenty, she was baptized Catherine or "Kateri." After a brief respite, the persecutions against her mounted. Abstaining from work on Sunday drew heavy reprimands; she was constantly ridiculed and at times deprived of food; and a young brave even threatened to kill her. Fearing for her safety, the priest arranged to send her to the mission of St. Francis Xavier at Caughnawaga on the south bank of the St. Lawrence opposite Montreal, where many Christian Indians had already sought refuge. The converted Chief Ganeagowa lived there with his family, and it became known far and wide as an exemplary community of "praying Indians."

Her escort to this locale would be a fiery chief known as Hot Cinders, one of St. Jean de Brébeuf's executioners, who had been converted and baptized with the name of Louis. A gifted orator, he had become a zealous catechist, who made regular missionary journeys on his own throughout Iroquois territory, teaching with the aid of pictures drawn by the Jesuits, who found this kind of native help indispensable. He was said to begin his instructions by informing his hearers, "I used to have no sense. I lived like an animal, but I was told about the Great Spirit, the true Lord of heaven and earth, and now I live like a man!" Apparently he, a Huron convert and a relative of Tekakwitha, happened to be on one such jaunt, when he came to her village and was prevailed upon to take her back with him. There were others like him. Fr. de Bruyas speaks of one Kinnonskouen as "that fervent preacher [who] gathered our Christians together in the evening (work in the fields not permitting him to do so by day) and spent two or three hours of the night instructing them and teaching them to sing. One man like him could do more than ten missionaries like me! Oh, holy the mission which possesses such perfect Christians, and holier yet the missionary who formed them by his cares and labors! *Crescent in millia millia!*"

There were other Canadian diamonds among the Indians, a few of whose names have come down to us. The extraordinary Catherine Ganneaktena, co-foundress of the St. Francis Xavier Mission, died only two years before Bl.Tekakwitha arrived there, and the fourteen-year-old Jeanne Ouendité, who had been permitted to make a formal vow of chastity, died in Quebec that very year. And there was the young hunter Martin Standekonraksen, who had been favored with three visions of Our Lady before his death at the age of twenty. True men of Nineveh, deeply ashamed of their former crimes, the Indian converts found an outlet for both their natural generosity and their penchant for extreme cruelty in ardent love of the Cross, thirsting for the martyrdom which was so often accorded them. One of the missionaries' greatest problems was curbing their penitential excesses. They indulged in bloody scourging as a matter of course, and some, like the Chief, wore iron girdles under their clothing. In winter, the women would roll in the snow in sub-zero temperatures, even cracking the ice of ponds in order to stand up to their necks in icy water, as they recited the Rosary. One mother, who nearly killed her three-year-old girl by such an immersion, maintained the child should be allowed to expiate her future sins in advance!

It was into such an atmosphere that Bl. Kateri was introduced after a ticklish escape from her former pagan surroundings, armed with a letter from Fr. de Lamberville to Fr. Cholenc at the Mission, which read, "We are sending you a treasure.... Guard it well!" Fr. Cholenc was not disappointed, for he would thrice write her biography. In her new, intensely Catholic environment, she spent the last three years of her life in a rapid spiritual ascent. Lodged with her adopted relations, she found herself with the saintly old Anastasia Tegonhatsiongo, who had been a friend of her mother and who now became her counselor and would prepare her for her First Holy Communion that Christmas. She formed a spiritual friendship with a fervent young widow by the name of Teresa Tegaiaquenta, and, according to Fr. Cholenc, the two became "one heart and soul in two bodies. They spoke only of God and of things which would draw them to God. Their talks were like spiritual conferences."

On a trip to Montreal, they saw nuns for the first time and yearned to form an Indian community of religious, but the Father judged this inopportune, and they had to rest content with membership in the Confraternity of the Holy Family. The Jesuit relates that they disappeared into the woods "several times a week to scourge their shoulders with birches, as Catherine had been doing privately for a long time." Kateri was foremost in the frightening austerities prevalent among her compatriots, but she joined hers to an extraordinary love for the Blessed Sacrament, unalterable sweetness and patience, and an unswerving obedience to her spiritual guide. She also possessed that saving sense of humor which so often accompanies a just appreciation of suffering, which in her case was not all self-inflicted. Her health, always poor, began to fail rapidly, and she was in constant pain.

To her great distress, her adopted sister and even old Anastasia began urging her to marry, and, as a final purification, God permitted her to be accused of adultery. Only a year before her death, was she allowed to make a private vow of virginity, consecrated to Our Lady. In 1680, she died in the odor of sanctity, promising the friends at her bedside, "In heaven I shall be nearer to you than during this life. I will watch over you...." The whole mission was inconsolable. Praying near her body, Fr. Cholenc was amazed to see that every pockmark had disappeared from her face, which became radiantly beautiful.

She who, like the Little Flower, had lived in near-total obscurity now became famous overnight through the flood of miracles she unleashed over the Sides. Among innumerable cures were those of Fr. de la Colombière, Vicar General at the time and brother of the Apostle of the Sacred Heart Bl. Claude de la Colombière. She also restored to health Captain du Luth, after whom the Minnesota city is named. Fr. Cholenc was constrained to paint as well as he could a likeness of Kateri, from which crude paper copies could be made, but these turned out to be so productive of miracles that the demand could not be met. Cures were reported even at the French court, whence devotion to Bl. Kateri began radiating throughout Europe. At the time, her beatification seemed imminent, but this was not to take place until the twentieth century.

Meanwhile, back at the old Mission, fervor reached fever pitch. Married couples began living in continence, widows renounced second marriages, and young people begged to be allowed to make vows of chastity. Following Kateri's example, women rolled themselves on thorns for whole nights. Even on her deathbed, Kateri had asked for extra penances, and to a friend who had taken the discipline for her intention in the woods, she said shortly before she died, "I know where you come from and what you did there. Go, take heart, rest assured you are pleasing to God and that I shall help you before Him." She appeared to many, among the first to Anastasia, to whom she said, "Mother, look at this Cross I am carrying. See, see how beautiful it is! Oh, how I loved it on earth! Oh, how I love it still in heaven!"

By 1744, Fr. François Xavier de Charlevoix, in his monumental *History of New France,* had to acknowledge that Kateri Tekakwitha, "a young neophyte almost unknown to the whole country during her life ... for more than sixty years ... has been regarded as Protectress of Canada, and it has been impossible to oppose a kind of cultus publicly rendered to her." Nonetheless, fiercely contested by the devils of the Sides, her beatification, like that of her Bishop and Marie de l'Incarnation, was delayed for three hundred years, and there would be much woe in the interval. According to her biographer, Fr. Edouard Lecompte, S.J., six days after her death on Easter Monday, Kateri appeared in glory to Fr. Chauchetière, one of the priests of the Mission, for the space of two hours, with "her eyes raised to heaven as if in ecstasy. On her right could be seen a toppled church, on her left a savage bound to a stake and burned alive." The vision was not understood at the time, but a few years later the village church was demolished by a hurricane, a Catholic Iroquois was captured and martyred, and there was much more to come.

Chapter X

TRAMPLING THE LILY

According to Bl. Marie de l'Incarnation, a vocation to Canada virtually created "a moral necessity of becoming a saint," because little short of sanctity was equal to the obstacles encountered there. It was not long before St. Tekakwitha's ominous vision began materializing, for despite appearances to the contrary, the Church would indeed topple, and Amerindia's martyrdom would begin. Whereas the Wasp was wont to hug the shorelines of the East, the Lily in her search for souls penetrated the interior, planting fur-trading posts and missions, from which some of the greatest American cities would germinate. Years before Tekakwitha's death, the French Jesuit Fr. Marquette and Louis Joliet had explored the Mississippi—designated on early Spanish maps as the River of the Holy Spirit—and two years after her death, French Catholic rule was carried by the Sieur de La Salle and three Franciscan Recollects as far as the Gulf of Mexico, on whose shores the city of New

Orleans would be founded in French Louisiana in 1718. Already in 1701, a hundred Canadians and a missionary, under the leadership of the Sieur de la Mothe-Cadillac, had founded Detroit. St. Louis and Chicago had similar beginnings. Even now, northwest Indiana is still known as St. Joseph's Valley, for Bishop Laval's little seminary in Quebec sent priests all the way down the Illinois and Ohio Rivers to minister and evangelize. Of major importance was the communications network maintained throughout the wilderness by traveling missionaries and *coureurs de bois* of the fur trade, who relayed supplies and vital information along with the Word of God. Expansion at so phenomenal a rate aroused the envy of the Wasp, never dormant except in the dead of winter and always fearful lest the pincers of France and Spain close from either side on his precarious position. Had the two Catholic powers succeeded in compromising their political differences and cooperated with each other in the Faith, the history of America would have taken a radically different turn.

There is hardly a better illustration of the basic incompatibility of Wasp and Catholic than the spirited correspondence which began in 1685 between Governor Denonville of Canada and Governor Thomas Dongan of the British colony of New York, newly acquired from the Dutch. Oddly enough, both men were Catholics, the French-speaking Dongan being a nephew of the Irish Earl of Tyrconnel and heir to the Earldom of Limerick. Although he had once commanded an Irish regiment for Louis XIV, he was apparently deeply committed to the service of the Wasp. The Marquis de Denonville, on the other hand, was an ardent devotee of St. Tekakwitha. He arrived in Canada on the same ship which brought Bishop de Laval's successor, Saint-Vallier, who formed so high an opinion of him in the course of the trip that he remarked later, "He spent nearly all his time in prayer and the reading of good books.... In all the voyages, I never saw him do anything wrong."

At the time he assumed office, the burning question was whether New France or New York would control the newly opened West. Both governors realized that whichever side managed to enlist the support of the Indians would be the ultimate winner. "They like the manners of the French," reported Denonville, "but they like the cheap goods of the English better.... The artifices of the English have reached such a point that it would be better if they attacked us openly and burned our settlements, instead of inciting the Iroquois against us for our destruction." He blamed Dongan for arousing them, "by telling them publicly that I meant to declare war against them," adding that "Mr. Dongan has written to me, and I have answered him as a man may do who wishes to dissimulate and does not feel strong enough to get angry."

In their correspondence, Denonville in fact appealed to Dongan as a fellow Catholic, pointing out, "Think you, sir, that religion will make any progress while your merchants supply *eau-de-vie* [brandy] in abundance, which, as you ought to know, converts the savages into demons and their cabins into counterparts and theaters of hell?" And again, "You love our holy religion. Can we not then come to an understanding to sustain our missionaries by keeping these fierce tribes in respect and fear?" At this distance from the seriousness of the events, the exchanges between the two aristocrats are often humorous in their veiled sarcasm. Dongan politely denies the charges, and in June of 1687 sends Denonville some oranges, "hearing they are a rarity in your parts." In August, Denonville replies, "I thank you, sir, for your oranges. It was a great pity that they should have been all rotten."

Begging his King next year to send troops, Denonville writes, "We should succumb if our cause were not the cause of God. Your Majesty's zeal for religion ... encourages me to hope that you will be the bulwark of the Faith in the New World as you are in the Old. I cannot give you a truer idea of the war we have to wage with the Iroquois than by comparing them to a great number of wolves ... issuing out of a vast forest to ravage the neighboring settlements.... Nobody can find their lair, for they are always in motion." There would be peace, says he, "but for the malice of the English and the protection they have given our enemies." He is seconded by the Bishop, who writes in his turn, "The glory of God is involved, for the Iroquois are the only tribe who oppose the progress of the Gospel."

The situation growing explosive, two years later Louis XIV ordered the aged Comte de Frontenac out of retirement to invade New York and New England. He burned Schenectady and attacked Albany, initiating the serial conflict now referred to generically as "the French and Indian Wars." The Catholic Indians, with many Iroquois among them, recognized the struggle as a crusade against God's enemies. While the squaws prayed the Rosary at home, the braves made vows to Our Lady and carried the fight into Maine, New Hampshire and Massachusetts. According to Fr. Thury, a Quebec seminary priest present at the battle for Pemaquid, these Indian converts took no scalps, tortured no prisoners and poured out whatever barrels of rum they came across.

For the Puritan Wasp also, it was a holy war, its issues racial and political as well as religious, sharpened by the fact that the French would recognize only James II as the legitimate King of England, and not the incumbent William of Orange. Numbers of women and children were certainly butchered by uncontrollable Indians on both sides, but the French saved many by offering money for captives, some of whom opted to become Canadians as a result. A retaliatory expedition was organized under Governor William Phipps of Massachusetts, a coarse, rapacious self-made man and an ardent democrat. He began by invading the neutral province of Acadia, forcing its surrender and not neglecting to imprison Governor Ménéval and appropriate his household silver, linens and wardrobe. At Port Royal, one of his men boasted, "We cut down the cross, rifled their church, pulled down their high altar and broke their images," thus, again, revealing the true nature of the battle for Amerindia. Thence the Wasp turned unsuccessfully against Quebec and Montreal. Bishop de Laval remarked later, "Our Lord's protection that year appeared miraculous.... Our greatest recourse was prayers and novenas.... This means was more efficacious than the power of arms."

He does not mention germ warfare, but a Sokoki Indian told the Canadians that the overland attack on Montreal failed only because smallpox had spread among the English from infected clothing they were preparing to use against the French and their allies. Perhaps the Wasp must be credited with the first use of this risky modern weapon, for some years later, when Canada was prostrate and the English were beset on all sides by Indian uprisings, an exchange took place between the English Commander-in-Chief, Sir Jeffrey Amherst, and his subordinate, Col. Henry Bouquet, which is preserved among the Haldimand Papers in the British Museum and reads thus: "Could it not be conceived," asks Amherst, "to send the *Small Pox* among those disaffected tribes of Indians?" To which Bouquet replies, "I will try to inoculate the _____ with some blankets that may fall into their hands, and take care not to get the disease myself..." And

Amherst rejoins, "You will do well to try to inoculate the Indians by means of blankets, as well as to try every other method that can serve to extirpate this execrable race."

Such was the Wasp response to St. Kateri Tekakwitha's humble, "Who will teach me what is most pleasing to God, that I may do it?" Very different was the pious Denonville's reaction, who warned Governor Dongan not to prevent the Jesuits from entering the Iroquois villages, "for until now they have held the country together by their skill in governing the spirits of these barbarians, *who are savages in name only.*"

+

While Frontenac was Governor, the New Englanders made little progress, despite two attacks by New York and one by Massachusetts. Frontenac died with the century, however, and the Wasp soon regained control. In 1713, the Treaty of Utrecht awarded the entire province of Acadia, with Newfoundland and Hudson Bay, to the English. A half-century of bloodletting ensued over the remaining French holdings, which Voltaire had referred to in *Candide* as "two nations at war for a few acres of Canadian snow." These few acres, remarks Fr. Zaratti in *The Work of the Catholic Church in America,* "were in point of fact twelve million square miles of land that could have developed into a Christian empire, the gem of the French colonial possessions, had it not been for the indifference of the politicians and anti-clerical philosophers like ... [Voltaire]."

Engrossed with her domestic problems and rife with heresy, France by then had all but abandoned Canada. Incredible as it may seem, in 1673 the *Jesuit Relations,* which had been published for fifty-seven years without intermission, since the days of St. Francis Xavier, was interdicted by the Roman Propaganda under pressure from the Gallican government. A generation later, emigration virtually ceased, and Canada was left largely to her own resources. Her population, held together almost exclusively by a faithful clergy, who maintained ties with the mother country, nevertheless contiued to increase, reaching forty-two thousand in the last census taken by the French. Unfortunately, their numbers were confronted by some two hundred and fifty thousand New England Wasps, whose ranks had been swelled indiscriminately by some of the worst elements of Europe.

Despite the English takeover, the Acadians numbered about fifteen thousand by 1750. Normally such prosperity would have rejoiced the hearts of their new masters, were it not that the whole province, both French and Indian, resisted to a man every effort on their part to assimilate them religiously and politically. The Micmacs and Abenakis, literally all converts to the Faith, publicly accused the English of impiety. When the Jesuits were expelled, these converts declared to the English, "You are too late to start teaching us your prayers after we have known you for so many years. The French were more far-seeing than you, and as soon as they knew us, they taught us how to pray to God. Now we pray better than you do!" Obviously Acadia, the base on which the Wasp depended for further penetration into Canada, had to be brought under control.

In 1755, Capt. Alexander Murray wrote John Winslow, the Lt. Colonel at Grand Pré, "You know our soldiers detest them [the Acadians] and would avail themselves of any excuse to kill them!" On July 28, the Governor's Council in Halifax therefore resolved to expel the inhabitants by force. This act of inconceivable barbarity, matched on this side of the Atlantic only by President Andrew Jackson's treatment of the Cherokees, became the backdrop for Henry Wadsworth Longfellow's epic *Evangeline.* In September, an unsuspecting, unarmed population was rounded up under false pretenses in the parish churches, surrounded by militia, herded onto leaky boats, and summarily deported from their native country. The humane Winslow confessed at the time to a fellow officer, "This affair is more grievous to me than any I was ever employed in."

An entry in his diary reads, "Began to embark the inhabitants, who went off very solentarily *(sic)* and unwillingly, the women in great distress, carrying their children in their arms; others carrying their decrepit parents in their carts with all their goods, moving in great confusion, and appeared a scene of woe and distress." From Nova Scotia alone, sixty-five hundred innocent persons were dispatched without warning or preparation to any settlement which would accept them, their lands confiscated and their houses burned to prevent their return. As more and more were dislodged as transports became available, many governors refused them entry. Massachusetts alone turned away five loads of these eighteenth-century "boat people" as late as 1762. Some died in flight, some from exposure and disease. Others managed to return to France or took to the woods with their Indian friends. As related in *Evangeline*, a considerable number opted for French Louisiana, where their descendants, still Catholic and, to a degree, French-speaking, subsist as "Cajuns."

A sleeper clause in the Treaty of Utrecht, awarding the English a protectorate over the Iroquois, provided all the Wasp needed to conquer the rest of the country. His affinity for the pagan Indians has been noted, and explains in large part the clandestine spread of Masonry among the Amerindians who remained savages. This is a facet of history often overlooked or purposely downplayed, yet much of the symbolism of the American Masonic lodges, not to mention the Boy Scouts and "white" Masonry, can be traced to Amerindian demonology. Patent similarities, especially the "Great Spirit" and the apron-loincloth, hark back to common origins in the Old Religion practiced at Babel, and now resurfacing in the new religion of the New Age.

Worthy of mention in this connection are the mysterious Tonkawas, a singular cannibal tribe, whose depredations against the Spanish missions, at the very time that France was losing her hold on her territories, drew the famous Fr. Junipero Serra to Texas in 1758, where the Tonkawas' cruelty was such that few soldiers dared confront them. First heard of in 1691, in Francisco de Jesus-Maria's enumeration of hostile tribes, they seemed to spring from nowhere, without natural affiliations. Exhibiting no common racial characteristics and regarding no part of the country as their own, they were not a tribe at all in the usual sense, but more like a secret brotherhood, similar to Freemasonry. Stranger yet, their one invariable target was the Catholic mission, and up to their last chief Placido, they proved unwavering allies of the Wasp and the United States. One exception only occurred: During the Civil War, the Luciferian Masonic Grand Master, the Yankee-born Albert Pike, enlisted them on the side of the Confederacy, in whose ranks the unspeakable atrocities committed by them served to alienate European sympathy for the Southern cause. Until they were finally relegated to an Oklahoma reservation, they served as Army Scouts, hunting, killing and eating Comanches and Apaches under the flag of the United States.

The formal union of the Wasp with the pagan Iroquois sealed New France's fate. The end came on September 13,

1759, on the Plains of Abraham above Quebec, where the frail, boyish English General Wolfe and eight thousand men scaled the heights and overcame the Marquis de Montcalm and fourteen thousand defenders. Anyone viewing those sheer cliffs today can only marvel that fortifications in such a location could ever be taken. There was talk of treachery and apathy among the troops, but mayhap the true cause lay deeper, for Our Lord had promised Louis XIV the defeat of all his enemies, if he would consecrate the nation to His Sacred Heart, and inasmuch as the consecration was not made, it was only to be expected that France's colonies would share the fate of the mother country. By the eighteenth century, many officials in the French government were Freemasons, and Montcalm, a friend of Louis XV's mistress Madame de Pompadour, was put in command of the colonial defense, summarily replacing the Marquis de Vaudreuil, an undefeated veteran, who was moreover a dedicated member of the Confraternity of the Sacred Heart.

Following the defeat, St. John's Day, a Masonic holiday traditionally enlivened with bonfires and high ritual, was openly celebrated for the first time in Catholic Quebec on December 27. Eventually a Masonic obelisk composed of thrice times thirteen courses of stone, the well-known "39 steps," was raised on the battle site to the joint memory of the opposing generals, both of whom fell in the fight. In 1763, the Treaty of Paris transferred the whole of France's claims to the Sides of the North, along with Spanish Florida, to the English conqueror.

+

The Indians were in consternation. Believing the Great Father in France had only fallen asleep and would soon waken, tribes rose almost to a man against the English, in a concerted effort at resistance, known in Wasp history books as the Pontiac Conspiracy, but which was in some respects a sort of Amerindian counterrevolution. An Ottawa chief allied to the French all his life, although not a Catholic, Pontiac is believed to have led his people against General Braddock when the latter unsuccessfully attacked Fort Duquesne. He was highly esteemed by Montcalm, who bestowed on him the full dress uniform of a French officer, which the chief wore on solemn occasions. The Indian Confederation correctly guessed that they were now at the mercy of a nation more interested in exterminating them than ruling them.

Laying siege to Detroit, Pontiac told the French remnant there, "It is not to revenge myself alone that I make war on the English. It is to avenge you, my brothers.... I know that they have taken away your arms and made you sign a paper which they have sent home to their country. Therefore you are left defenseless, and now I mean to avenge your cause and my own together. I mean to destroy the English and leave not one upon our lands." At the very least, he hoped to retain France's western outposts. The cost to the English was high, but his project quixotic, for help could come no more from France. "Hitherto," writes Parkman, "the two rival European nations had kept each other in check ... and the Indians had in some measure held the balance of power between them. To conciliate their good will and gain their alliance, to avoid offending them by injustice, was the policy of both the French and the English. But now ... the English had gained an undisputed ascendancy, and the Indians, no longer important allies, were treated as mere barbarians who might be trampled upon with impunity.... The doom of the race was sealed, and no human power could avert it."

The inestimable legacy of the Faith remained to them, however, for according to Fr. Zaratti, writing in 1956, "Today the following tribes in North America are either wholly or partly Catholic: Abenaki, Black Feet, Coeur d'Alene, Chippewa, Crow, Gros Ventre, Huron, California Diggers, Flatheads, Mohawk, Pottawatomie, Iroquois, Passamaquoddy, Pueblo, Sioux and Yakima, to mention only the best-known. The Iroquois, responsible for the sacrifice of so many Jesuit lives, now count four thousand souls dedicated to the Catholic cause, despite their vastly diminished numbers. Where they once appeared indomitable, they have become deeply faithful. In 1831, their Catholic leaders sent a gift to Pope Gregory XVI of moccasins and a handmade belt, accompanied by this message: 'You are our Father, never will we recognize another. If our descendants forget you and fall into error, show them this belt, and they will return immediately to the fold.' "

Although rarely heard from until today, when "ethnicity" has found favor as a political posture, the Catholic Amerindians still constitute a slumbering hope for the revival of the Faith. On June 24, 1980, the Mohawk Andrew Delisle, Grand Chief of the

Confederation of the Indians of Quebec, recited a prayer of thanksgiving before Pope John Paul II in Rome, at the Beatification of St. Kateri Tekakwitha. Long ago, his forebears had told the Baptist and Methodist missionaries sent to convert them to Protestantism, "Go and learn. Do as the Blackrobes did, and then we will believe what you tell us!"

+

After the English conquest, Canada found herself scalped, if not actually decapitated. Their Catholic officials gone and most of the aristocracy having returned to France, the people were left a headless body. For the most part, peasants with no experience in self-government, much less any inclinations to "democracy," they shifted for themselves as well as they could. Parochial structures alone continued to function in the vacuum, and social collapse was averted by a heroic lower clergy, who faithfully discharged their stewardship. Protestantism, which sought to take over in the wake of the English conquest, only served to unify the faithful, who till then had had to contend only with carefully chaperoned French heresies. Now, over and beyond racial and national altercations, began open religious warfare.

Although the peace treaty guaranteed religious liberty, it was soon evident that the newly installed Anglican hierarchy sought to replace the Catholic, and that the young were to be educated in Protestant schools. The Catholic clergy suffered every vexation. Religious communities were marked for extinction, forbidden to accept novices, and their property confiscated. To the Bishop was conceded only the title of Superintendent of Catholic Worship. A supernatural glance into this area of history would suggest that it was not so much Valley Forge as the expulsion of Catholic missionaries which cost England her own colonies a generation later in divine retribution, for total suppression of the Faith on the Eastern seaboard was indeed averted only by the threatening American Revolution. Realizing that French Canada must be pacified at any cost lest she join forces with the rebels to the south, the British Crown found it expedient to grant relative religious freedom by the Quebec Act of 1774.

A year later, the American revolutionaries invaded Canada as anticipated. Led by Richard Montgomery, twenty-one hundred men easily took Montreal, whose defenders numbered one hundred and fifty. Trois-Rivières fell next. Proceeding to join Benedict Arnold in the siege of Quebec, the attackers left their prey in the hands of the tyrannical, anti-Catholic General David Wooster, who threatened to send the Vicar General into exile because, "The clergy refuse absolution to all who have shown themselves our friends, and preach damnation to all those that will not take up arms against us!" Labeling the Catholic French "but a small remove from the savages," he did much to harden their resistance. With defeat at Quebec and the death of Montgomery, the American putsch began to collapse. The Revolution, which could be more properly defined as a civil war between Englishmen, never enjoyed widespread support, even among the thirteen colonies, and of the three hundred American prisoners taken, ninety-four decided to enlist in the British forces. As we know, before the close of hostilities, thousands of Loyalists who wished to remain faithful to their English sovereign would sell their property in the Colonies, swarm over New Brunswick, and populate Ontario.

With an aim at securing allies, a commission headed by Benjamin Franklin was sent to Canada with a formal invitation to become the fourteenth colony of the rebel confederation. Accompanying him on this venture to incite their neighbors to rebellion were two prominent Catholics, the millionaire Charles Carroll, one of the Masonic signers of the Declaration of Independence, and his cousin Fr. John Carroll, destined to become the first Catholic bishop of the United States, on Franklin's recommendation. The commission was entertained in Montreal at the home of the merchant-agitator Thomas Walker, who hopefully suggested, "We must have blood, and then in a few years everything will be set right." He and other Yankee businessmen of the city made every effort to foment an uprising among the French Canadians, who certainly had no love for their British conquerors, but as Catholics they respected legitimate authority and were not disposed to forcible overthrow. The commissioners held many clandestine meetings with French ecclesiastics and dignitaries in the garden of the secret revolutionary Pierre Calvet, but all came to nothing.

The spine of the resistance was provided by the Catholic clergy, who showed plainly what they thought of the American proposal. One Canadian priest was severely disciplined for allowing Fr. Carroll to say Mass in a chapel, and another, Fr.

François de la Lotbinière, was suspended for accepting the chaplaincy of a French Canadian regiment recruited to help the American cause. The previous year the French bishop had ordered loyalty to Britain, even forbidding his clergy to marry American soldiers to French-Canadian girls. In a letter to one of his priests, Bishop Briand wrote at the time, "They are saying about me what they are saying about you, that I am English. As a matter of fact I am. So should you be, and so should they, inasmuch as they have pledged their allegiance, and every law, natural, divine and human, requires it of them. But neither you nor I must partake of the English religion. They are under English domination in civil matters. Where their souls and their salvation are concerned, they are under the lovable law of Jesus, of his Vicar on earth, the Sovereign Pontiff, and of the priests and bishops." Bishop Briand did not scruple to excommunicate accomplices of the Americans, exacting a public retraction from them before he would reconcile them to the Church. His successor, Bishop Hubert, would beg Sir Guy Carleton, Canada's second British governor, to discourage the immigration of Anglo-Saxon priests, knowing them to be infected with democratic ideas and eager to infect their charges.

In any case, ordinary Catholics were not disposed to trust the revolutionaries' Continental Congress, which only the year before had passed the Suffolk Resolves, declaring George III's tolerant Quebec Act "dangerous in an extreme degree to the Protestant religion and to the civil rights and liberties of all Americans: and therefore, as men and as Protestant Christians, we are indispensably obliged to take all proper measures for our security." Who could place any confidence in rebels, who by definition set themselves against existing law and order? Having seen for themselves, however, how effective religious liberty was in generating political cooperation, these rebels were not slow to exhibit the same tolerance as had the monarch they repudiated. In due time, freedom of worship would be espoused as a basic principle of the Masonic U.S. Constitution, and the Catholics, under the leadership of their liberal Bishop, would be among the most enthusiastic supporters of the new democratic government.

Although defeated in his immediate objective of winning Canada to the American cause, the astute Franklin left behind him in Montreal a useful fifth columnist in the person of the revolutionary propagandist Fleury Mesplet, a Frenchman personally trained by him, first in London and later in Philadelphia. Besides doing commercial printing, Mesplet produced Montreal's earliest books and pamphlets and founded the *Montreal Gazette*, leaving a well-organized media operation, which continued to function effectively in the hands of a series of able succesors. One of the most prominent in the 1870's was Joseph Guibord, who was responsible for introducing stereotyping into Canada. He was also the moving force behind the liberal Catholic *Institut Canadien*, which not only launched the spellbinding Prime Minister Wilfred du Laurier's political career, but distributed quantities of modernist propaganda and condemned books throughout the dominions. Excommunicated along with the *Institut* 's entire membership for such activities, he opted to die without the Sacraments rather than renounce his affiliations, so that his body remained unburied for six years, while Church and state battled over his right to a plot in the Catholic cemetery of Côte-des-Neiges. The courts finally decided against the Church, but Bishop Bourget had the last word, for after the funeral he quietly deconsecrated the gravesite where the troublesome remains lay, encased in cement.

There is no necessity to pursue the history of Canada further in any detail, for the forces at work remain the same as they were in the beginning. English control grew ever tighter, but despite every inducement, the Wasp succeeded in eradicating neither French nationalism nor the Faith. In 1829, England's Emancipation Act accorded full civil rights to Catholics, although it was not applied in many provinces until 1851. By then Canada had experienced the same "Irish invasion" which took place in the United States after the Potato Famine, and the added numbers of English-speaking Catholics should have provided powerful leverage against the Anglican bloc, but what actually occurred was in many respects the counterpart of what transpired in the U.S. under Bishop Carroll's leadership. Many Irish Catholics, no doubt drawn by the common English language, allied themselves only too easily with the Wasp establishment, so that the Irish clergy acquired an ascendancy over their French co-religionists, which in many instances produced tensions far more debilitating to the Faith than those with the Anglican divines. What should have been a cooperative effort to defeat the Serpent became a family feud inviting treacherous "coalitions" with Anglo-Masonry, which not only weakened the unity of the faithful, but immeasurably

187

strengthened the Wasp.

The atheist Paul Blanshard, certainly no friend of Catholics, wrote in *The Irish and the Catholic Power,* "Irish Catholicism is particularly important for the West because its compromise with democracy in the Republic is the most advanced form of church-state adjustment in any completely Catholic country. It represents the utmost compromise which the Papacy can make with Western society and still be true to its principles." The end result of such a policy is visible today in Ireland and wherever the Irish have exported it. It is therefore not surprising that "Quebec has the same educational pattern as Ireland: not public schools, but Catholic and Protestant systems supported by the public treasury. Newfoundland has four denominational school systems ... Ontario, Saskatchewan and Alberta grant public funds to separate denominational schools." Hard put to conceal his admiration, Blanshard continues, "In all English-speaking Canada, the fight for segregation is led by the Irish priests, who control the Catholic Church as completely as they control it in the United States. 'Outside of Quebec,' says the *Irish World,* 'nearly every priest and nun in Canada is Irish.' This is an exaggeration, but it is close to the truth. The outside world has tended to think of Canadian Catholicism as exclusively French; it is time to realize it is both French and Irish."

One of the first fruits of the new influx was Laval University, inaugurated in Quebec in 1854 and canonically erected with a branch in Montreal in 1876. Operating on lines similar to the Americanist Catholic University in Washington, D.C., and Maynooth in Ireland, it began injecting modernism into Canadian Catholic education under the liberal Archbishop Taschereau. A clear indication of its spirit is that it refused an honorary degree to that excellent Wasp historian Francis Parkman, to whom so much of this writing is indebted. He was not discriminated against because of his Protestant prejudices, but on the contrary, because of his avowed admiration of the old French regime and the Jesuits! A bitter struggle ensued between Archbishop Taschereau and the French ultramontane Bishops Taché and Laflèche, who had the staunch support of Pius IX, the Pope of the *Syllabus.;* but the victory was thrown definitively to the modernists in 1886 when his successor Leo XIII elevated Taschereau to the cardinalate and primacy of Canada. Nature took its course with the able help of Masonry behind the scenes, and today, in the wake of the Second Vatican Council, the formation of a new "American Church" is openly advocated by Canadian and USan clergy in concert.

+

Meanwhile, the pastor at Cap de la Madeleine had remained true to his vow to Our Lady. The primitive church was renovated after the miracle of the ice, obtained by recital of the Rosary and appropriately dedicated to Our Lady of the Rosary. In 1888, the statue of Notre Dame du Cap, her eyes and hands lowered in the attitude in which she had appeared to St. Catherine Labouré, was solemnly placed on its high altar. On the evening of June 22, according to the witness of the pastor and that of a Franciscan priest and an invalid who had dropped by to pray, the eyes of the statue were suddenly raised and opened wide. "The look of the Virgin was that of a living person," testified the Franciscan. "It wore an expression of severity mingled with sorrow." What fell beneath Our Lady's scrutiny as she gazed mournfully westward?

At the time, Canada's western expansion was carrying the battle for Amerindia by horse and canoe, sled and snowshoe ever deeper into the Serpent's hinterlands. France's civil militia may have been forced to surrender to the Wasp, but not her Church Militant. In 1845, the immense Northwest Territory boasted one bishop and six priests; by 1908, there were seven bishops and some four hundred clergy. The Oblates of Mary Immaculate were among the most zealous. Bishop Taché's coadjutor, the Ven. Vital Grandin, labored a half-century in a diocese twice the size of France, struggling against desperate poverty and Wasp interference, in order to reach the Indians and prairie settlers, of whom many of the latter were Ukrainian Byzantines. "And I hope to continue after my death," quoth he. To him was reserved the joy of ordaining the first half-breed priest, Fr. Cunningham, on the Feast of St. Joseph in 1890. He died in the odor of sanctity in 1902, as Alberta's first Bishop. Another Oblate, the humble Brother Anthony Kowalczyk, a Canadian diamond imported from Poland, died in Alberta in 1947, with graces and cures pouring from his grave in St. Albert.

From her pedestal at the Cap de la Madeleine, Our Lady may well have been contemplating the plight of her beloved

Amerindians in Manitoba and Saskatchewan, where three years before her manifestation at the Cap, Louis Riel had been executed for high treason, defending his people against the Wasp. A Catholic half-breed, or *métis*, whose paternal grandmother was a Chippewa, Riel was the son of Julie de Lajimondine, the first white woman born in the Canadian Northwest. A protégé of the good Bishop Taché, he was educated by the Jesuits at St. Mary's College in Montreal, but his home was the vast territorial empire which after the British conquest was controlled by the Hudson Bay Company. With the formation of the Dominion of Canada in 1867, these lands were arbitrarily sold to the new government in Ottawa without the slightest consultation with the native inhabitants, regarded as little more than serfs, or as the press put it, "a herd of buffaloes."

The *métis*, both French- and English-speaking, had for a long time lived under a loose traditional government of their own, which had continued to function well under the paternal eyes of their Bishop and the overseas Governor of the Company. Before the transfer became law, however, Wasp Orangemen from Ontario entered illegally and set up a regime of terror. In view of imminent annexation and immense profits, innocent persons were plundered and killed and lands appropriated without jurisdiction. Acting with singular prudence, Riel established a legally constituted provisional government to stem the engulfing anarchy. Its wise recommendations resulted in the Manitoba Act of 1870, which erected the Red River area as a separate province, where the rights of the Lily were at least acknowledged on paper. From the scaffold, Riel could rightly declare, "I know that by the grace of God I am the founder of Manitoba." He is so regarded today, with monuments to his memory both in Winnipeg and in Regina.

Bishop Taché saw only too clearly that Riel's confrontation was no mere Indian uprising, but one more stage of the struggle between the Wasp and the Lily. As he wrote to the statesman Georges Etienne Cartier, "It's really for Lower Canada [Quebec Province] as well as for us that our poor *Métis* took up arms." All considered themselves simply French Canadians. Unfortunately, Riel's provisional government had been forced to convict and execute a flagrant offender named Thomas Scott, who happened to be a rabid Orangeman.

Overnight he became a Wasp martyr, and the government later used his execution as an excuse for refusing the *Métis* a promised amnesty. Although twice properly elected to Parliament, Riel was expelled from that body, a heavy bounty placed on his head, and he was hounded for the rest of his life.

Anything but a rebel, he had in fact refused large offers of money and troops from the American Fenians, led by O'Donoghue, a former member of the provisional government. Like Franklin and his commission before them, they invaded Canada from the United States at this time, foolishly expecting to win the *Métis* to their cause. At St. Norbert, Riel told Bishop Taché there was "not the slightest danger that I or any of my friends would join the Fenians. We detest them, for they are condemned by the Church." Accepting a five-year exile in the interests of peace and to insure free elections, Riel retired to the U.S. By this time, however, his mind had unfortunately given way in the face of his terrible sufferings, and at various times his friends had to have him confined to institutions.

He was teaching school in Montana when the *Métis* appealed to him once more. Many had long since abandoned Manitoba, now filling with vengeful Wasps supported by government troops. Some had fled to the States, others to Saskatchewan, where they suffered the same old injustices. The government offering no redress, they unfortunately broke into open rebellion, with the now unstable Riel at their head, and sealed their fate politically. In the full throes of a messianic mania, Riel by then had wandered from the Faith, seeing himself as the Great Prophet of a gigantic half-breed America. A theocratic republic composed of half-breeds of the various immigrant nationalities would rule the continent, with each ethnic segment occupying its own section of land.

He believed it had been revealed to him that Amerindians were the true Chosen People, who had come to America after the birth of Moses. The Papacy would be transferred from Rome to the Sides, and there would be a new Eucharist of bread and milk. These delusions ended abruptly in a skirmish with the Mounted Police and the Army, and, despite a well-founded plea of insanity, he was sacrificed to the gods of the Wasp. Disregarding his brilliant early services, establishment historians prefer to dwell on his pathetic later aberrations. Sir Adolphe Chapleau could applaud Riel's execution before the House of Commons by citing the shining example of the precedent set by the United States, where, "they have given fomenters of the Indian wars and hostile Indians no kind of trial except bringing them before the military authorities, shooting them or hanging them by the dozen or the four dozens, as was done after the Custer Massacre. The government of the United States, that model government, ... [does] not allow any scruple to interfere." The Wasp, as we have said, is not always English.

On April 17, 1982, Canada took full responsibility for her own Constitution, although the British Crown still makes a show of signing its formal acts. Much like the United States after the Revolution, the Dominion is free to run its own affairs without interference from England, but without actually severing their ties, for its finances and foreign policy remain under the control of the Wasp. There is a growing Separatist movement, dating from the days of Benjamin Franklin, which would divide French- speaking Canadians politically from their English compatriots, but whatever civil adjustments are made only serve to cloak the tension between the same two opponents, set at odds by Almighty God at the beginning in Eden. Call them France and England or the Lily and the Wasp, those really at war in the Battle for Amerindia are always the Woman and the Serpent. Albert Pike tells us that a Masonic medal of the sixteenth or seventeenth century displayed a sword cutting off the stalk of a lily, and that Cagliostro had on his personal seal the letters L. P. D., standing for the motto, *Lilia pedibus destrue,* "Trample the lilies!" The lilies of France are those specifically referred to, but behind them always stands the one "Lily among thorns" (Cant. 2:2), who declared her Immaculate Conception first in Mexico and then in France. Not only will she never be trampled, but she will inevitably crush the head of the Serpent, even now "lying in wait for her heel." (Gen. 3:15)

In the face of every setback, the Sides of the North have continued to produce Canadian diamonds. Mother Caouette, foundress of the Institute of the Precious Blood, died in 1905. She was followed seven years later in Sherbrooke, Quebec, by Bl. Mother Marie Léonie Paradis, who founded the Little Sisters of the Holy Family to provide domestic help for the clergy, and whose cause was introduced in 1966. Among diamonds exported abroad was Mother Joseph of the Sisters of Providence. Responsible for hospitals and schools along the West Coast of the United States in the last century, she was actually granted the honor of a statue in the U.S. Capitol.

Another export, Marie "Little Rose" Ferron, a saintly stigmatic, died in Woonsocket, Rhode Island in 1936.

And there is Marie Louise Brault, an Anglo-French descendant of one of Maisonneuve's men and a grandniece of St. Marguerite Bourgeoys, who sometimes appeared to her. A victim soul of a high order, who lived at Pointe Claire near Montreal, she successfully combined the life of a model wife and mother of nine children with the hidden life of an extraordinary mystic. According to her biographer, Fr. Louis Bouhier, Pastor of Notre Dame de Montreal, she manifested heroic humility and overflowing charity, along with visions, stigmata, unexplainable physical suffering, diabolic persecutions, prophecy, miracles, bilocations and constant communication with souls in Heaven and Purgatory, not to mention the ability to go without food or sleep. Even in Canada, she remains largely unknown, but St. Joseph of Montreal's apostle, Bl. Brother André, whose confidante she was, stated emphatically to two intimate friends after her death in 1910, "She is a saint, a great saint. You may invoke her!"

Explaining to Madame Brault on one occasion how His Passion continues on earth in the Eucharist, Our Lord said, "The world is full of crimes. Sin sweeps over it as a sea gone out of its bed.... The Sacred Host in which I give Myself as food to men is profaned and disdained. The justice of My Heavenly Father cries for vengeance. If His arm does not fall, it is because in the midst of this impure and cruel world, there are still pure hearts, souls of good will, to weep, to love and to atone." One of the more recent was another descendant of New France's earliest settlers, the young Bl. Dina Bélanger, in religion Sr. Marie Sainte-Cécile de Rome of the Congregation of Jesus and Mary. A gifted pianist destined to spend most of her nine years of religious life as an invalid, she had soon realized, "My sole occupation is to suffer." To her, Our Lord had confided, "You will not possess Me more fully in heaven, for I have absorbed you entirely." Following the publication of the *Autobiography* she wrote under obedience, numerous graces were attributed to the intercession of this victim of expiation, who became so closely identified with her Savior that He called her "My little Myself." Dying hidden from the world at the age of thirty-two in her convent in Quebec in 1929, she was beatified by John Paul II.

These are the true combatants for Amerindia. So

unconcerned was the Wasp with liberating the Sides from its demon masters that he himself has become their prey, sinking day by day into savagery deeper than that of the savages he despised. Astrologers and mediums flourish in all ranks of government, as magicians and sorcerers once controlled the Indian councils. Where the sexes slept together in the longhouses, they now indulge in promiscuity in coed dormitories. Parental failure to control children, so deplored by the Catholic missionaries, is more prevalent than ever it was among the savages. Devotees of resurging satanism now practice the old ritual cannibalism, not on enemies captured in battle, but on victims whose organs are harvested for transplant. The innocent unborn are slaughtered by the millions in the scientific rites of modern hospitals. Animal mutilations continue to take place, but under cover of laboratory experimentation, no longer partly excused by winter hunger, as when the Indians boiled dogs alive, their feet weighted by stones, or sat down to the harvest feast of "Iroquois stew," whose main ingredients were five dogs, plenty of squash and one Frenchman.

Has the Battle of Amerindia been lost to the Serpent? On June 22, 1993, the Dalai Lama, welcomed by Canada's Cardinal Turcotte as "our brother," arrived from Tibet to preside over an interfaith prayer meeting at St. Joseph's Oratory. Where were the troops of Christ the King? Fr. Antonio Pacios answers that question in *La Pasion de la Iglesia,* where he writes: "When the handful of leaven is thrown into the dough, the dough is flat and insipid, and that leaven is powerful; but as it dissolves into the dough, it loses its strength, and there comes a time when neither the leaven any longer appears as such, nor is the dough completely leavened, albeit modified. The whole has become a shapeless mass, neither leavened nor without leavening, neither leaven nor dough. But when the leaven, thus weakened, seems to have lost its strength, it exercises its full efficacy. Then is precisely when the hour is near in which the entire dough will be leavened, and will have power to leaven other masses of dough in its turn.... As Christ wished to associate us in His redemptive work, in order to hasten the coming of the Kingdom, it is most important that particles of pure leaven be everywhere multiplied. Such are the holy souls who, united with the Eucharistic Christ, have complete faith in Him and surrender themselves totally into His hands as instruments of redemption: *victim souls.* "
LONG LIVE CATHOLIC AMERICA!

Seven Other Titles by Solange Strong Hertz

- Utopia, "Nowhere"—Now Here
- Apostasy in America
- The Star-Spangled Heresy
- On The Contrary
- Beyond Politics: A Meta-Historical View
- Sin Revisited
- The Thought of Their Heart

All titles available from:
*The Remnant Press, 2539 Morrison Ave., St. Paul,
Minnesota 55117 **Telephone: 651-484-4206***